Under-standing Macro-economics

ROBERT L. HEILBRONER

Under-standing Macro-economics

SECOND EDITION

PRENTICE-HALL, INC.
ENGLEWOOD CLIFFS, NEW JERSEY

PRENTICE-HALL INTERNATIONAL, INC., London
PRENTICE-HALL OF AUSTRALIA, PTY. LTD., Sydney
PRENTICE-HALL OF CANADA, LTD., Toronto
PRENTICE-HALL OF INDIA PRIVATE LTD., New Delhi
PRENTICE-HALL OF JAPAN, INC., Tokyo

for Hans Neisser

Preface

The purpose of this book is to present the main themes of macroeconomics as simply and lucidly as possible, not only so that its readers can pass their exams, but in the more ambitious hope that long after these exams have faded into oblivion, something of the central ideas and conclusions of contemporary economics will remain.

The problem in a book of this kind is not just how to present the material, but where to draw the line—a matter than cannot, I fear, be resolved to everyone's satisfaction. The instructor who has spent years acquiring a knowledge of the subtleties and complexities of economic relationships is sure to feel that too much has been left out. The student who has a semester or two to absorb all the formal economic instruction he is likely to receive in his life is apt to feel just the opposite. By way of apology to both, I can say only that I have thought hard about where I *have* drawn the line, emphasizing and highlighting certain basic processes of great conceptual and practical importance and minimizing side issues of secondary interest. Whether I will now succeed either in helping my readers over their exams or in giving them an understanding of economics that will "stick" are questions to which I shall be just as eager as they are to learn the answers.

Let me add that this volume, with some emendations, comprises Part II of a larger text, *The Economic Problem*. That larger book represents an attempt not only to teach the elements of macro- and microeconomics, but to present both in a setting of economic history. The text was many years in the making, however, and parts of it appeared separately and independently, as *The Making of Economic Society* and as this book. To my pleasure, both volumes were received warmly enough to allow me to think that a useful purpose would be served by continuing them in their separate existences as well as in their originally intended union in a larger text. I should add, though, that this second edition of

Understanding Macroeconomics is considerably altered from the first edition, both in substance and sequence, and that a concise summary and question section has been added to each chapter. If this edition is better than the first, as I think it is, most of the credit belongs to my reading public, I will be happy to hear from my readers, as in the past, if there are still pages that they wish to see changed or improved.

A number of people have helped me very greatly in this book, and I should like to thank them for their pains. Hans Neisser of the Graduate Faculty of the New School for Social Research strengthened the manuscript substantially with his critical comments. In gratitude for this and previous assistance, and in partial payment of a long-standing debt of student to teacher and of colleague to friend, I am happy to dedicate this book to him. I am deeply indebted also to another New School colleague and devoted friend, Peter L. Bernstein, who read the manuscript twice with meticulous care. There is not a page that has not benefited from his searching criticism and good advice. Harry G. Johnson of the University of Chicago gave me generously of his time and provided an invaluable critique. Eli Ginzberg of Columbia University pointed out several weak points in the text and was especially helpful in regard to the chapter on employment, and Carey Thompson of the University of Texas performed a similarly useful task, with particular emphasis on the chapter on money. Finally, I am happy to acknowledge the counsel of Adolph Lowe, now Professor Emeritus at my teaching institution. Quite aside from his discerning comments, this book, like all my previous ones, is an expression of an interest in, and orientation toward, economics that I received in large measure from him. It remains only to add that usual proviso, absolving all the above from the errors of omission and commission from which even their combined thoughtful efforts could not save me.

New York and Chilmark   ROBERT L. HEILBRONER

Contents

8 *The government sector*   *109*

Government in the expenditure flow · The government
sector in historical perspective · The composition of public
spending · Classifying public expenditure · Characteristics
of the public sector · Fiscal policy · Taxes, expenditures,
and GNP · Automatic stabilizers · A diagram of
government spending · Another view of equilibrium,
again · Deficit spending · Deficits and losses · Debts and
assets · Real corporate debts · Total business debts ·
Government deficits · Sales vs. taxes · Internal and
external debts · Problems of a national debt · Expenditures
vs. tax cuts · Perpetual public debts · Real burdens ·
Indirect effects · Personal debts and public debts · The
public sector again in perspective · Public and private
assets · Political problems · Political vs. economic
considerations

9 *Money*   *137*

The supply of money · Currency · Bookkeeping money ·
The Federal Reserve System · The banks' bank ·
Fractional reserves · Loans and investments · Increasing
the supply of money · New money · The expansion of
deposits · Why banks must work together · Investments
and interest · Creating reserves · Monetary control
mechanisms · Federal Reserve notes · The gold cover ·
Gold and money · Money and belief

10 *Money and the macro system*   *157*

The quantity equation · The quantity theory · Changes
in V · Changes in T · Output and prices · Inflation and
public finance · Full employment vs. underemployment ·
Bottlenecks · Inflation vs. unemployment · Money and
sticky prices · Money and interest rates · The financial
demand for money · Liquidity preference · Liquidity
preference and interest rates · Liquidity preference and
money management · Fiscal policy and monetary policy ·
Monetary policy in perspective

Under-standing Macro-economics

1

Introduction

When I first studied economics (in the late 1930's), my textbook, which was large and fat, covered Prices and the Factors of Production and Distribution and expounded in its 700 pages, the bulk of what was then considered to be "economics." Yet, amazing as it may seem, in those pages was nothing whatsoever about National Income or Unemployment or Economic Growth. There was, to be sure, a chapter headed "Business Cycles," which concluded in a half-page section entitled "Desirability of Elimination of the Business Cycle" (this, in 1936, with 10,000,000 unemployed!); but taking the text as a whole, it is fair to say that the subject of the book you are about to read simply did not exist.

This was not, let me hasten to say, because the author of the text in question was singularly blind. It was, rather, typical of a kind of myopia that affected all economists in those days. For more than a century they had developed economics into a supposedly powerful tool of social inquiry. Yet, in retrospect, it was as if they had studied every part of the social vehicle except what went on under the hood. Hence, when the economic mechanism came to a grinding halt in the Great Depression, the result was not only an immense social tragedy but an absolutely numbing intellectual shock.

More than thirty years have passed since those terrifying days *in which no one could explain why the economic mechanism was not working.* They have been the most important years for the development of economic thought since Adam Smith first laid down the classical outlines of the subject in 1776. For in the very year in which I started to study economics, a new understanding of economic problems began to shoulder aside the old. Within a year of my entrance into college, fierce debates were raging in the corridors; a year later, the textbook on which I had cut my teeth was being busily revised; and by the time I

1

graduated, the man who had written it had himself become the most distinguished American advocate of the new ideas themselves—ideas that would have been totally foreign to him four years before.

In those days we called the revolution in economic thought Keynesianism, after the name of the brilliant Englishmen, John Maynard Keynes, who was its originator.* For a while, Keynes and his economic ideas seemed dangerously close to heresy; I remember faces empurpled and voices shaking over such blasphemies as that, under certain circumstances, the attempt to save might redound to the disbenefit of a nation, or that wage cuts might not result in an increase in employment. Today those passionate debates seem very distant. The shock has gone out of Keynesianism, the awkwardly formulated ideas have been refined, the unfamiliar terminology accepted. We are all Keynesians now, as one frequently hears said, except that we call the new approach macroeconomics.

What is macroeconomics? As the name suggests, it is the study of large-scale economic problems: employment and unemployment, prosperity and recession, growth and decline—in short, the very problems that were so egregiously lacking from the text of my freshman days. Another way of describing it is to say that it represents the distillation of thirty odd years of very intent work under the hood. Still another way is to call it our best assurance that the tragedy of the Great Depression will never recur.

Is that assurance well-founded? Or could it be that another generation will find the concerns of this text as remote and irrelevant as those of my first were to me? It is possible. Already it is clear that the great economic issues of the future are likely to be the struggle of the backward countries, the rescue (or the death) of our cities, the uses and the abuses of our affluence. These are all issues that are only tangentially macroeconomic. That is to say, we could solve the problem of a high level of production and employment and still fail to solve the problems of underdevelopment, of urban poverty and decay, of a high standard of living as well as a high standard of life. These failures could be equally as catastrophic as that of the Depression itself.

Nonetheless, I think it is also true that a successful solution to these looming problems of the future must assume that we will keep our economy moving ahead at a fast rate of speed—that we will not suffer another Depression or even a series of smaller recessions. Macroeconomics may not provide many of the answers we need in order to cope with the future, but it provides the precondition without which the answers are not likely to be found. Understanding macroeconomics is not the last, but it is the indispensable first step toward controlling our social destiny.

*The name is pronounced to rhyme with Kanes, not Keenes.

2

The feeling that great matters are at stake gives the subject its special excitement, an excitement that it deserves—for they are.

Yet it is just because macroeconomics is so concerned with our collective destiny that I must add one more word before we come to grips with the subject itself. Most students who first approach economics are motivated by a desire to know more about the particular problems with which it is concerned—riches and poverty, prosperity and depression, automation or whatever. This is precisely the right attitude with which to approach it. Yet it is well to make clear at the outset that the *method* of economics is not that of description. Someone who wants a telling account of what life is like for the poor, or of the ways in which technology is entering our lives, must turn to books other than this one. This is not because the description of these problems is not of great value and importance. It is rather that very few economic problems will yield to our efforts to correct them if we can do no more than describe them. However urgent these problems may be, until we have understood their roots, our efforts to ameliorate them will be, as often as not, in vain; and the effort to understand their roots forces us to look away from their particular circumstances to the underlying system out of which they arise.

Hence this book is directed first of all at giving us a picture of society as a vast, intricate—and yet comprehensible—social mechanism. What we will try to learn about that mechanism are not the facts and figures of particular economic issues or of a particular year's problems, but the meshing of the gears that power and the construction of the girders that sustain the whole. Processes and relationships will command our attention first; then issues and problems. For once we have acquired a systematic grasp of the way our economy is constructed, it will not be difficult to fit the newspaper headlines into our over-all knowledge, nor to infuse our intelligence with feeling.

Yet, to learn something of the grand mechanics of a society requires a special effort, perhaps even a touch of a special gift. It is seemingly a very small effort, a very minor gift; but on it, more than anything else, hinges the ability to understand how the economic system operates. That effort is the willingness to abandon our familiar vantage point on economic life for a new and sometimes disconcerting one. It is our capacity to leave behind an acquaintance with the economic scene as individual participants, and to enter upon a new view from which we can see all our economic activities at once, simultaneously and collectively—a view that embraces not the actions of a single person or firm or town, but that looks out over an entire society. Of all the intellectual demands made by economics, this first leap to the economist's perch is perhaps the most difficult. But it is also the most necessary, for only after we have gained this lofty vantage point can we begin to see the extraordinary panorama with which economics deals.

3

2

Wealth and output

What is "macroeconomics"? The word derives from the Greek *macro* meaning "big," and the implication is therefore that it is concerned with bigger problems than in microeconomics (*micro* = small). Yet, the difference is really not one of scale. It is one of approach, of original angle of incidence. *Macroeconomics begins from a viewpoint that initially draws our attention to aggregate economic phenomena and processes,* such as gross national product or saving and investment. Microeconomics begins from a vantage point that first directs our analysis to the individual constituents of economic behavior, mainly the actions of individuals and firms. Both views are needed to comprehend the economy as a whole, just as it takes two different lenses to make a stereophoto jump into the round. But we can learn only one view at a time, and so, in this book, let us turn to the exciting spectacle of the entire national economy as it unfolds to the macroscopic gaze.

What does the economy look like from this perspective? The view is not unlike that from a plane. What we see first is the fundamental tableau of nature—the fields and forests, lakes and seas, with their inherent riches; then the diverse artifacts of man—the cities and towns, the road and rail networks, the factories and machines, the stocks of half-completed or unsold goods; and finally the human actors themselves with all their skills and talents, their energies, their social organization.

Thus our perspective shows us a vast panorama from which we single out for our special attention those elements and activities having to do with our worldly well-being, with our capacity to provide ourselves with the necessaries and luxuries of material life. It need hardly be said that this is at best only a partial view of society. An economist does not examine the flux of social goings-on, the quality of intellectual life, the spirituality or crassness of a community. Initially, at any rate, he

5

concerns himself with only those aspects of society that bear on its *material provisioning*, and even here he often limits himself to things that he can measure in some fairly objective way.

The national wealth

Let us, then, begin to set our first economic impressions in order by directing our attention to an attribute of the landscape below us that is clearly important in the provisioning process, and that should be subject to roughly accurate measurement—our national wealth. By our wealth, we mean the very objects—or at least many of them—that have already caught our eye. Table 2-1 is a preliminary estimate made of the national wealth of the United States for the year 1966.

Let us note immediately that this is not a full valuation of the riches of our society. No monetary worth is put on our human skills or even on the presence of so many head of population. Nor does this table pretend

TABLE 2 • 1   UNITED STATES NATIONAL WEALTH: 1966 VALUE*

	(Billions of dollars)
Structures	
Residential	603
Business	317
Government	300
Equipment	
Producers (machines, factories, etc.)	285
Consumers durables (autos, appliances)	290
Inventories, business	182
Monetary gold and silver	17
Land	
Farm	145
Residential	113
Business	96
Public	59
Net foreign assets	49
TOTAL	2,456

Source: Goldsmith and Lipsey, *Studies in the National Balance Sheet of the United States,* I. Table 1, extended to 1966 by J. W. Kendrick in *Finance* magazine (Jan., 1967), p. 13.
*Rather than encumber each table with sources that are, for the most part, identical, I have added the source only if the figures might be difficult to find or if they are the result of considerable arithmetical manipulation. All unidentified figures will be found in one or more of the following basic sourcebooks: *Historical Statistics of the United States* and *Statistical Abstract of the United States,* 1965, both published by the Bureau of the Census, Washington, D.C., and "Revised Estimates of the United States Income and Product Accounts," as reported in *Survey of Current Business* (August, 1965), Department of Commerce, and in subsequent *Economic Indicators,* Joint Economic Committee.

to embrace, much less measure, all our material possessions. Such immense economic treasures as the contents of the Library of Congress or the Patent Office cannot be accurately valued. Nor can works of art, nor military equipment—neither of which is included in the total. Much of our public land is valued at no more than nominal amounts. Hence at best this is the roughest of estimates. Nonetheless, it gives us an idea of the magnitude of the economic endowment that we have at our disposal.

It would perhaps be a much more meaningful idea if we could now compare our own national wealth with that of a poor nation, such as India, or more precisely, compare the *per capita* value of our wealth —that is, the share of our wealth that is available to each of us—to the *per capita* wealth of India. Alas, as is so often the case with the less-developed countries, such statistics do not exist for India. But perhaps we can get a glimmering of what such a comparison might show by comparing a few items for which we do have figures.

It is clear enough that if we could total up all the items in both nations, the scales would tilt overwhelmingly in favor of the United States. That

TABLE 2 • 2   COMPARATIVE WEALTH STATISTICS, INDIA AND UNITED STATES, RECENT YEARS*

	United States	India
	Per 1,000 people	
Rooms, residential	1430	340
Motor vehicles in use	422	1
Telephones	430	1
Radios	944	5

*Years vary; see source: *Statistical Abstract,* 1965.

this has an immense significance for the relative well-being of the two countries is apparent. However, let us defer a consideration of exactly what that significance is, until we look a little more closely into the nature of national wealth itself.

Capital

One portion of the endowment of a nation's wealth has a special significance. This is its national *capital*—the portion of its productive wealth that is *man-made* and therefore *reproducible.* If we look back at the table, we can see that our own national capital in 1966 consisted of the sum total of all our structures, our producers' equipment and our consumer durables, our inventories, our monetary gold and silver, and our foreign assets—$2043 billions in all.

We can think of this national capital as consisting of whatever has been preserved out of the sum total of everything that has ever been produced from the very beginning of the economic history of the United States up to a certain date—here December 31, 1966. Some of that capital—inventories for example—might be used up the very next day. On the other hand, inventories might also be increased. In fact, our national capital changes from date to date, as we do add to our inventories or to our stocks of equipment or structures, etc., or, more rarely, as we consume them and do not replace them. But at any date, our capital still represents *all that the nation has produced*—yesterday or a century ago—*and that it has not used up or destroyed.*

The reason that we identify our national capital within the larger frame of our wealth is that it is constantly changing and usually growing. Not that a nation's inheritance of natural resources is unimportant; indeed, the ability of a people to build capital depends to no small degree on the bounties or obstacles offered by its geography and geology—think of the economic limitations imposed by desert and ice on the Bedouin and the Eskimo. But the point in singling out our capital is that it represents the portion of our total national endowment over which we have the most immediate control. As we shall later see, much of a nation's current economic fortunes is intimately related to the rate at which it is adding to its capital wealth.

Wealth and claims

There remains to be noted one more thing before we leave the subject of wealth. In our table of national wealth, two items are missing that would be the very first to be counted in an inventory of our personal wealth: our bank accounts and our financial assets, such as stocks or bonds or deeds or mortgages. Why are these all-important items of personal wealth excluded from our summary of national wealth?

The answer to this seeming paradox is not hard to find. We have already counted the *things*—the houses, factories, machines, etc.,—that constitute the real assets behind stocks, bonds, deeds, and the like. Indeed these certificates tell us only who *owns* the various items of our national capital. Stocks and bonds and mortgages and deeds are *claims* on assets, but they are not those assets in themselves. The reality of General Motors is its physical plant and its going organization, not the shares of stock that organization has issued. If by some curious mischance all its shares disintegrated, General Motors would still be there; but if the plants and the organization disintegrated instead, the shares would not magically constitute for us another enterprise.

So, too, with our bank accounts. The dollars we spend or hold in our accounts are part of our personal wealth only insofar as they command goods or services. The value of coin or currency as "objects" is much less than their official and legal value as money. But most of the goods over which our money exerts its claims (although not, it must be admitted, the services it also buys) are already on our balance sheet. To count our money as part of national wealth would thus be to count a claim as if it were an asset, much as in the case of stocks and bonds.

Why, then, do we have an item for monetary gold and silver (mainly gold) in our table of national wealth? The answer is that under existing international arrangements, foreigners will accept gold in exchange for their own real assets (whereas they are not bound to accept our dollar bills) and that, therefore, monetary gold gives us a claim against *foreign* wealth.* In much the same way, the item of *net foreign assets* represents the value of real assets located in other nations but owned by U.S. citizens, less the value of any real wealth located in the United States and owned by foreigners.

Thus we reach a very important final conclusion. *National wealth is not quite the same thing as the sum of personal wealth*. When we add up our individual wealth, we include first of all our holdings of money or stocks or bonds—all items that are excluded from our national register of wealth. The difference is that as individuals we properly consider our own wealth to be the *claims* we have against one another, whereas as a society we consider our wealth to be the stock of material *assets* we possess, and the only claims we consider are those that we may have against other societies. National wealth is a *real* phenomenon, the tangible consequence of past production. Financial wealth, on the other hand—the form in which individuals hold their wealth—is only the way the claims of ownership are established vis-à-vis the underlying real assets of the community. The contrast between the underlying, slow-changing reality of national wealth and the overlying, sometimes fast-changing financial representation of that wealth is one of the differences between economic life viewed from the vantage point of the economist and that same life seen through the eyes of a participant in the process. We shall encounter many more such contrasts as our study proceeds.

Wealth and output

But why is national wealth so important? Exactly what is the connection between the wealth of nations and the well-being of their citizens?

The question is not an idle one, for the connection between wealth and well-being is not a matter of direct physical cause and effect. After all, India has the largest inventory of livestock in the world, but its contribution to Indian living standards is far less than that of our live-

*Gold has, of course, a value in itself—we can use it for jewelry and for dentistry. However, in the balance sheet of our national wealth, we value the gold at its international exchange price, rather than merely as a commodity.

stock wealth. Or again, our national capital in 1933 was not significantly different from that in 1929, but one year was marked by widespread misery and the other by booming prosperity. Clearly then, the existence of great physical wealth by itself does not guarantee—it only holds out the possibility of—a high standard of living. It is only insofar as wealth interacts with the working population that it exerts its enormous economic leverage, and this interaction is not a mechanical phenomenon that we can take for granted, but a complex *social* process, whose motivations we must explore.

As the example of Indian livestock indicates, local customs and beliefs can effectively sterilize the potential physical benefits of wealth. Perhaps we should generalize that conclusion by observing that the political and social system will have a primary role in causing an effective or ineffective use of existing wealth. Compare the traditional hoarding of gold or gems in many backward societies with the possibility of their disposal to produce foreign exchange for the purchase of machinery.

In a modern industrial society, we take for granted some kind of effective social and political structure. Then why do we at times make vigorous use of our existing material assets and at other times seem to put them to little or no use? Why do we have "good times" and "bad times"? The question directs our attention back to the panorama of society to discover something further about its economic operation.

The factors of production

This time, our gaze fastens on a different aspect of the tableau. Rather than noticing our stock of wealth, we note the result of our use of that wealth, a result we can see emerging in the form of a *flow of production.*
How does this flow of production arise? We can see that it comes into being as man combines his energies with his natural and man-made environment. To assist us in understanding this crucial process, we classify the cooperating elements in the production process into three categories.

Into the first of these we put the resources of nature itself—the land and waters and their riches—and to this essential element in production we give the name Land. Into a second category we place those man-made artifacts that are of such vital importance in nearly every economic activity. To these we give the name Capital. And finally, to human activity in the economic process, however simple or complicated, we give the title Labor. These three categories, Land, Capital, and Labor, we call the *factors of production. It is* a useful term, for it enables us to sum up in a phrase the component agencies needed to bring about production.

The social meaning of the factors of production

We will be speaking of the factors of production throughout this book, but we should not leave them in this introduction without making clear one further point. When we speak of combining land, labor, and capital, we are really talking about two related, and yet distinct, things. Partly we refer to the *physical* combination of the soil or its wealth, of machines, buildings, and so on, and of human effort. This engineering aspect of production is, needless to say, of great importance. But when we talk about "the factors of production," we do not mean only this technical side of things. We mean also that different *social* functions have to be combined in various ways, if the production process is to be carried out.

For in our society, land, labor, and capital are all privately owned. This is not true in every society. In some tribal societies, for instance, land is communally owned and not available for purchase or rent from a single owner. In many societies in history, labor has been performed by serfs or slaves who did not "own" their labor in the sense of being able to offer it as free agents for a price. Today, in the communist countries, capital and land are both usually owned by the state, and not by a private person. Only in our kind of economic society—capitalism—are the great bulk of the physical agencies of production privately owned.

Hence when we speak of combining the factors of production, we are speaking not only of a process of engineering, but also of a *social process* —a system of rewards and penalties, sanctions and inducements that motivates the owners of the physical agencies to offer their services for use in the production process.

Micro- and macroeconomics

Much of economics is an attempt to analyze how a society of privately owned land, labor, and capital (each possessing its particular physical attributes) will in fact be combined into production. When economics focuses its study on the individual agents of the process, the individual owner of labor or capital or land, or when it highlights the manner in which a typical entrepreneur organizes land, labor, and capital in his firm, we call the resulting study *microeconomics*. When, however, economics opens its lens to the widest possible extent, to study not so much the individual participant in the production process but the total activity of all participants, we call the study *macroeconomics*.

We will not venture into the world of microeconomics, the world of the individual entrepreneur or the individual consumer or worker, but we must understand something of the background against which both the micro- and the macroeconomic processes work. This is the presence of an *all-embracing market* on which the factors can offer their services —the landowner offering the use of his land; the capitalist, the use of his capital; the worker, the use of his labor—a market on which, as well, the entrepreneur can bid for these services. On this vast market, not only are the *services* of the factors bought and sold, as entrepreneurs hire labor, rent land, and borrow capital; but the *products* created by these employed factors are also sold here by the entrepreneurs.

This ubiquitous market network, where both factors of production, and goods and services are bought and sold, is an essential feature of our economic system. Like private property, however, it should not be too easily taken for granted. Many economies do not have a highly developed market network. Traditional societies in the underdeveloped world, for instance, often have no real market for labor, so that village laborers do not earn *wages* determined by the supply of, and demand for, their labor, but are paid a sum determined by long-standing custom or by some powerful personage. In the same way, some societies do not have a market for land—feudalism, for instance, did not—so that landlords do not earn a rent determined by the supply and demand for land, but simply expropriate a traditional share of the crops grown on their holdings. Or again, markets for capital may not exist (as in the U.S.S.R.), so that no one will earn interest or profit for making his capital available to an entrepreneur.

Our introduction to the factors of production has thus given us insight into much more than just the possibility of classifying the variety of economic activity into the simple categories of land, labor, and capital. In turn, these categories have told us something of the historic evolution of our society and have alerted us to its all-important institutions of private property and the market.

The flow of production

We have lingered long enough over the factors. Now let us move on to watch the process for whose clarification we originally stopped to classify the factors themselves.

We have learned, in our new vocabulary, that production takes place by the combination of the services of the factors of production organized through the marketplace. Now what happens to that flow of production as it leaves the hands of the entrepreneurs who brought it into existence?

It may help us picture the flow as a whole if we imagine that each and every good and service that is produced—each loaf of bread, each nut and bolt, each doctor's call, each theatrical performance, each car, ship, lathe, or bolt of cloth—can be identified in the way that a radioactive isotope allows us to follow the circulation of certain kinds of cells through the body. Then if we look down on the economic panorama, we can see the continuous combination of land, labor, and capital giving off a continuous flow of "lights" as goods and services emerge in their saleable form.

Where do these lights go? Many, as we can see, are soon extinguished. The goods or services they represent have been incorporated into other products to form more fully finished items of output. Thus from our aerial perspective we can follow a product such as cotton from the fields to the spinning mill, where its light is extinguished, for there the cotton disappears into a new product: yarn. In turn, the light of the yarn traces a path as it leaves the spinning mill by way of sale to the textile mill, there to be doused as the yarn disappears into a new good: cloth. And again, the cloth leaving the textile mill lights a way to the factory where it will become part of an article of clothing.

The consumption flow

And what of the clothing? Here at last we have what the economist calls a *final good*. Why "final"? Because once in the possession of its ultimate owner, the clothing passes out of the active economic flow. As a good in the hands of a consumer, it is no longer an object on the marketplace. Its light is now extinguished permanently — or if we wish to complete our image, we can imagine it fading gradually as the clothing "disappears" into the use and pleasure, the so-called utility, of the consumer. In the case of consumer goods like food, or of consumer services like recreation, the light goes out faster, for these items are literally "consumed" when they reach their final destination.

We shall have a good deal to learn in later chapters about the behavior of consumers. What we should notice in this first macroeconomic view is the supreme importance of this flow of production into consumers' hands. This is the vital process by which the population replenishes or increases its energies and ministers to its wants and needs; it is a process that, if halted for very long, would cause a society to perish. That is why we speak of consumption as the ultimate end and aim of all economic activity.

The investment flow

Nevertheless, for all the importance of consumption, if we look down on the illuminated flow of output we see a surprising thing. Whereas the greater portion of the final goods and services of the economy is bought by the human agents of production for their consumption, we also find that a lesser but still considerable flow of final products is not. What happens to it?

If we follow an appropriate good, we may find out. Let us watch the destination of the steel that leaves a Pittsburgh mill. Some of it, like our cotton cloth, will become incorporated into consumers' goods, ending up as cans, automobiles, or household articles of various kinds. But some steel will not find its way to a consumer at all; instead, it will end up as part of a machine or an office building or a railroad track.

Now in a way, these goods are not "final," for they are used to produce still further goods or services—the machine producing output of some kind, the building producing office space, the rail track producing transportation. Yet there is a difference between such goods, used for production, and consumer goods, like clothing. The difference is that the machine, the office building, and the track are goods that are used by business enterprises as part of their productive equipment. As a result, they are usually carefully maintained and replaced as they wear out. In terms of our image, these goods slowly lose their light-giving powers as their services pass into flows of production, but usually they are replaced with new goods before their light is totally extinguished. That is why we call them *capital goods* in distinction to consumers' goods. As part of our capital, they will be preserved, maintained, and renewed, perhaps indefinitely. Hence *the stock of capital, like consumers, constitutes a final destination for output.* *

Gross and net investment

We call the great stream of output that goes to capital *gross investment.* The very word *gross* suggests that it conceals a finer breakdown; and looking more closely, we can see that the flow of output going to capital does indeed serve two distinct purposes. Part of it is used to replace the capital—the machines, the buildings, the track, or whatever—that has been used up in the process of production. Just as the human agents of production have to be replenished by a flow of consumption goods, so the material agents of production need to be maintained and renewed if their contribution to output is to remain undiminished. We call the part of gross investment, whose purpose is to keep society's stock of capital intact, *replacement investment,* or simply *replacement.*

Sometimes the total flow of output going to capital is not large enough to maintain the existing stock—for instance, if we allow inventories (a form of capital) to become depleted, or if we simply fail to replace

*We might note that some products, like automobiles, possess characteristics of both consumption goods and capital goods. We call such goods *consumer durables;* and unlike ordinary goods (such as clothing) held by consumers, we include them in our inventory of national wealth (see Table 2-1. p. 2).

worn-out equipment or plant. We call this running-down of capital *disinvestment*, meaning by the phrase the very opposite of investment: instead of building up capital, we are literally consuming it.

Not all gross investment is used for replacement purposes, however. Some of the flow may *increase* the stock of capital, adding machines, buildings, track, and so on. If the total output consigned to capital is sufficiently great not only to make up for wear and tear, but to increase the capital stock, we say there has been *new* or *net investment*, or *net capital formation.**

One last important point. Who normally buys these additions to our capital wealth? In the main, the purchasers are business firms who seek to increase their holdings of machines and buildings and equipment of various kinds. Since additions to business capital are additions to our nation's wealth, and since with more wealth we would expect to be able to produce still more goods and services, the act of business investment immediately stands out as a key element in the study of macroeconomics. In-fact, as we shall see, in many ways the process and the problems of business investment will be a central point of focus in macroeconomic analysis.

Consumption and investment

A simple diagram may help us picture the flows of output we have been discussing.

Figure 2-1 calls to our attention three important attributes of the economic system.

1. It emphasizes the essential *circularity*, the self-renewing, self-feeding nature of the production flow. This circularity is a feature of the macroeconomic process to which we will return again and again.

2. It illumines a basic choice that all economic societies must make: *a choice between consumption and investment.* For the split flow of production reveals that every good entering the capital stream cannot

---

*Sometimes it helps to have a homely picture in mind to keep things straight. The difference between replacement and net investment is made clear by using as an example the paving of streets. Each year some streets wear out, and we have to repave them to keep them passable. This is clearly *investment*, but it does not add to our ability to enjoy surface transportation. Hence it is solely *replacement* investment. Only when we build *additional* streets do we undertake new or net investment. Also, sometimes we build a new street but allow an old one to deteriorate beyond usability. Now we have to offset the new investment with the *disinvestment* in our now unpassable road. Whether or not we have any net investment in street building as a whole depends on whether we have added or subtracted from street capacity when we consider the net investment and the disinvestment together.

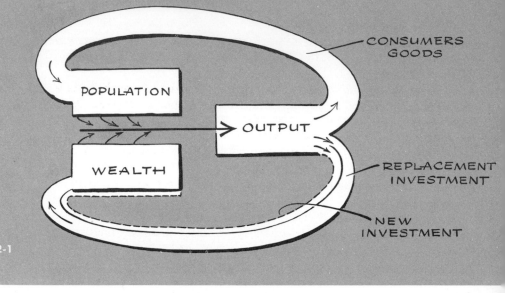

FIG. 2-1

also be in the consumption stream. At any given level of output, consumption and investment are, so to speak, rivals for the current output of society.

3. Finally, it makes clear that *society can invest* (that is, add to its capital) *only the output that it refrains from consuming.* We call this relinquishing of consumption *saving*, and saving thus becomes an economic act located at the very core of the wealth-creation process. For the economic meaning of saving, as our diagram shows, is to release resources from consumption so that they can be used for the building of capital. Whether they *will* be so used is a matter that will occupy us through many subsequent chapters.

Gross national product

There remains but one preliminary matter before we proceed to a closer examination of the actual determinants of the flow of production. We have seen that the annual output of the nation is a revealing measure of its well-being, for it reflects the degree of interaction between the population and its wealth. Later we shall also find output to be a major determinant of employment. Hence it behooves us to examine the nature and general character of this flow and to become familiar with its nomenclature and composition.

We call the dollar value of the total annual output of final goods and services in the nation its gross national product. The gross national product (or GNP as it is usually abbreviated) is thus nothing but the dollar value of the total output of all consumption goods and of all investments goods. As such we are already familiar with its general meaning. At this juncture, however, we must define GNP a little more precisely.

1. GNP *includes only final goods*. We are interested, through the concept of GNP, in measuring the value of the *ultimate* production of the economic system—that is, the total value of all goods and services *enjoyed by its consumers or accumulated as new or replacement capital*. Hence we do not count intermediate goods. For example, we do not add up the value of the cottom *and* the yarn *and* the cloth *and* the final clothing when we compute the value of GNP. That kind of multiple counting might be very useful if we wanted certain information about our total economic activity, but it would not tell us accurately about the final value of output. For when we buy a shirt, the price we pay already includes the cost of the cloth to the shirtmaker; and in turn, the amount the shirtmaker paid for his cloth already included the cost of the yarn; and in turn, again, the seller of yarn included in his price the amount he paid for raw cotton. Embodied in the price of the shirt, therefore, is the value of all the intermediate products that went into it. Thus in figuring the value for GNP, we add only the values of all final goods, both for consumption and for investment purposes. Note as well that GNP only includes a given year's production of goods and services. Therefore sales of used car dealers, antique dealers, etc., are not included, because the value of these goods was already picked up in the GNP of the year they were produced.

2. *There are four categories of final goods*. In our first view of macroeconomic activity we divided the flow of output into two great streams: consumption and gross investment. Now, for purposes of a closer analysis, we impose a few refinements on this basic scheme.

First we must pay heed to a small flow of production that has previously escaped our notice. This is the net flow of goods or services that leaves this country; that is, the total flow going abroad minus the flow that enters. This international branch of our economy has its proper name: *net exports*. Because these net exports are a kind of investment (they are goods we produce but do not consume), we must now rename the great bulk of investment that remains in this country. We will henceforth call it *gross private domestic investment*.

The word *private* brings us to a second refinement. It concerns a subflow of goods and services within both the great consumption stream and the investment branch of activity. These are the goods and services bought or produced by the government (as contrasted with consumers or businesses). Some of these may be consumers' goods—policemen's services, say—and some may be investment goods, such as roads or schools or dams. Conventionally, however, we include all public pur-

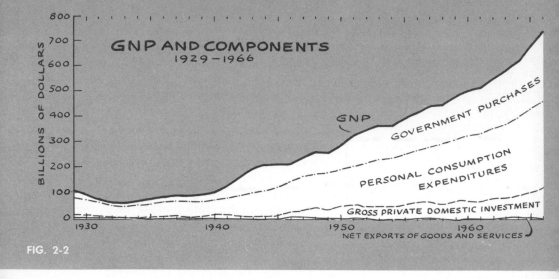

FIG. 2-2

GNP AND COMPONENTS
1929–1966

BILLIONS OF DOLLARS

GNP

GOVERNMENT PURCHASES

PERSONAL CONSUMPTION EXPENDITURES

GROSS PRIVATE DOMESTIC INVESTMENT

NET EXPORTS OF GOODS AND SERVICES

chases, whether for consumption or investment purposes, in a category called *government purchases of goods and services.*

This gives us four streams of "final" output, each going to a final purchaser of economic output. Therefore we can speak of gross national product as being the sum of consumption goods and services, gross private domestic investment, government purchases, and net exports, or (to abbreviate a long sentence) we can write that $\boxed{\text{GNP} = C + I + G + E.}$ This is a descriptive equation that should be remembered.

It helps, at this juncture, to look at GNP over the past decades. In Figure 2-2 we show the long irregular upward flow of GNP from 1929 to the present, with the four component streams of expenditures visible. Later we will be talking at length about the behavior of each stream, but first we need to be introduced to the over-all flow itself.

Cautions about GNP

GNP is an indispensable concept in dealing with the performance of our economy, but it is well to understand the weaknesses as well as the strengths of this most important single economic indicator. There are four of them.

1. *GNP deals in dollar values, not in physical units.* That is, it does not tell us how many goods and services were produced, but only what their sales value was. Trouble then arises when we compare the GNP of one year with that of another, to determine whether or not the nation is better off. For if prices in the second year are higher, GNP will be higher, even though the actual volume of output is unchanged.

We can correct for this price change very easily when all prices have moved in the same degree or proportion. Then it is easy to speak of

18

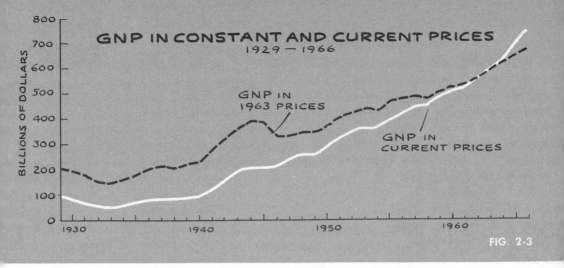

GNP IN CONSTANT AND CURRENT PRICES
1929 — 1966

GNP IN 1963 PRICES

GNP IN CURRENT PRICES

BILLIONS OF DOLLARS

FIG. 2-3

"real" GNP—that is, the current money value of GNP adjusted for price changes—as reflecting the actual rise or fall of output. The price problem becomes more difficult, however, when prices change in different degrees or even in different directions, as they often do. Then a comparison of "real" GNP from one year to the next, and especially over a long span of years, is unavoidably arbitrary to some extent.

Figure 2-3 shows us the previous totals for GNP corrected as best we can for price changes. In this chart, 1963 is used as the "base," and the GNP's of other years are raised or lowered so that price changes are eliminated to the greatest possible extent. One can, of course, choose any year for a base. Although the basic dollar measuring rod will then change, the profile of "real" changes year to year will be the same.

2. *GNP does not reflect changes in the quality of output*. The second weakness of GNP also involves its inaccuracy as an indicator of "real" trends over time. This time the difficulty revolves around the changes in the utility (or use and pleasure-producing capabilities) of goods and services. In a technologically advancing society, goods are usually improved from one decade to the next, or even more rapidly; and in an urbanizing, increasingly high-density society, the utility of other goods may be lessened over time. An airplane trip today, for example, is certainly highly preferable to one taken twenty or thirty years ago; a subway ride is not. Thus, to the extent that the quality of most goods and services improve, and as some deteriorate, GNP misrepresents the true value of output, especially over long stretches of time.

3. *GNP does not reflect the purpose of production*. A third difficulty with GNP lies in its blindness to the ultimate use of production. If in one year GNP rises by a billion dollars owing to an increase in expenditure on education, and in another year it rises by the same amount because of a rise in cigarette purchases, the figures in each case show

19

the same amount of "growth" of GNP. Even output that turns out to be wide of the mark or totally wasteful—such as the famous Edsel car that no one wanted or military weapons that are obsolete from the moment they appear—all are counted as part of GNP.

Thus, GNP gives us only a very rough indication of the *quality* of life. That is why comparisons of GNP today and fifty or one hundred years ago—comparisons that show Americans today enjoying a vastly greater output than did their forebears—should not be interpreted to mean that life is therefore that much "better."

4. *GNP does not include most goods and services that are not for sale.* Presumably GNP tells us how large our final output is. Yet it does not include one of the most important kinds of work and sources of consumer pleasure—the labor of wives in maintaining their households. Yet, curiously, if this labor were paid for—that is, if we engaged cooks and maids and babysitters instead of depending on our wives for these services, GNP *would* include their services as final output, since they would be purchased on the market. But the labor of wives being unpaid, it is excluded from GNP.*

The difficulty here is that we are constantly moving toward purchasing "outside" services in place of home services—laundries, bakeries, restaurants, etc., all perform work that used to be performed at home. Thus the process of *monetizing* activity gives an upward trend to GNP statistics which is not fully mirrored in actual output.

A related problem is that some parts of GNP are paid for by some members of the population and not by others. Rent, for example, measures the services of landlords for homeowners and is therefore included in GNP, but what of the man who owns his own home and pays no rent? Similarly, what of the family that grows some part of its food at home, and therefore does not pay for it? In order to include such items of "free" consumption into GNP, the statisticians of the Commerce Department add an "imputed" value figure to include goods and services like these not tallied on a cash register.

These problems lead economists to treat GNP in a gingerly fashion. We should remember that comparisons between GNP's are more trustworthy for two close years than for two distant ones (prices and qualities are not apt to have changed so much in the shorter span of time); and that GNP is, at best, an imperfect measure of real final output and a still less dependable indicator of ultimate well-being.

With all these cautions we have found no better way of summarizing

---

*This gives rise to an amusing anomaly. Every time a man marries his cook, GNP declines by the amount of the wages he formerly paid her, even though her cooking may continue, and even if he pays her an allowance as large as her wages. Allowances are not presumed to cover "productive services" and therefore are not picked up in GNP.

the over-all performance of the economy. GNP is a yardstick of economic activity used by every nation in the world. It has become a term familiar to every congressman and editorial writer, although not many of them could describe very clearly exactly what it means. Hence, let us turn to a closer study of the gross national product by examining how it is actually generated and maintained.

Summary

1. *Macroeconomics* is not a separate part of economics, but an *approach to economic problems* through the study of certain aggregate processes.
2. We begin the study of macroeconomic processes by observing how a *flow of output comes from human resources interacting with our national wealth* (the most important part of which is our capital).
3. We note that capital consists *of real things,* and *not of the financial claims against those things.*
4. The flow of output shows us *the circular nature of the process of production.* From the interaction of population and wealth emerges a stream of goods going back to replenish consumers (consumption goods) and a stream to replenish and add to our capital wealth (gross investment).
5. A study of the flow of output and its division into consumption and investment emphasizes the essential choice that must be made between these *two basic uses of output.*
6. The investment flow can be subdivided into two: one flow *replaces or renews capital* that has been worn out or used up. This is *replacement investment.* The other flow *adds to the stock of capital wealth,* and is called *new* or *net capital* or *investment.* The two flows together are called *gross investment.*
7. The name for the total flow of output is *gross national product.* It is usually divided into four major categories:
   - *Consumption* (C), or the goods and services going to consumers.
   - *Gross private domestic investment* (I), or that portion of output going to private businesses as replacements for, and additions to, their real domestic capital.
   - *Government purchases* (G), or those goods, both consumers' and capital, bought by all public agencies.
   - *Net exports* (E), the net outflow of goods to other countries.
   - The formula $GNP = C + I + G + E$ conveniently summarizes these four subdivisions.
8. Note that GNP counts only the dollar value of *final goods* and services in each of these categories. Intermediate goods are not counted, since their value is included in the value of final goods.
9. GNP is an indispensable concept in macroeconomics. Nonetheless, it must be used with caution.
   - GNP deals in *dollar values, not physical units.* This can lead to problems in adjusting price changes from year to year so that GNP accurately reflects changes in output.
   - GNP does not show changes in the *quality* of output.

- GNP does not reveal the composition of output.
- GNP figures do not include output that is not for sale.

Thus, comparisons from year to year should be made with caution, especially when the years are very far apart.

Questions

1. Why is capital so important a part of national wealth? Why is money not considered capital?

2. What is meant by the "circularity" of the economic process? Does it have something to do with the output of the system being returned to it as fresh inputs?

3. What is meant by net investment? by gross investment? What is the difference?

4. Write the basic formula for GNP and state *carefully* the exact names of each of the four constituents of GNP.

5. Suppose we had an island economy with an output of 100 tons of grain, each ton selling for $100. If it is the only product sold, what is the value of GNP? Now suppose that production stays the same, but that prices rise to $150. What is GNP now? How could we "correct" for the price rise? If we didn't, would GNP be an accurate measure of output from one year to the next?

6. Presumably, the quality of most products improves over time. If their price is unchanged, does that mean that GNP understates or overstates the real value of output?

7. When more and more consumers buy "do-it-yourself" kits, does the value of GNP (which includes the sale price of these kits) under- or overstate the true final output of the nation?

8. Do you think that we should develop measures other than GNP to indicate changes in our basic well-being? What sorts of measures?

9. What is an intermediate good, and why are such goods not included in the value of GNP? Is coal sold to a utility company an intermediate good? Coal sold to a consumer? Coal sold to the army? What determines whether a good will or will not be counted in the total of GNP?

3

Output and income

So far, we have talked about output as it emerges from the interaction of wealth and labor, but we have not inquired very deeply into the manner in which that interaction takes place. Yet the output of our economy does not spring forth "automatically" by the pursuit of changeless tradition, as is the case in simple preindustrial societies. Nor is it brought into being because the labor force is more or less forcibly combined with material resources, as is the case in collectivized economics. Rather, in our kind of society, output results from innumerable activities and decisions on the marketplace where men buy and sell, largely as they wish. What we must now understand is precisely how this daily activity of the marketplace gives rise to the flow of gross national product.

Output and demand

How does the market actually bring output into existence? How does it effect the combination of land, labor, and capital under the guidance of an entrepreneur? Any businessman will give you the answer. He will tell you that the crucial factor enabling him to perform his economic task (or in his language, "to run a business") is *demand* or *purchasing power;* that is, the presence of buyers who are willing and able to buy some good or service at the price for which he is willing to sell it.

But how does demand or purchasing power come into existence? If we ask any buyer, he will tell us that his dollars come to him because they are part of his *income* or his cash receipts.

But where, in turn, do the dollar receipts or incomes of buyers come from? If we inquire again, most buyers will tell us that they have money in their pockets because in one fashion or another they have contributed to the process of production; that is, because they have helped to make the output that is now being sold.

Thus our quest for the motive force behind the flow of production leads us in a great circle through the market system. We can see this in Fig. 3-1.

At the top of the circle we see payments flowing from the public to firms, thereby creating the demand that brings forth production. At the bottom of the circle, we see more payments, this time flowing from firms back to the public, as businesses hire the services of the various factors in order to carry out production. Thus we can see that there is a constant regeneration of demand as money is first spent by the public on the output of firms, and then in turn spent by firms for the services of the public.

An economic model

We must examine this chain of payments and receipts in great detail, for it contains the key to the operation of our economic system. First, however, we need a reminder about our method of inquiry. It must be obvious that it is impossible to depict the flux of buying and selling as it actually occurs on the marketplace of the nation. It would require us to fix in our minds more details than can be reported on all the financial pages of all the newspapers in the nation every day. Hence, to compre-

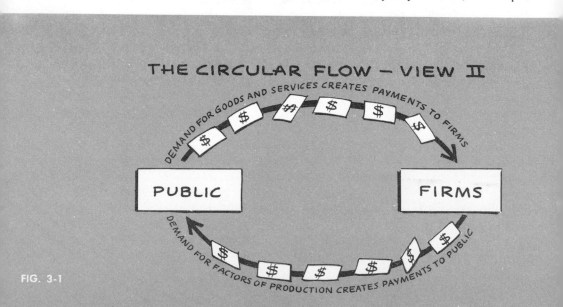

THE CIRCULAR FLOW — VIEW II

DEMAND FOR GOODS AND SERVICES CREATES PAYMENTS TO FIRMS

PUBLIC

FIRMS

DEMAND FOR FACTORS OF PRODUCTION CREATES PAYMENTS TO PUBLIC

FIG. 3-1

hend the basic processes of the economy, we must use a special method of reducing its confusion to understandable dimensions. This we do by extracting from the actual happenings of economic life those aspects that experience and analysis have taught us to regard as central and critical. From these crucial links and processes we then create an imaginary *model* of an economy that exhibits, in its operation, all the essential movements of its real-life counterpart. We shall find our model to be an indispensable guide to the complicated reality of economic life around us.

Our model, to begin with, will be a very simple one. We must, of course, exclude from it all the variety of life itself: the differences in personality of one man and another, the peculiar ways that one market differs from another, the distinctions that separate one firm from its competitor. We reduce our economy, in other words, to a colorless and abstract reproduction of life in which we can speak of general *kinds* of relationships without having to qualify each and every statement to accommodate each and every existing situation. Thus our model will call upon our capacity to think in that abstract manner which is so much a part of economic reasoning.

But our model will be simple not only in its disregard of "life." We must also simplify it, at first, by ruling out some of the very events to which we will later turn as the climax of our study. For instance, we shall ignore changes in *people's tastes,* so that we can assume that everyone will regularly buy the same kinds of goods. We shall ignore differences in the *structure of firms* or *markets,* so that we can forget about differences in competitive pressures. We shall rule out *population growth* and, even more important, *inventive progress,* so that we can deal with a very stable imaginary world. For the time being, we will exclude even *saving* and *net investment* (although of course we must permit replacement investment), so that we can ignore growth. Later, of course, we are to be deeply concerned with just such problems of dynamic change. But we shall not be able to come to grips with them until we have first understood an economic world as "pure" and changeless as possible.

Cost and output

The very abstract model we have created may seem too far removed from the real world to tell us much about its operation. But if we now go back to the circle of economic activity, in which payments to firms and factors become their incomes, and in turn reappear on the marketplace as demand, our model will enable us to explain a very important problem. *It is how an economy that has produced a given GNP is able to buy it back.*

This is by no means a self-evident matter. Indeed, one of the most common misconceptions about the flow of economic activity is that there will not be enough purchasing power to buy everything we have produced—that somehow we will fail to generate enough demand to keep up with the output of our factories. So it is well to understand once and for all how an economy can sustain a given level of production through its purchases on the market.

We start, then, with an imaginary economy in full operation. We can, if we wish, imagine it as having just produced its year's output, which is now sitting on the economic front doorstep looking for a buyer. What we must now see is whether it will be possible to *sell* this gross national product to the people who have been engaged in producing it. In other words, *we must ask whether there is enough income or receipts generated in the process of production to buy back all the products themselves.*

How does production create income? Businessmen do not think about "incomes" when they assemble the factors of production to meet the demand for their product. They worry about *cost.* All the money they pay out during the production process is paid under the heading of *cost,* whether it be wage or salary cost, cost of materials, depreciation cost, tax cost, or whatever. Thus it would seem that the concept of cost may offer us a useful point of entry into the economic chain. For *if we can show how all costs become incomes,* we will have taken a major step toward understanding whether our gross national product can in fact be sold to those who produced it.

A cost summary

It may help us if we begin by looking at the kinds of costs incurred by business firms in real life. Here is a hypothetical expense summary of General Manufacturing, which will serve as an example typical of all business firms, large or small. (If you will examine the year-end statements of any business, you will find that their costs all fall into one or more of the cost categories below.)

TABLE 3 • 1   GENERAL MANUFACTURING COST SUMMARY

Wages, salaries, and employee benefits	$100,000,000
Rental, interest, and profits payments	5,000,000
Materials, supplies, etc.	50,000,000
Taxes other than income	15,000,000
Depreciation	20,000,000

Factor costs and national income

Some of these costs we recognize immediately as payments to factors of production. The item for "wages and salaries" is obviously a payment to the factor *labor*. The item "interest" (perhaps not so obviously) is a payment to the factor *capital*—that is, to those who have lent the company money in order to help it carry on its productive operation. The item for rent is, of course, a payment for the rental of *land* or natural resources from their owners.

Note that we have included profits with rent and interest. In actual accounting practice, profits are not shown as an expense; for our purposes, however, it will be quite legitimate and very helpful to regard profits as a special kind of factor cost going to entrepreneurs for their risk-taking function. In our next chapter, we shall go a little more thoroughly into the matter of profits.

Two things strike us about these factor costs. First, it is clear that they represent payments that have been made to secure production. In more technical language, they are payments for factor inputs that result in commodity outputs. All the production actually carried on within the company, all the value it has added to the economy, has been compensated by the payments the company has made to land, labor, and capital. To be sure, the company has incurred other costs, for materials and taxes and depreciation, and we shall soon turn to these. But whatever production, or assembly, or distribution the company itself has carried out during the course of the year has required the use of land, labor, or capital. Thus *the total of its factor costs represents the value of the total new output that General Manufacturing by itself has given to the economy.*

From here it is but a simple step to add up all the factor costs paid out by *all* the companies in the economy, in order to measure the total new *value added* by all productive efforts in the year. This measure is called *national income* (or sometimes national income at factor cost).* As we can see, it is less than gross national product, for it does not include other costs of output; namely, certain taxes and depreciation.

Factor costs and household incomes

A second fact that strikes us is that *all factor costs are income payments*. The wages, salaries, interest, rents, etc., that were costs to the

---

*It might be well to add that not all production (and therefore not all national income) originates with companies. Governments also produce value, such as the output of firemen's services or of roads, and private individuals, like farmers or doctors, produce output as "proprietorships." For the purposes of exposition, however, we can think of government units or individual proprietorships as "companies" since they incur exactly the same kinds of costs.

company were income to its recipients. So are the profits, which will accrue as income to the owners of the business.

Thus, just as it sounds, national income means the total amount of earnings of the factors of production within the nation. If we think of these factors as constituting the households of the economy, we can see that *factor costs result directly in incomes to the household sector.* Thus, if factor costs were the only costs involved in production, the problem of buying back the gross national product would be a very simple one. We should simply be paying out to households, as the cost of production, the very sum needed to buy GNP when we turned around to sell it. But this is not the case, as a glance at the General Manufacturing expense summary shows. There are other costs, besides factor costs. How shall we deal with them?

Costs of materials

The next item on the expense summary is puzzling. Called payments for "materials, supplies, etc.," it represents all the money General Manufacturing has paid, not to its own factors, but to other companies for other products it has needed. We may even recognize these costs as payments for those intermediate products that lose their identity in a later stage of production. How do such payments become part of the income available to buy GNP on the marketplace?

Perhaps the answer is already intuitively clear. When the General Manufacturing sends its checks to, let us say, U.S. Steel, or General Electric, or to a local supplier of stationery, each of these recipient firms now uses the proceeds of General Manufacturing's checks to pay its own costs. (Actually, of course, they have probably long since paid their own costs and now use General Manufacturing's payment only to reimburse themselves. But if we want to picture our model economy in the simplest way, we can imagine U.S. Steel and other firms sending their products to General Manufacturing and waiting until checks arrive to pay their own costs.)

And what are those costs? What must U.S. Steel or all the other suppliers now do with their checks? The answer is obvious. They must now reimburse their own factors and then pay any other costs that remain.

Figure 3-2 may make the matter plain. It shows us, looking back down the chain of intermediate payments, that what constitutes material costs to one firm is made up of factor and other costs to another. Indeed, as we unravel the chain from company to company, it is clear that all the contribution to new output must have come from the contribution of factors somewhere down the line, and that all the costs of new output

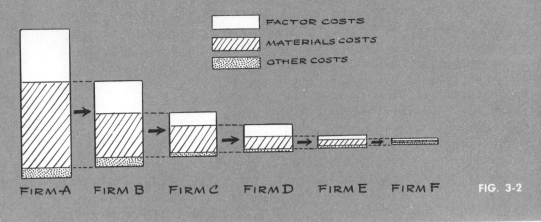

HOW MATERIALS COSTS BECOME OTHER COSTS

FACTOR COSTS
MATERIALS COSTS
OTHER COSTS

FIRM A   FIRM B   FIRM C   FIRM D   FIRM E   FIRM F   FIG. 3-2

—all the value added—must ultimately be resolvable into payments to land, labor, and capital.

Another way of picturing the same thing is to imagine that all firms in the country were bought up by a single gigantic corporation. The various production units of the new supercorporation would then ship components and semifinished items back and forth to one another, but there would not have to be any payment from one division to another. The only payments that would be necessary would be those required to buy the services of factors—that is, various kinds of labor, or the use of property or capital—so that at the end of the year, the supercorporation would show on its expense summary only items for wages and salaries, rent, and interest (and as we shall see, taxes and depreciation) but it would have no item for materials cost.

We have come a bit further toward seeing how our gross national product can be sold. To the extent that GNP represents new output made during the course of the year, the income to buy back this output has already been handed out as factor costs, either paid at the last stage of production or "carried along" in the guise of materials costs. But a glance at the General Manufacturing expense summary shows that entrepreneurs incur two kinds of costs that we have still not taken into account: taxes and depreciation. Here are costs employers have incurred that have not been accounted for on the income side. What can we say about them?

Tax costs

Let us begin by tracing the taxes that General Manufacturing pays, just as we have traced its materials payments. In the first instance, its taxes will go to government units—federal, state, and local. But we need not stop there. Just as we saw that General Manufacturing's checks to supplier firms paid for the suppliers' factor costs and for still further interfirm transactions, so we can see that its checks to government agencies pay for goods and services that these agencies have bought — goods such as roads, buildings, or defense equipment; or services such as teaching, police protection, and the administration of justice. General Manufacturing's tax checks are thus used to help pay for factors of production — land, labor, and capital — that are used in the *public sector*.

In many ways, General Manufacturing's payments to government units resemble its payments to other firms for raw materials. Indeed, if the government *sold* its output to General Manufacturing, charging for the use of the roads, police services, or defense protection it affords the company, there would be *no* difference whatsoever. The reason we differentiate between a company's payment to the public sector and its payments for intermediate products is important, however, and worth looking into.

The first reason is clearly that, with few exceptions, the government does *not* sell its output. This is partly because the community has decided that certain things the government produces (education, justice, or the use of public parks, for instance) should not be for sale but should be supplied to all citizens without charge. In part, it is also because some things the government produces, such as defense or law and order, cannot be equitably charged to individual buyers, since it is impossible to say to what degree anyone benefits from — or even uses — these communal facilities. Hence General Manufacturing, like every other producer, is billed, justly or otherwise, for a share of the cost of government.

There is also a second reason why we consider the cost of taxes as a new kind of cost, distinct from factor payments. It is that when we have finished paying the factors we have not yet paid all the sums that employers must lay out. Some taxes, in other words, are an addition to the cost of production.

Indirect vs. direct taxes

These taxes — so-called *indirect taxes* — are levied on the productive enterprise itself or on its actual physical output. Taxes on real estate, for instance, or taxes that are levied on each unit of output, regardless of whether or not it is sold (such as excise taxes on cigarettes), or taxes levied on goods sold at retail (sales taxes) are all payments that entrepreneurs must make as part of their costs of doing business.

Note that not all taxes collected by the government are costs of production. Many taxes will be paid, not by the entrepreneurs as an expense of doing business, but by the factors themselves. These so-called *direct* taxes (such as income taxes) are *not* part of the cost of production. When General Manufacturing adds up its total cost of production, it naturally includes the wages and salaries it has paid, but it does not include the taxes its workers or executives have paid out of their incomes. Such direct taxes transfer income from earners to government, but they are not a cost to the company itself.

In the same way, the income taxes on the profits of a company do *not* constitute a cost of production. General Manufacturing does not pay income taxes as a regular charge on its operations, but waits until a year's production has taken place, and then pays income taxes on the profits it makes *after* paying its costs. If it finds that it has lost money over the year, it will not pay any income taxes — although it will have paid other costs, including certain other kinds of taxes. Thus direct taxes are not a cost that is paid out in the course of production and must be recouped, but a payment made by factors (including owners of the business) from the incomes they have earned through the process of production.

Thus we can see two reasons why taxes are handled as a separate item in GNP and are not telescoped into factor costs, the way materials costs are. One reason is that taxes are a payment to a *different sector* from that of business and thus indicate a separate stream of economic activity. But the second reason, and the one that interests us more at this moment, is that certain taxes — indirect taxes — are an entirely new kind of cost of production, not previously picked up. As an expense paid out by entrepreneurs, over and above factor costs (or materials costs), these tax costs must be part of the total selling price of GNP.

Will there be enough incomes handed out in the process of production to cover this item of cost?

We have seen that there will be. The indirect tax costs paid out by entrepreneurs will be received by government agencies who will use these tax receipts to pay incomes to factors working for the government. Thus the new item of tax costs will eventually become income to factors working in the public sector, and will be available, together with all other factor incomes, to create demand on the marketplace.

Depreciation

But there is still one last item of cost. At the end of the year, when the company is totting up its expenses to see if it has made a profit for the period, its accountants do not stop with factor costs, material costs, and taxes. If they did, the company would soon be in serious straits. In producing its goods, General Manufacturing has also used up a certain amount of its assets — its buildings and equipment — and a cost must now be charged for this wear and tear if the company is to be able to preserve the value of its physical plant intact. If it did not make this cost allowance, it would have failed to include all the resources that were used up in the process of production, and it would therefore be overstating its profits.

Yet, this cost has something about it clearly different from the other costs General Manufacturing has paid. Unlike factor costs, or taxes, or materials costs, the company does not have to send anybody a check when its accountants make an allowance for depreciation. In fact, all they do is to make an entry on the company's books, stating that plant and equipment are now worth so-and-so much less than in the beginning of the year.

At the same time, however, General Manufacturing *includes* the amount of depreciation in the price it intends to charge for its goods. As we have seen, part of the resources used up in production was its own capital equipment, and it is certainly entitled to consider the depreciation as a cost. Yet, it has not paid anyone a sum of money equal to this cost! How, then, will there be enough income in the marketplace to buy back its product?

The answer lies in the fact that we are not dealing with a single company but with a vast assemblage of companies, all of which are depreciating their assets—that is, adding to their costs sums equal to the wear and tear on their equipment—and *some of which are also busy replacing their equipment as it becomes completely worn out.*

Suppose we had 10 companies, each with machines worth $1,000 which deteriorated at a rate of $100 a year. If these companies originally bought their machines in different years, then we can see that each year the sum of depreciation costs would be $1,000 (10 companies each adding $100 to their costs), but that this would be nicely offset by the actual expenditure of $1,000 as, each year, one company bought itself a new machine to take the place of the unit that had finally worn out. Ten companies might not space their replacement expenditures so evenly. But when we deal with the thousands of companies in the economy and with the widely varying "lifetimes" of their equipment, we can make the quite realistic assumption that there will be a steady flow of replacement spending.*

This enables us to see that insofar as there is a steady stream of expenditures going to firms that make replacement capital, there will be

---

*But wait, some bright student will object. Suppose one of the 10 companies decides not to replace its machine, but to junk it, or suppose it decides to go out of business or to go into some other line. Then there won't be a flow of replacement spending equal to depreciation costs! Our student is quite right. But that brings us ahead of ourselves to consider a highly dynamic economy. In our calm model, we just ignore such complexities of the actual economic world. Furthermore, we are not too unrealistic in doing so. Save for the most severely depressed years, the economy as a whole *does* replace its depreciated assets.

payments just large enough to balance the marking-up of costs due to depreciation. As with all other payments to firms, these replacement expenditures will, of course, become incomes to factors, etc., and thus can reappear on the marketplace.

The three streams of expenditure

Our analysis is now essentially complete. Item by item, we have traced each element of cost into an income payment, so that we now know there is enough income paid out to buy back our GNP at a price that represents its full cost.

Perhaps this was a conclusion we anticipated all along. After all, ours would be an impossibly difficult economy to manage if somewhere along the line purchasing power dropped out of existence, so that we were always faced with a shortage of income to buy back the product we made. But our analysis has also shown us a most unexpected thing. We are accustomed to thinking that all the purchasing power in the economy is received and spent through the hands of "people" — by which we usually mean households. Now we can see that this is not true. There is not only one, but there are *three* streams of incomes and costs, all quite distinct from one another. The first is the factor cost — household — consumers goods stream. Another is the tax — government agency — government goods stream. A third is the depreciation — business — replacement stream.

To help visualize these three flows, imagine for an instant that our money comes in colors (all of equal value): green, red, and blue. Now suppose that firms always pay their factors in green money, their taxes in red money, and their replacement expenditures in blue money. In point of fact, of course, the colors would soon be mixed. A factor paid in green bills will be paying some of his green income for taxes; or a government agency will be paying out red money as factor incomes; or firms will be using blue dollars to pay taxes or factors, and red or green dollars to pay for replacement capital.

But at least in our mind we could picture the streams being kept quite separate. A red tax dollar paid by General Manufacturing to the Internal Revenue Service for taxes could go from the government to another firm, let us say in payment for office supplies, and we can think of the office supply firm keeping these red dollars apart from its other receipts, to pay its taxes with. Such a red dollar could circulate indefinitely, from government agencies to firms and back again, helping to bring about production but never entering a consumer's pocket! In the same way, a blue replacement expenditure dollar going from General Manufacturing to, let us say U.S. Steel, could be set aside by U.S. Steel to pay for *its* replacement needs; and the firm that received this blue dollar might, in turn, set it aside for its own use as replacement expenditure. We could, that is, imagine a circuit of expenditures in which blue dollars went from firm to firm, to pay for replacement investment, and never ended up in a pay envelope or as a tax payment.

There is a simple way of explaining this seemingly complex triple flow. Each stream indicates the existence of a *final taker* of gross national product: consumers, government, and business itself.* Since output has final claimants other than consumers, we can obviously have a flow of purchasing power that does not enter consumers' or factors' hands.

The crucial role of expenditures

The realization that factors do not get paid incomes equal to the total gross value of output brings us back to the central question of this chapter: can we be certain that we will be able to sell our GNP at its full cost? Has there surely been generated enough purchasing power to buy back our total output?

We have thus far carefully analyzed and answered half the question. *We know that all costs will become incomes to factors or receipts of government agencies or of firms making replacement items.* To sum up again, factor costs become the incomes of workers, managements, owners of natural resources and of capital; and all these incomes together can be thought of as comprising the receipts of the household sector. Tax costs are paid to government agencies and become receipts of the government sector. Depreciation costs are initially accrued within business firms, and these accruals belong to the business sector. But as long as worn-out capital is regularly replaced, these accruals will be matched by equivalent new receipts of capital-goods-making firms.

What we have not yet established, however, is that these sector receipts will become sector *expenditures*. That is, we have not demonstrated that all households will now *spend* all their incomes on goods and services, or that government units will necessarily *spend* all their tax receipts on public goods and services, or that all firms will assuredly *spend* their depreciation accruals for new replacement equipment.

What happens if some receipts are not spent? The answer is of key importance in understanding the operation of the economy. A failure of the sectors to spend as much money as they have received means that some of the costs that have been laid out will *not* come back to the

*Here we can satisfactorily think of net exports as a component of gross private investment.

original entrepreneurs. As a result, they will suffer losses. If, for instance, our gross national product costs $600 billion to produce, but if the various sectors in all spend only $590 billion, then some entrepreneurs will find themselves failing to sell all their output. Inventories of unsold goods would begin piling up, and businessmen would soon be worried about "over-producing." The natural thing to do when you can't sell all your output is to stop making so much of it, so that businesses would begin cutting back on production. As they did so, they would also cut back on the number of people they needed to employ. As a result, businessmen's costs would go down; but so would factor incomes, for we have seen that costs and incomes are but opposite sides of one coin. As incomes fall, the expenditures of the sectors might very well fall further, bringing about another twist in the spiral of recession.

This is not yet the place to go into the mechanics of such a downward spiral of business. But the point is clear. *A failure of the sectors to bring all their receipts back to the marketplace as demand can initiate profound economic problems.* In the contrast between an unshakable equality of costs and incomes on the one hand, and the uncertain connection between receipts and expenditures on the other, we have come to grips with one of the most important problems in macroeconomics.

The complete circuit

We shall have ample opportunity later to observe exactly what happens when receipts are not spent. Now let us be sure that we understand how the great circle of the economic flow is closed when the sectors *do* spend their receipts. Figure 3-3 shows how we can trace our "red, blue, and green" dollars through the economy and how these flows suffice to buy back GNP for its total cost.

We can trace the flow from left to right. We begin on the left with the bar representing the total cost of our freshly produced GNP. As we know, this cost consists of all the factor costs of all the firms and government units in the nation, all the indirect tax costs incurred during production, and all the depreciation charges made during production. The bar also shows us the amount of money demand our economy must generate in order to buy back its own output.

The next bars show us the transmutation of costs into sector receipts for householders, government units, and business firms (who retain their own depreciation accruals). This relationship between costs and sector receipts is one of *identity* — all costs *must* be receipts. Hence we use the sign $\equiv$ to indicate that this is a relation of identities — of definitional differences only.

Thereafter we notice the crucial link. Each sector dutifully spends all its receipts, as it is supposed to. Our household sector buys the kinds of goods and services householders do in fact buy—consumption goods and services. Our government sector buys government goods and services, and our business sector buys replacement investment. This time we use an arrow (→) because this is emphatically *not* a relationship of identity.

Now note the next bar. Here we see what happens to these expenditures when they are received by the firms who make consumer goods, or by the firms or individuals who make goods and services bought by governments, or by the manufacturers of capital equipment. Each of these recipients will use the money he has received to cover factor payments, taxes, and depreciation for his own business. (What we show in our diagram are not these costs for each and every firm, but the aggregate costs for all firms selling to each sector.)

We are almost done. It remains only to aggregate the sector costs; that is, to add up all the factor costs, all the taxes, and all the depreciation accruals of *all* firms and government agencies—to reproduce a bar just like the one we started with. A circle of production has been completed. Firms and government units have received back on the marketplace a sum just large enough to cover their initial costs, including their profits for risk. The stage is set for another round of production, similar to the last.

GNP as a sum of costs and a sum of expenditures

Our bar graph also enables us to examine again the concept of gross national product, for now we can see that GNP can be looked at in one of two ways. We can think of a year's gross national product as a sum of all the costs that have been paid out during that year—factor costs, indirect taxes and depreciation. Or we can think of the same GNP as the sum of the expenditures that brought this output—that is, consumption expenditure, government expenditure, and gross private investment expenditure. Since the final output is one and the same, we can see that the two methods of computing its value must also be the same. One method merely separates total output into various categories of cost, while the other tells us who bought the output as it finally emerged.*

Generally we analyze the causes for changes in GNP from the point of view of changes in expenditures since, as we have already seen, expenditure is the key activity in a monetary economy. But not until we

---

*And what if no one bought it? Then it would pile up in warehouses as unsold inventories, and count as investment—that is, as part of output that has not been consumed. Its "buyers" would be the business firms who (unwillingly) were stuck with these inventories. Needless to say, this is a very unwanted form of investment. More about this later.

THE CIRCULAR FLOW — VIEW III

≡ SECTOR INCOMES OR RECEIPTS

→ EXPENDITURES (DEMAND) ≡ RECEIPTS (USED TO COVER COSTS)

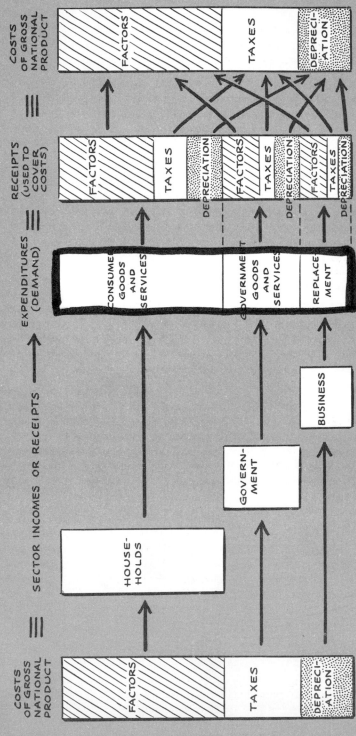

COSTS OF GROSS NATIONAL PRODUCT

FACTORS

TAXES

DEPRECI-ATION

HOUSE-HOLDS

GOVERN-MENT

BUSINESS

CONSUMER GOODS AND SERVICES

GOVERNMENT GOODS AND SERVICES

REPLACE-MENT

FACTORS

TAXES

DEPRECIATION

FACTORS

TAXES

DEPRECIATION

FACTORS

TAXES

DEPRECIATION

COSTS OF GROSS NATIONAL PRODUCT

FACTORS

TAXES

DEPRECI-ATION

FIG. 3-3

understand how costs become incomes (and thus become *available* for expenditure) can we really understand how it is possible for the system to maintain its ongoing level if expenditures do not change.

Net national product and national income

It is now also very easy to understand the meaning of two other less frequently used measures of output. One of these is called *net national product* (NNP). As the name indicates, it is exactly equal to gross national product *minus depreciation*. The other measure, national income, we have already met. It is GNP *minus depreciation and indirect taxes*. This makes it equal to the sum of factor costs only. Figure 3-4 should make this relationship clear.

The circular flow

The "self-reproducing" model economy we have now sketched out is obviously still very far from reality. Nevertheless, the particular kind of unreality that we have deliberately constructed serves a highly useful purpose. An economy that regularly and dependably buys back everything it produces gives us a kind of bench mark from which to begin our subsequent investigations. We call such an economy, whose internal relationships we have outlined, an economy in *stationary equilibrium,* and we denote the changeless flow of costs into business receipts and receipts back into costs a *circular flow.*

We shall return many times to the model of a circular flow economy for insights into a more complex and dynamic system. Hence it is well

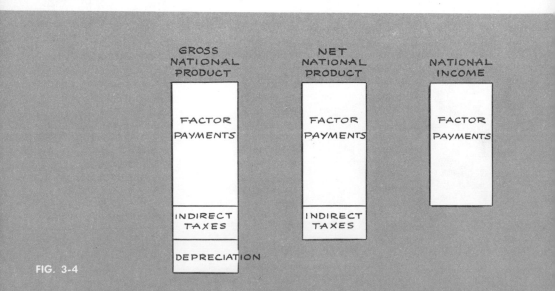

GROSS NATIONAL PRODUCT

FACTOR PAYMENTS

INDIRECT TAXES

DEPRECIATION

NET NATIONAL PRODUCT

FACTOR PAYMENTS

INDIRECT TAXES

NATIONAL INCOME

FACTOR PAYMENTS

FIG. 3-4

that we summarize briefly two of the salient characteristics of such a system.

1. *A circular flow economy will never experience a "recession."* Year in and year out, its total output will remain unchanged. Indeed, the very concept of a circular flow is useful in showing us that an economic system can maintain a given level of activity *indefinitely,* so long as all the sectors convert all their receipts into expenditure.

2. *A circular flow economy also will never know a "boom."* That is, it will not grow, and its standard of living will remain unchanged. That standard of living may be high or low, for we could have a circular flow economy of poverty or of abundance. But in either state, changelessness will be of its essence.

In the chapters that follow, we must successively reintroduce the very elements that we have so carefully excluded. First, saving and net investment, then technological change and population growth must one by one find their way back into our model. Thus, gradually it will approximate itself to the realities around us, allowing us to return from the abstract world of ideas to the concrete world of reality.

Summary

1. A great circle of payments and receipts constantly renews the demand that keeps the economy going. Income is pumped out to the participants in the production process, who then spend their incomes to buy the output they have helped to make, thereby returning money to the firms that again pump it out.

2. We seek to elucidate this circle by constructing a *model*—an economy stripped of everything that is not essential to the process we seek to understand. Our model simplifies and therefore highlights the relationships that underlie the macroeconomic process.

3. We use our model to show *how an economy can in fact buy back all of its own output*—how enough demand can be created to keep the economy going. To do so, we must show that *every item of cost to business firms can become demand* for them on the marketplace.

4. The first item of cost is *factor payments* (wages, rent, profits, interest). These payments for factor services are *the source of household income.* In turn, households can spend their incomes for *consumption goods.*

5. *Indirect taxes* are costs paid by firms to government agencies. In turn, these agencies spend their tax receipts for *government purchases.*

   (Note that direct taxes—income taxes—are not a cost of production, but a levy imposed on factors after they have been paid.)

6. *Depreciation costs* are costs incurred by *businesses* for the wear and tear of capital. They are accrued by business firms, who, in turn, are able to use them to purchase *replacement investment.*

7. *Materials costs* are payments to other firms. Ultimately, they can all be broken down into factor costs, indirect tax costs, and depreciation costs.

8. *The total value of output (GNP) can be seen not only as a sum of expenditures (C + I + G + E), but as a sum of costs (F + T + D).*

9. *All costs thus become sector receipts:* factor costs become household incomes; indirect tax costs become government receipts; depreciation costs become business receipts. In turn, *these sector receipts can be returned to the market as new expenditures* (demand).

10. This gives us *three streams of cost – income – expenditure (demand):*
    - factor costs – household incomes – consumption expenditure
    - indirect taxes – government receipts – government expenditure
    - depreciation – business receipts – replacement expenditure

11. *The key linkage is that between receipts and expenditure. All costs must become receipts. But not all receipts need necessarily be spent.*

12. When all receipts are spent, then we have a perfect *circular flow.* In such a situation, the economy generates an unchanging flow of demand, and therefore experiences neither boom, recession, nor growth.

13. NNP ← GNP – depr. (pg. 38)

Questions

1. How can a model elucidate reality when it is deliberately stripped of the very things that make reality interesting?

2. Why do we need a model to show that an economy can buy back its own production?

3. What are factor costs? What kinds of factor costs are there? To what sector do factor costs go?

4. What are direct taxes? What are indirect taxes? Which are considered part of production costs? Why?

5. To whom are materials costs paid? Why are they not part of the sum total of costs in GNP?

6. What is depreciation? Why is it a part of costs? Who receives the payments or accruals made for depreciation purposes?

7. Show in a carefully drawn diagram how costs become income or receipts of the different sectors.

8. Show in a second diagram how the incomes of the various sectors can become expenditures.

9. Why is the link between expenditure and receipt different from that between receipt and expenditure?

10. What is meant by a circular flow economy? Why does such an economy have neither growth nor fluctuation?

11. Explain the two different ways of looking at GNP and write the simple formula for each.

12. Can we have demand without expenditure?

4

Saving and investment

Let us return for a moment to our original perspective overlooking the economic flow. We will remember that we could see the workings of the economy as an interaction between the factors of production and their environment, culminating in a stream of production — some private, some public — that was used in part for consumption and in part for the replacement or the further building up of capital. Now in our model of a circular flow economy we have seen how such an economy can be self-sustaining and self-renewing, as each round of disbursements by employers found its way into a stream of purchasing power just large enough to justify the continuation of the given scale of output.

The meaning of saving

Yet we all know that such a circular flow is a highly unreal depiction of the world. Indeed, it omits the most important dynamic factor of real economic life — the steady accumulation of new capital (and the qualitative change in the nature of the capital due to technology) that characterizes a *growing* economy. What we must now investigate is the process by which society adds each year to its stock of real wealth — and the effect of this process on the circuit of production and purchasing.

We begin by making sure that we understand a key word in this dynamic analysis — saving. We have come across saving many times by now, and so we should be ready for a final mastery of this centrally important economic term. In Chapter 3, when we spoke of saving it was in *real* terms, as the act by which society relinquished resources that might have been used for consumption, thereby making them available for the capital-building stream of output. Now we must translate that underlying real meaning of saving into terms corresponding with the buying and selling, paying and receiving discussed in the preceding chapter.

What is saving in these terms? It is very simply *not spending all or part of income for consumption goods or services.** It should be very clear then why saving is such a key term. In our discussion of the circular flow, it became apparent that expenditure was the critical link in the steady operation of the economy. If saving is not-spending, then it would seem that saving could be the cause for just that kind of downward spiral of which we caught a glimpse in our preceding chapter.

And yet this clearly is not the whole story. We also know that the act of investing—of spending money to direct factors into the production of capital goods—requires an act of saving; that is, of not using that same money to direct those factors instead into the production of consumers goods. *Hence, saving is clearly necessary for the process of investment.* Now, how can one and the same act be necessary for economic expansion and a threat to its stability? This is a problem that will occupy us during much of this book.

The demand gap

It will help us to understand the problem if we again have recourse to our now familiar diagram of the circular flow. But this time we must introduce into it the crucial new fact of net saving. Note *net* saving. Quite unnoticed, we have already encountered gross saving in our circular flow, together with gross investment. After all, in our model economy, replacement expenditures for capital goods used money that might have been paid out to stockholders or workers. Thus there was a regular non-spending on the part of businesses (whose owners might have taken the depreciation accruals as part of their own income), offset by an equally regular spending for replacement investment. But this saving did not buy *additional* capital; it merely replaced worn-out equipment with identical new equipment. That is why we call it gross saving, rather than net.

In this look at our model economy, however, we assume that when

---

*Note "for consumption goods and services." Purchasing stocks or bonds or life insurance is also an act of saving, even though you must spend money to acquire these items. What you acquire, however, are assets, not consumption goods and services. Some acts of spending are difficult to classify. Is a college education, for instance, a consumption good or an investment? It is probably better thought of as an investment even though in the statistics of GNP it is treated as consumption.

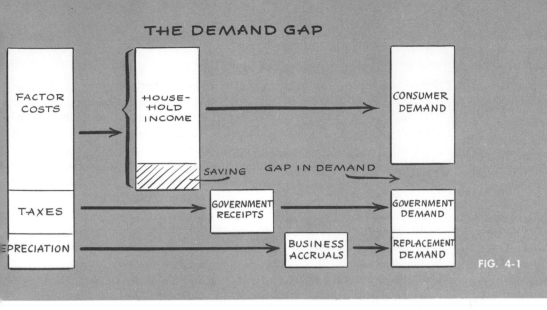

THE DEMAND GAP

FACTOR COSTS

HOUSE-HOLD INCOME

CONSUMER DEMAND

SAVING GAP IN DEMAND

TAXES

GOVERNMENT RECEIPTS

GOVERNMENT DEMAND

DEPRECIATION

BUSINESS ACCRUALS

REPLACEMENT DEMAND

FIG. 4-1

employers pay out their factor costs, householders will save a portion of their incomes. The result is shown in Fig. 4-1.

What we see is precisely what we would expect. There is a gap in demand introduced by the deficiency of consumer spending. This means that the total receipts of employers who make consumer goods will be less than the total amounts they laid out. It begins to look as if we were approaching the cause of economic recession and unemployment.

Yet, whereas we have introduced saving, we have forgotten about its counterpart, investment. Cannot the investment activity of a growing economy in some way close the demand gap?

The dilemma of saving

This is indeed, as we shall soon see, the way out of the dilemma. But before we trace the way in which investment compensates for saving, let us draw two conclusions from the analysis we have made up to this point.

1. *The act of saving, in and by itself, creates a gap in demand, a shortage of spending. Unless this gap is closed, there will be trouble in the economic system, for employers will not be getting back as receipts all the sums they laid out.*
2. *The presence of a demand gap forces us to make a choice. If we want a dynamic, investing economy, we will have to be prepared to cope with the problems that saving raises. If we want to avoid these problems, we can close the gap by urging consumers not to save. Then we would have a dependable circular flow, but we would no longer enjoy economic growth.*

The offset to savings

How, then, shall we manage to make our way out of the dilemma of saving? The previous diagram makes clear what must be done. If a gap in demand is due to the savings of households, then that gap must be closed by the expanded spending of some other sector. There are only two other such sectors: government or business. Thus in some fashion or other, the savings of one sector must be "offset" by the increased activity of another.

But how is this offset to take place? How are the resources that are relinquished by consumers to be made available to entrepreneurs in the business sector or to government officials? In a market economy there is only one way that resources or factors not being used in one place can be used in another. Someone must be willing and able to hire them.

Whether or not government and business *are* willing to employ the factors that are not needed in the consumer goods sector is a very critical matter, soon to command much of our attention. But suppose that they are willing. How will they be able to do so? How can they get the necessary funds to expand their activity?

There are four principal methods of accomplishing this essential increase in expenditure.

1. The business sector can increase its expenditures by *borrowing* the savings of the public through the sale of new corporate bonds.
2. The government sector can increase its expenditures by *borrowing* savings from the other sectors through the sale of new government bonds.
3. The business sector can increase its expenditures by attracting household savings into partnerships, new stock, or other *ownership or equity*.
4. Both business and government sectors can increase expenditures by *borrowing* additional funds from commercial banks.

There are other possibilities. Government has a very important means of increasing its command over resources, through taxing the household or business sectors. Business can also increase its expenditures by using its own savings to finance new spending.

Claims

But the four important methods itemized above all have one attribute that calls them especially to our attention. Without exception they give rise to *claims* that reveal from whom the funds have been obtained and to whom they have been made available, as well as on what terms. Bonds, corporate or government, show that savings have been borrowed from individuals or banks by business and government units. Shares of stock reveal that savings have been obtained on an equity (ownership) basis, as do new partnership agreements.

We can note a few additional points about claims, now that we see how many of them arise in the economy. First, many household savings are first put into banks and insurance companies—so-called financial intermediaries—so that the transfer of funds from households to business or government may go through several stages; e.g., from household to insurance company and then from insurance company to corporation.

Second, not *all* claims involve the offsetting of savings of one sector by expenditures of another. Many claims, once they have arisen, are traded back and forth and bought and sold, as is the case with most stocks and bonds. These purchases and sales involve the *transfer of existing claims*, not the creation of new claims.

Finally, not every new claim necessarily involves the creation of an asset. If A borrows $5 from B, bets it on the races, and gives B his note, there has been an increase in claims, but no new asset has been brought into being to match it.

Public and private claims

Now let us look at Fig. 4-2. This time we show what happens when savings are made available to the business sector by direct borrowing from households. Note the claim (or equity) that arises.

If the government were doing the borrowing, rather than the business sector, the diagram would look like Fig. 4-3. Notice that the claim is now a government bond.

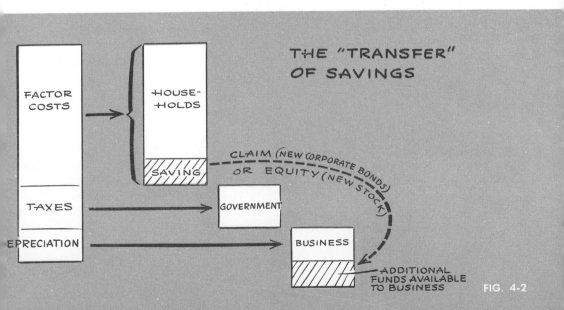

FIG. 4-2

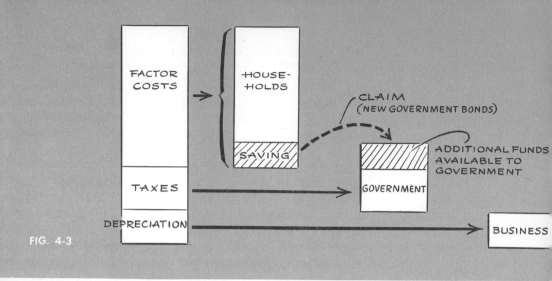

FIG. 4-3

We have not looked at a diagram showing business or government borrowing its funds from the banking system. (This process will be better understood when we take up the problem of money and banking, in Chapter 9.) The basic concept, however, although more complex, is much the same as above.

The completed act of offsetting savings

There remains only a last step, which must by now be fully anticipated. We have seen how it is possible to offset the savings in one sector, where they were going to cause an expenditure gap, by increasing the funds available to another sector. It remains only to *spend* those additional funds in the form of additional investment or, in the case of the government, for additional public goods and services. The two completed expenditure circuits now appear in Fig. 4-4.

Intersectoral offsets

We shall not investigate further at this point the differences between increased public spending and increased business investment. What we must heed is the crucial point at issue: *if saving in any one sector is to be offset, some other sector (or sectors) must spend more than its income. A gap in demand due to insufficient expenditure in one sector can be compensated only by an increase in demand—that is, in expenditure—of another.*

Once this simple but fundamental point is clearly understood, much of the mystery of macroeconomics disappears, for we can then begin to see that an economy in movement, as contrasted with one in a stationary

46

circular flow, is one in which sectors must *cooperate* to maintain the
closed circuit of income and output. In a dynamic economy, we no
longer enjoy the steady translation of incomes into expenditure which,
as we have seen, is the key to an uninterrupted flow of output. Rather,
we are faced with the presence of net saving and the possibility of a gap
in final demand. Difficult though the ensuing problems are, let us not
forget that saving is the necessary condition for the accumulation of
capital. The price of economic growth, in other words, is the risk of
economic decline.

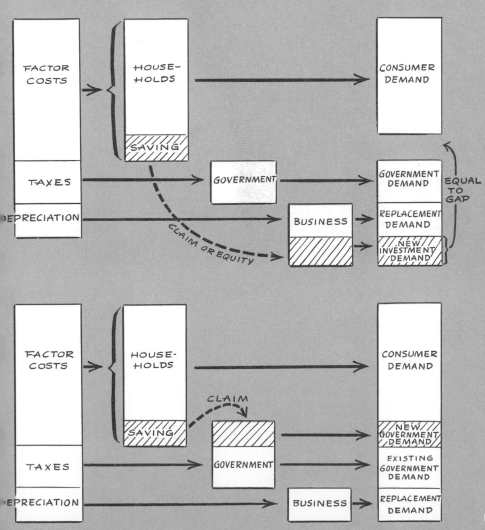

TWO WAYS OF CLOSING THE DEMAND GAP

FIG. 4-4

Real and money saving

This central importance of saving in a growing economy will become a familiar problem. At this juncture, where we have first encountered the difficulties it can pose, we must be certain that we understand two different aspects that saving assumes.

One aspect, noticed in our initial overview of the economy, is the decision to relinquish *resources* that can then be re-deployed into capital-building. This is the real significance of saving. But this "real" aspect of saving is not the way we encounter the act of saving in our ordinary lives. We think of saving as a monetary phenomenon, not a "real" one. When we save, we are conscious of not using all our incomes for consumption, but we scarcely, if ever, think of releasing resources for alternative employments.

There is a reason for this dichotomy of real and money saving. In our society, with its extraordinary degree of specialization, the individuals or institutions that do the actual saving are not ordinarily those that do the actual capital-building. In a simple society, this dichotomy between saving and investing need not, and usually does not, occur. A farmer who decides to build new capital—for example, to build a barn—is very much aware of giving up a consumption activity—the raising of food—in order to carry out his investment. So is an artisan who stops weaving clothing to repair his loom. Where the saver and the investor are one and the same person, there need be no "financial" saving, and the underlying real phenomenon of saving as the diversion of activity from consumption to investment is immediately apparent.

In the modern world, savers and investors are sometimes the same individual or group—as in the case of a business management that spends profits on new productive capacity rather than on higher executive salaries. More often, however, savers are not investors. Certainly householders, though very important savers, do not personally decide and direct the process of capital formation in the nation. Furthermore, the men and materials that households voluntarily relinquish by not using all their incomes to buy consumers goods have to be physically transferred to different industries, often to different occupations and locations, in order to carry out their investment tasks. This requires funds in the hands of the investors, so that they can tempt resources from one use to another.

Hence we need an elaborate system by which money saving can be "transferred" directly or indirectly into the hands of those who will be in a position to employ factors for capital construction purposes. Nevertheless, underlying this complex mechanism for transferring purchasing power remains the same simple purpose that we initially witnessed. Resources that have been relinquished from the production of consumption goods or services are now employed in the production of capital goods. Thus, *saving and investing are essentially real phenomena*, even though it may take a great deal of financial manipulation to bring them about.

A final important point. *The fact that the decisions to save and the decisions to invest are lodged in different individuals or groups alerts us to a basic reason why the savings-investment process may not always work smoothly.* Savers may choose to consume less than their total incomes at times when investors have no interest in expanding their capital assets. Alternatively, business firms may wish to form new capital when savers are interested in spending money only on themselves. This separation of decision-making can give rise to situations in which savings are not offset by investment, or in which investment plans race out ahead of savings capabilities. In our next chapters we will be investigating what happens in these cases.

Transfer payments

We have talked about the transfer of purchasing power from savers to investors, but we have not yet mentioned another kind of transfer, also of great importance in the over-all operation of the economy. This is the transfer of incomes from sector to sector (and sometimes within sectors).

Income transfers (called *transfer payments*) are a very useful and important means of reallocating purchasing power in society. Through transfer payments, members of the community who do not participate in production are given an opportunity to enjoy incomes that would otherwise not be available to them. Thus Social Security transfer payments make it possible for the old or the handicapped to be given an "income" (not, to be sure, a currently *earned* income) of their own, or unemployment benefits give purchasing power to those who cannot get it through employment.

Not all transfers are in the nature of welfare payments, however. The distribution of money *within* a household is a transfer payment. So is the payment of interest on the national debt.* So is the grant of a subsidy to a private enterprise, such as an airline, or of a scholarship to a college student. Any income payment that is not earned by selling one's productive services on the market falls in the transfer category.

It may help to understand this process if we visualize it in our flow diagram. Figure 4-5 shows two kinds of transfers. The upper one, from

*Curiously, the payment of interest on corporate debt is not considered a transfer payment, but a payment to a factor of production. Actually, much government interest should also be thought of as a factor payment (for the loan of capital for purposes of public output); but by convention, all government interest is classified as a transfer payment.

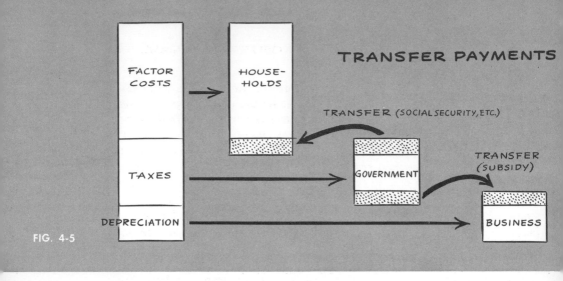

FIG. 4-5

the government to the household sector, shows a typical transfer of incomes, such as veterans' pensions or Social Security; the transfer below it reflects the flow of income that might be illustrated by a payment to agriculture for crop support. Transfers *within* sectors, such as household allowances, are not shown in the diagram.

One thing we may well note about transfers is that they can only *rearrange* the incomes created in the production process; they cannot increase those incomes. Income, as we learned in the last chapter, is inextricably tied to output — indeed, income is only the financial counterpart of output.

Transfer payments, on the other hand, are a way of arranging individual claims to production in some fashion that strikes the community as fairer or more efficient or more decorous than the way the market process allocates them through the production process. As such, transfer payments are an indispensable and often invaluable agency of social policy. But it is important to understand that no amount of transfers can, in itself, increase the total that is to be shared. That can happen only by raising output itself.

Transfer payments and taxes

We have mentioned, but only in passing, another means of transferring purchasing power from one sector to another: taxation. Heretofore, however, we have often spoken as though all government tax receipts were derived from indirect taxes that were added onto the cost of production.

In fact, this is not the only source of government revenue. Indirect taxes are an important part of state and local revenues, but they are only a minor part of federal tax receipts. Most federal taxes are levied on the incomes of the factors of production or on the profits of businesses after the other factors have been paid.

50

Once again it is worth remembering that the government taxes consumers (and businesses) because it is in the nature of much government output that it cannot be *sold*. Taxes are the way we are billed for our share — rightly or wrongly figured — of government production that has been collectively decided upon. As we can now see, taxes — both on business and on the household sector — also finance many transfer payments. That is, the government intervenes in the distribution process to make it conform to our politically expressed social purposes, taking away some incomes from certain individuals and groups, and providing incomes to others. Figure 4-6 shows what this looks like in the flow of GNP.

As we can see, the exchanges of income between the household and the government sectors can be very complex. Income can flow from households to government units via taxation, and return to the household sector via transfer payments; and the same two-way flows can take place between government and business.

Profits and demand

The last diagram has already introduced a new element of reality in our discussion. Taxes on business *income* presuppose that businesses make *profits*. Let us see how these profits fit into the savings-investment process.

During our discussion of the circular flow, we spoke of profits as a special kind of factor cost — a payment to the factor capital in return for its contribution of risk-taking. But since we are no longer in a changeless circular flow economy, we can introduce a much more dynamic conception of profits. Now we can think of profits not merely as a factor cost (although there is always a certain element of risk-remuneration in

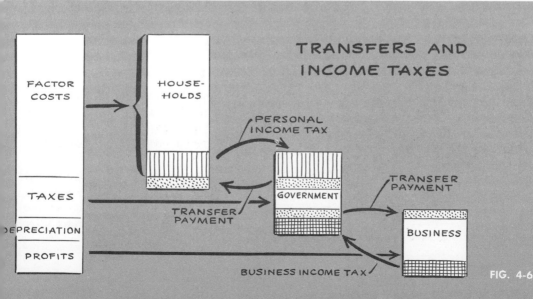

TRANSFERS AND INCOME TAXES

FACTOR COSTS

HOUSE-HOLDS

PERSONAL INCOME TAX

TAXES

GOVERNMENT

TRANSFER PAYMENT

TRANSFER PAYMENT

DEPRECIATION

BUSINESS

PROFITS

BUSINESS INCOME TAX

FIG. 4-6

profits), but as a return to especially efficient or forward-thinking firms who have used the investment process to introduce profitable new products or processes ahead of the run of their industries. We can think of profits, too, as being in part the return accruing to powerful firms who exact a semimonopolistic return from their customers.

What matters in our analysis at this stage is not the precise explanation we give to the origin of profits, but a precise explanation of their role in maintaining a "closed-circuit" economy in which all costs are returned to the marketplace as demand. A commonly heard diagnosis for economic maladies is that profits are at the root of the matter, in that they cause a "withdrawal" of spending power or income from the community. If profits were "hoarded," or kept unspent, this might be true. In fact, however, profits can be spent in three ways:

1. They may be distributed as income to the household sector as dividends or profit shares, to become part of household spending.
2. They may be spent by business firms for new plant and equipment.
3. They may be taxed by the government and spent in the public sector.

All three methods of offsetting profits appear in Fig. 4-7.

We can see that profits need not constitute a withdrawal from the income stream. Indeed, unless profits are adequate, businesses will very likely not invest enough to offset the savings of the household sector. They may, in fact, even fail to make normal replacement expenditures, aggravating the demand gap still further in this way.

Thus the existence of profits, far from being deflationary — that is, far from causing a fall in income — is, in fact, essential for the maintenance of a given level of income or for an advance to a higher level. Nonetheless,

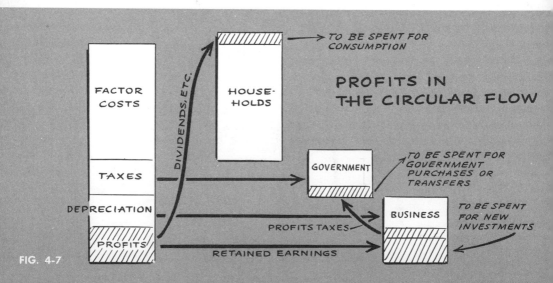

FIG. 4-7

there is a germ of truth in the contentions of those who have maintained that profits can cause an insufficiency of purchasing power. *For unless profits are returned to the flow of purchasing power as dividends that are spent by their recipients, or as new capital expenditures made by business, or as taxes that lead to additional public spending, there will be a gap in the community's demand.* Thus we can think of profits just as we think of saving—an indispensable source of economic growth or a potential source of economic decline.

Saving, investment, and growth

We are almost ready to leave our analysis of the circle of production and income, and to proceed to a much closer study of the individual dynamic elements that create and close gaps. Before we do, however, it is well that we take note of one last fact of the greatest importance. In offsetting the savings of any sector by investment, we have closed the production and income circuit, much as in the stationary circular flow, but there is one crucial difference from the circular flow. Now we have closed the flow by diverting savings into the creation of *additional* capital. Unlike the stationary circular flow where the handing around of incomes did no more than to maintain unchanged the original configuration of the system, in our new dynamic saving-and-investing model *each closing of the circuit results in a quantitative change—the addition of a new "layer" of capital.* Hence, more and more wealth is being added to our system; and thinking back to our first impressions of the interaction of wealth and population, we would expect more and more productiveness from our human factors. Bringing with it complications with which we shall have to deal in due course, *growth* has entered our economic model.

Summary

1. The critical element missing from the concept of the circular flow is *saving*. The key question is how an economy can buy back all its output when some of its receipts are saved rather than returned to the market through expenditure.
2. Saving poses a dilemma. On one hand, it breaks the circular flow and creates a *demand gap*. On the other hand, if there is *no saving,* there can be *no investment*.
3. The answer to the dilemma is that *saving*, which is essential for growth, *must be offset by additional expenditure*. This means that another sector must spend more than its income.
4. There are four main ways in which a sector can spend more than its income:
   • The *business sector can borrow* from the household sector.

- The *government sector can borrow* from the household sector.
- The *business sector* can attract household savings into *equities.*
- Business and government can borrow from the *commercial banks.*

5. Although saving involves money, it is essentially a "real" process (as is investment). That is, its real meaning is that resources are released from consumption.
   The acts of releasing resources (saving) and the acts of employing them (investment) are usually performed by different groups in modern society.

6. *Transfer payments,* from one sector to another or within one sector, play an
   important part in *redistributing* income, but do not increase the total GNP.

7. Profits can be returned to the expenditure flow by being: (1) paid out as dividends, etc., to the household sector (where they are used for consumption);
   (2) spent by business firms for new investment; or (3) taxed by the government
   and spent by it.

8. Saving thus requires investment to assure that all payments will be returned to
   the market as demand. Note, however, that the process of *investment adds to
   capital* and thereby increases productivity. Saving and investment are therefore
   an integral part of the *process of growth.*

Questions

1. What do we mean by a demand gap? Show diagrammatically.
2. How is a demand gap filled by business investment? Show diagrammatically.
3. Why is saving indispensable for growth?
4. Can we have planned business investment without saving? Saving without
   planned business investment?
5. Draw carefully a diagram that shows how savings can be offset by government
   spending.
6. How is it possible for a sector to spend more than its income? How does it get
   the additional money?
7. What is a transfer payment? Draw diagrams of transfers from government to
   consumers, from government to business. Is charity a transfer? Is a lottery?
8. Diagram the three ways in which profits can be returned to the expenditure
   flow. What happens if they are not?
9. Why is a problem presented by the fact that those who save and those who
   make the decision to invest are not the same people?
10. In what way is a circular flow economy different from an economy that saves
    and invests?

8

The consumption sector

With a basic understanding of the crucial role of expenditure and of the complex relationship of saving and investment behind us, we are in a position to look more deeply into the question of the determination of gross national product. For what we have discovered heretofore is only the *mechanism* by which a market economy can sustain or fail to sustain a given level of output through a circuit of expenditure and receipt. Now we must try to discover the *forces* that dynamize the system, creating or closing gaps between income and outgo. Hence, beginning with this chapter, we devote our attention to the actual behavior of the household, government, and business sectors and to their respective motivations for consumption, government purchases, and investment.

The household sector

Largest, most familiar, and in many respects more important of all the sectors in the economy is that of the nation's households — that is, its families and single-dwelling individuals (the two categories together called consumer units) considered as receivers of income and transfer payments, or as savers and spenders of money for consumption.

How big is this sector? In 1966 it comprised nearly fifty million families and some twelve million independent individuals who collectively gathered in $584 billion in income and who spent $479 billion.* As Fig. 5-1 shows, the great bulk of receipts was from factor earnings, and transfer payments played only a relatively small role. As we can also see, we must subtract personal tax payments from household income (or *personal income* as it is officially designated) before we get *disposable personal income* — income actually available for spending. It is from disposable personal income that the crucial choice is made to spend or save. Much of this chapter will focus on that choice.

Subcomponents of consumption

Finally we note that consumer spending itself divides into three main streams. The largest of these is for *nondurable* goods, such as food and clothing or other items whose economic life is (or is assumed to be) short. Second largest is an assortment of expenditures we call consumer *services,* comprising such things as rent, doctors' or lawyers' or barbers' ministrations, theater or movie admissions, bus or taxi or plane transportation, etc., where we buy not a physical good but the work performed by someone or by some equipment. Last is a substream of expenditure for consumer *durable* goods which, as the name suggests, includes items such as cars or household appliances whose economic life is considerably greater than that of most nondurables. We can think of these goods as comprising consumers' capital.

There are complicated patterns and interrelations among these three major streams of consumer spending. As we would expect, consumer spending for durables is extremely volatile. In bad times, such as 1933, it has sunk to less than 8 per cent of all consumer outlays; in the peak of good times in the 1960's, it has risen to nearly double that. Meanwhile, outlays for services have been a steadily swelling area for consumer spending in the postwar economy. As a consequence of the growth of consumer buying of durables and of services, the relative share of the

---

*The Department of Commerce has recently redefined some categories of the national income accounts, and the word *consumption* today applies, strictly speaking, only to personal expenditures for goods and services. Included in total consumer spending, however, are sizeable amounts for interest (mainly on installment loans) and for remittances abroad, neither of which sums are included in the amount for goods and services. The proper nomenclature for the total of consumer spending (goods and services plus interest and remittances) is now *personal outlays.* We shall, however, continue to use the simpler term consumption, although our figures will be those for personal outlays.

Note, also, that the compilation of these figures is a time-consuming process in which earlier estimates are frequently subject to revision. Hence, figures for the components of consumption, or, for that matter, for almost all magnitudes in the economic process, are apt to vary slightly in successive printed statistics until, eventually, the "final" figures are arrived at.

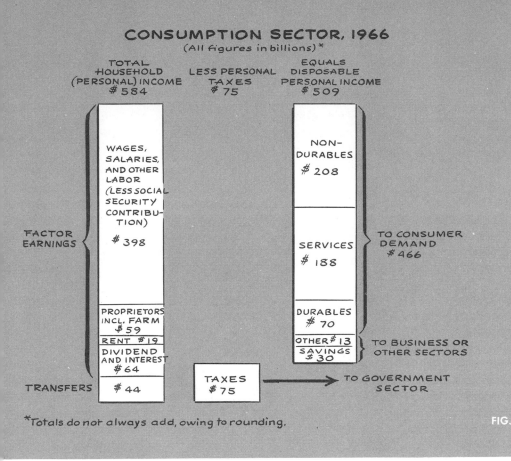

CONSUMPTION SECTOR, 1966
(All figures in billions)*

TOTAL HOUSEHOLD (PERSONAL) INCOME $584	LESS PERSONAL TAXES $75	EQUALS DISPOSABLE PERSONAL INCOME $509

FACTOR EARNINGS

WAGES, SALARIES, AND OTHER LABOR (LESS SOCIAL SECURITY CONTRIBUTION) $398

PROPRIETORS INCL. FARM $59

RENT $19

DIVIDEND AND INTEREST $64

TRANSFERS $44

TAXES $75

NON-DURABLES $208

SERVICES $188

DURABLES $70

OTHER $13

SAVINGS $30

TO CONSUMER DEMAND $466

TO BUSINESS OR OTHER SECTORS

TO GOVERNMENT SECTOR

*Totals do not always add, owing to rounding.

FIG. 5-1

consumer dollar going to "soft goods" has been slowly declining. It is interesting to note, for example, that between 1950 and 1963, consumer spending for food, beverages, and tobacco fell from 31 per cent of all consumption to 25 per cent and that expenditures for apparel fell from 12 per cent to 10. Conversely, consumer spending on recreation and foreign travel and remittances climbed from 6.4 per cent to 8.0 per cent, while household items increased from 11 to 13 per cent.

Consumption and GNP

These internal dynamics of consumption are of the greatest interest to someone who seeks to project consumer spending patterns into the future—perhaps as an aid to merchandising. But here we are interested in the larger phenomenon of the relationship of consumption as a whole to the flow of gross national product.

Figure 5-2 shows us this historic relationship since 1929. Certain things stand out.

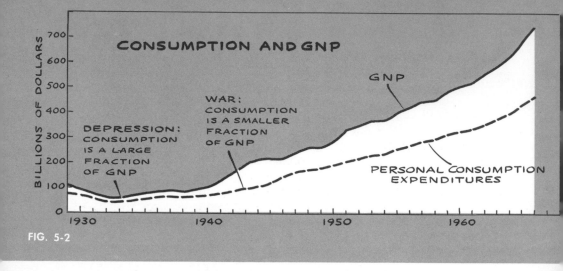

FIG. 5-2

1. *Consumption spending is by far the largest category of spending in GNP.* Total consumer expenditures—for durable goods, such as automobiles or washing machines; nondurables, like food or clothing; and services, such as recreation or medical care—account for approximately two-thirds of all the final buying in the economy.

2. *Consumption is not only the biggest, it is also the most stable, of all the streams of expenditure.* For consumption, as we have mentioned, is the essential economic activity. Unless there is a total breakdown in the social system, households will consume some bare minimum. Further, it is a fact of common experience that even in adverse circumstances, households seek to maintain their accustomed living standards. Thus consumption activities constitute a kind of floor for the level of over-all economic activity. Investment and government spending, as we shall see, are capable of sudden reversals; but the streams of consumer spending tend to display a measure of stability over time.

3. *Consumption is nonetheless capable of considerable fluctuation as a proportion of GNP.* Recalling our previous discussion, we can see that this proportionate fluctuation must reflect changes in the relative importance of investment and government spending. And indeed this is the case. As investment spending fell in the Depression, consumption bulked relatively larger in GNP; as government spending increased during the war, consumption bulked relatively smaller. The changing *relative* size of consumption, in other words, reflects broad changes in *other* sectors rather than sharp changes in consuming habits.

4. *Despite its importance, consumption alone will not "buy back" GNP.* It is well to recall that consumption, although the largest component of GNP, is still *only* two-thirds of GNP. Government buying and business buying of investment goods are essential if the income-expenditure circuit is to be closed. During our subsequent analysis it will help to remember that consumption expenditure by itself does not provide the only impetus of demand.

Saving in historic perspective

This first view of consumption activity sets the stage for our inquiry into the dynamic causes of fluctuations in GNP. We already know that the saving-investment relationship lies at the center of this problem, and that much saving arises from the household sector. Hence, let us see what we can learn about the saving process in historic perspective.

We begin with Fig. 5-3 that shows us the relationship of household saving to disposable income—that is, to household sector incomes after the payment of taxes.

What we see here are two interesting facts. First, during the bottom of the Great Depression there were *no* savings in the household sector. In fact, under the duress of unemployment, millions of households were forced to *dissave*—to borrow or to draw on their old savings (hence the negative figure for the sector as a whole). By way of contrast, we notice the immense savings of the peak war years when consumers' goods were rationed and households were urged to save. Clearly, then, the *amount* of saving is capable of great fluctuation, falling to zero or to negative figures in periods of great economic distress and rising to as much as a quarter of income during periods of goods shortages.

In Fig. 5-4, however, we are struck by another fact. However variable the amounts, the savings *ratio* shows a considerable stability in "normal" years. This steadiness is particularly noteworthy in the postwar period. From 1950 to the present, consumption has ranged between roughly 92 to 95 per cent of disposable personal income—which is, of

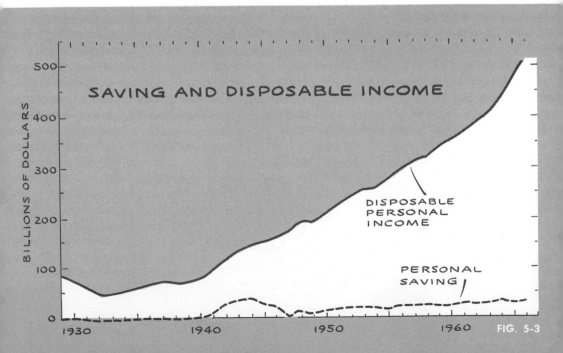

SAVING AND DISPOSABLE INCOME

BILLIONS OF DOLLARS

DISPOSABLE PERSONAL INCOME

PERSONAL SAVING

1930   1940   1950   1960   FIG. 5-3

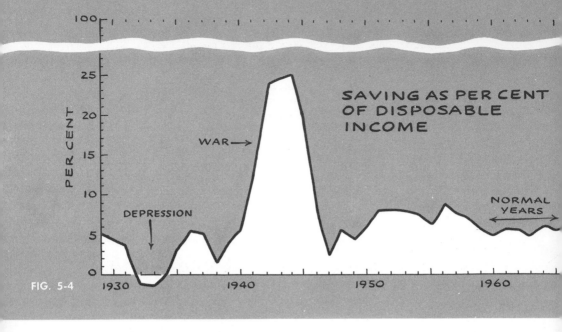

FIG. 5-4

course, the same as saying that savings have ranged between 8 and 5 per cent; and during the 1960's the range has been even smaller, averaging, from year to year, variations of less than half of 1 per cent around a persistent value of about 5.7 per cent. *That is, in an average recent year we have consumed a little more than 94 cents of each dollar of income, and this ratio has stayed very steady as our incomes have risen.*

Long-run savings behavior

This stability of the long-run savings ratio is an interesting and important phenomenon, and something of a puzzling one, for we might easily imagine that the savings ratio would rise over time. Statistical investigations of cross sections of the nation show that rich families tend to save not only larger amounts, but larger *percentages* of their income, than poor families do. Thus as the entire nation has grown richer, and as families have moved from lower income brackets to higher ones, it would seem natural to suppose that they would also take on the higher savings characteristics that accompany upper incomes.

Were this so, the economy would face a very serious problem. In order to sustain its higher levels of aggregate income, it would then have to invest an even larger *proportion* of its income to offset its growing ratio of savings to income. As we shall see in our next chapter, investment is always a source of potential trouble because it is so much riskier than any other business function. If we had to keep on making propor-

60

tionally larger investments each year to keep pace with our proportion-ally growing savings, we should live in an exceedingly vulnerable eco-nomic environment.

Fortunately, we are rescued from this dangerous situation, because our long-run savings ratio, as we have seen, displays a reassuring steadiness. In fact, there has been no significant upward trend in the savings ratio for the nation's households since the mid-1800's, and there may have been a slight downward trend.*

Short- vs. long-run savings behavior

How do we reconcile this long-run stability with the fact that statistical studies always reveal that rich families *do* save a larger percentage of their incomes than poor families? As the nation has moved, en masse, into higher income brackets, why has it not also saved proportionately more of its income?

The answer hinges on important differences between the savings behavior of typical families over a short period of time and over a longer period. In the short run, families in every income bracket do indeed increase their savings sharply as their incomes rise. Much of a salary raise or a windfall is likely to be used *at first* for savings purposes. Debts may be quickly paid off. Money may be allowed to pile up in the bank while plans are made to readjust living standards. Even when the in-crease in income is used for a splurge such as the purchase of a new car, income may be allowed to lie idle for a short period. Thus, in the short run, savings ratios for additions to income are typically higher than they were before the increase was received.

What is true for the short run, however, is not true for the long run. From decade to decade, and even from year to year, powerful pressures and pervasive changes in our environment seem to operate on families at all levels, giving rise to a slow, secular decline in the desire to save. The growth of Social Security and pension plans, the impingement of higher income taxes, the steady expansion of advertising and consumer credit, the temptations of affluence, and the spirit of keeping up with the Joneses —all these influences appear to have worked a gradual decline in the long-run desires of *all* income groups. In addition, despite the statistics that show a steady rise in savings-ratios from income class to income class, it is likely that families in different income groups save much more

---

*Economists maintain a certain tentativeness about their assertions as to long-run trends, since the statistical information on which they are based is inevitably subject to some error and uncertainty.

nearly equal proportions of their incomes than our "cross section" data show.*

As a result of these and still other motivations, savings behavior in the long run differs considerably from that in the short run. Over the years, American households have shown a remarkable stability in their rate of over-all savings. Its importance has already been mentioned. In a shorter period of time, however—over a few months or perhaps a year—households tend to save higher fractions of increases in their incomes than they do in the long run. The very great importance of this fact we shall subsequently note.

The consumption-income relationship

What we have heretofore seen are some of the historical and empirical relationships of consumption and personal saving to income. We have taken the trouble to investigate these relationships in some detail, since they are among the most important causes of the gaps that have to be closed by investment. But the statistical facts in themselves are only a halfway stage in our macroeconomic investigation. Now we want to go beyond the facts to a generalized understanding of what they mean. Thus our next task is to extract from the facts certain *relationships* that are sufficiently regular and dependable for us to build into a new dynamic model of the economy.

If we reflect back over the data we have examined, one primary conclusion comes to mind. This is the indisputable fact that the *amount* of saving generated by the household sector depends in the first instance upon the income enjoyed by the household sector. Despite the stability of the savings ratio, we have seen that the volume of saving in the economy is susceptible of great variation from negative amounts in the Great Depression to very large amounts in boom times. Now we must see if we can find a systematic connection between the changing size of income and the changing size of saving.

---

*For instance, Professor Milton Friedman has suggested that middle-class families who have suffered temporary reverses (and who are therefore counted in lower than their "regular" income brackets) will typically maintain their living standards and reduce their savings, thereby causing a lower savings ratio for these lower brackets than would be found if we included only "permanent" members of it. Conversely, families that have had a lucky year and are temporary residents of a higher bracket may save more than is customary for regular residents of that bracket, thereby exaggerating the saving propensities of the upper groups. The motivation to save, in order to provide future well-being, may well result in surprisingly similar savings ratios, at least in the broad spectrum of income brackets between the very low and the very high.

The propensity to consume

There is indeed such a relationship which lies at the heart of macro-economic analysis. We call it the *consumption schedule*, or more formally, the *propensity to consume*, the name invented by John Maynard Keynes who first formulated it.   What is this "propensity" to consume? We mean by it that the relationship between consumption and income is sufficiently dependable so that we can actually *predict* how much consumption (or how much saving) will be associated with a given level of income.

We base such predictions on a *schedule* that enables us to see the income-consumption relationship over a considerable range of variation. Table 5-1 is such a schedule—a purely hypothetical one—for us to examine.

TABLE 5 • 1   CONSUMPTION SCHEDULE (IN BILLIONS OF DOLLARS)

Income	Consumption	Savings
100	80	20
110	87	23
120	92	28
130	95	35
140	97	43

One could imagine, of course, innumerable different consumption schedules; in one society a given income might be accompanied by a much higher propensity to consume (or propensity to save) than in another. But the basic hypothesis of Keynes—a hypothesis amply confirmed by research—was that the consumption schedule in all modern industrial societies had a particular basic configuration, despite these variations. The propensity to consume, said Keynes, reflected the fact that on the average, *men tended to increase their consumption as their incomes rose, but not by as much as their income.* In other words, as the incomes of individuals rose, so did both their consumption *and their savings.*

Note that Keynes did not say that the proportion of saving rose. We have seen how involved is the dynamic determination of savings ratios. Keynes merely suggested that the *amount* of saving would rise as income rose—or to put it conversely again, that families would not use *all* their increases in income for consumption purposes alone. It is well to remember that these conclusions hold in going down the schedule as well as up. Keynes' basic "law" implies that when there is a decrease in income, there will be some decrease in the *amount of saving,* or that a family will not absorb a fall in its income entirely by contracting its consumption.

What does the consumption schedule look like in the United States? We will come to that shortly. First, however, let us fill in our understanding of the terms we will need for our generalized study.

The average and marginal propensity to consume

The consumption schedule gives us two ways of measuring the fundamental economic relationship of income and saving. One way is simply to take any given level of income and to compute the percentage relation of consumption to that income. This gives us the *average propensity to consume.* In Table 5-2, using the same hypothetical schedule as before, we make this computation.

The average propensity to consume, in other words, tells us how a society at any given moment divides its total income between consumption and saving. It is thus a kind of measure of long-run savings behavior, for the ratios in which households divide their income between saving and consuming reflect established habits and, as we have seen, do not ordinarily change rapidly.

TABLE 5 • 2 CALCULATION OF THE AVERAGE PROPENSITY TO CONSUME

Income	Consumption	Consumption divided by income (Average propensity to consume)
	(Billions of dollars)	
100	80	.80
110	87	.79
120	92	.77
130	95	.73
140	97	.69

But we can also use our schedule to measure another very important aspect of saving behavior: the way households divide *increases* (or decreases) in income between consumption and saving. This *marginal propensity to consume* is quite different from the average propensity to consume, as the figures in Table 5-3 (still from our original hypothetical schedule) demonstrate.

Much of economics, in micro- as well as macroanalysis, is concerned with studying the effects of *changes* in economic life. It is precisely here that marginal concepts take on their importance. When we speak of the average propensity to consume, we relate all consumption and all income from the bottom up, so to speak, and thus we call attention to behavior covering a great variety of situations and conditions. But when

**TABLE
5 • 3**   CALCULATION OF THE
MARGINAL PROPENSITY TO CONSUME

Income	Consumption (Billions of dollars)	Change in income	Change in consumption	(Marginal propensity to consume) = Change in consumption divided by change in income
100	80	—	—	—
110	87	10	7	.70
120	92	10	5	.50
130	95	10	3	.30
140	97	10	2	.20

we speak of the marginal propensity to consume, we are focusing only on our behavior toward *changes* in our incomes. Thus the marginal approach is invaluable, as we shall see, in dealing with the effects of short-run fluctuations in GNP.

A diagram of the propensity to consume

The essentially simple idea of a systematic relationship between income and consumption will play an extremely important part in the model of the economy we shall soon construct. But the relationships we have thus far defined are too vague to be of much usefulness. We want to know if we can extract from the facts of experience not only a general dependence of consumption on income, but a *fairly precise method of determining exactly how much saving will be associated with a given amount of income.*

Here we reach a place where it will help us to use diagrams and simple equations rather than words alone. So let us begin by transferring our conception of a propensity to consume schedule to a new kind of diagram directly showing the interrelation of income and consumption.

The *scatter diagram* (Fig. 5-5) on page 66 shows precisely that. Along the vertical axis on the left we have marked off intervals to measure total consumer expenditure in billions of dollars; along the horizontal axis on the bottom we measure disposable personal income, also in billions of dollars. The dots tell us, for the year that the numerals indicate, how large consumption and income were. For instance, if we take the topmost dot (for 1966) and look directly below it to the horizontal axis, we can see that disposable personal income for that year was roughly $510 billion. The same dot measured against the vertical consumption axis tells us that consumption for 1966 was a little more than $475 billion.

The actual values for the rounded-off figures shown in the scatter diagram are: $508.8 billion for disposable income and $479.0 billion for

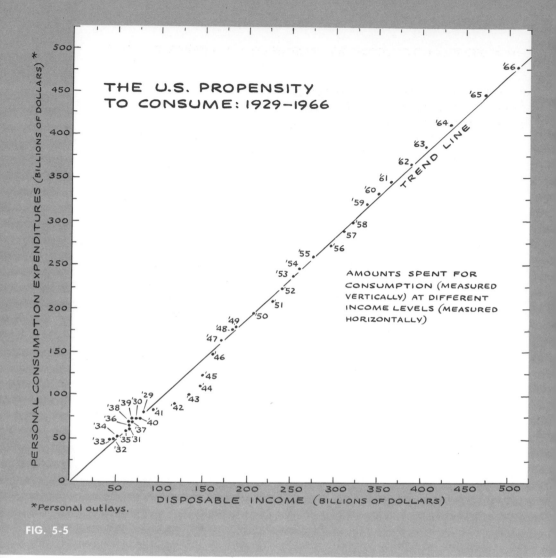

THE U.S. PROPENSITY
TO CONSUME: 1929–1966

PERSONAL CONSUMPTION EXPENDITURES (BILLIONS OF DOLLARS) *

AMOUNTS SPENT FOR
CONSUMPTION (MEASURED
VERTICALLY) AT DIFFERENT
INCOME LEVELS (MEASURED
HORIZONTALLY)

TREND LINE

DISPOSABLE INCOME (BILLIONS OF DOLLARS)

*Personal outlays.

FIG. 5-5

consumption. If we divide the figure for consumption by that for income, we get a value of 94.1 per cent for our propensity to consume. If we subtract that from 100, our propensity to save must have been 5.9 per cent.

Returning to the diagram itself, we notice that the black line which "fits" the trend of the dots does not go evenly from corner to corner. If it did, it would mean that each amount of income was matched by an *equal* amount of consumption—in other words, that there was no saving. Instead, the line leans slightly downward, indicating that as income goes higher, consumption also increases, but not by quite as much. If we now measure the *angle* of the "trend line" that fits the dots most accurately up to whatever end year we are interested in (and this line will be ever so slightly different as we alter our terminal years), we have our average propensity to consume for that year.

Does the chart also show us our marginal propensity to consume?

66

Indeed it does. If you take any single year and look at the changes in consumption and income from that year to the next, you will be considering the marginal propensity to consume.

Note that for many years, especially in the 1950's and 1960's, the marginal propensity to consume (if we drew it as a line connecting each pair of dots) would virtually coincide with the average propensity to consume.

Not so, however, for all years, as an inspection of the chart will show. During the war years, for instance, as the result of a shortage of many consumer goods and a general exhortation to save, the marginal propensity to consume was unusually low. That is why the dots during those years form a bulge below the main trend line. After the war, we can also see that increases in income resulted in a very high proportional increase in consumption. As a matter of fact, for a few years consumption actually rose *faster* than income, as people drew down their wartime savings to make up for wartime shortages. Between 1946 and 1947, for example, disposable income rose by some $9.8 billion, but personal outlays rose by almost $18 billion! By 1950, however, the consumption–income relationship was back to virtually the same ratio as during the 1930's.

The propensity to consume in simple mathematics

There is another way of reducing to shorthand clarity the propensity to consume idea, at least for those who find simple mathematics an expressive language. Even those who do not should try to follow the very simple formulas presented, if only because we shall often use the letters as abbreviations in our subsequent chapters.

We begin by giving letters to the words we use again and again.

$$C = \text{consumption}$$
$$I = \text{investment}$$
$$S = \text{saving}$$
$$Y = \text{income}$$

Finally, we use the symbol $f(\ )$ to express the idea of relationship. Read it "function of (whatever is included in the parentheses)."

Now when we talk of $C = f(Y)$, we read it aloud as "consumption is a function of income." What this means is that consumption is related to income in some manner that can be described by a mathematical relationship.

What kind of relationship? Highly sophisticated and complex formulas have been tried to "fit" the values of C and Y. Their economics and their mathematics both are beyond the scope of this book. But we can at least get a clearer idea of what it means to devise a *consumption function* by trying to make a very simple one ourselves. If we look at Fig. 5-5 on p. 66, we can see that during the Depression years, at very low levels of income, around $50 billion, consumption was just as large as income itself. (In some years it was actually bigger; as we have seen, there was net dissaving in 1933.) Hence, we might hypothesize that a consumption function for the United States might have a fixed value representing this "bottom," and some regular fraction designating the amount of income that would be saved for all income over that amount. Furthermore, recalling the stability of the savings ratio of 5.7 per cent (at least in postwar years) we might hypothesize that we will consume 94.3 per cent of all income over the "bottom."

In point of fact, such a formula would yield roughly accurate results. For 1966, for instance, it would predict that total consumption would equal $50 billion plus 94.3 per cent of all disposable income over $50 billion. This gives us a figure of $483 billion for consumption in 1966 — not very far from the actual figure of $479 billion. Let the reader be warned, however, that devising a reliable consumption function is much more difficult than this simple and uncritical test would indicate. Nonetheless, it gives one an idea of what the economist hopes to find — a precise way of expressing the relationship between C and Y, which can then be used for *predicting* changes in C in the future.*

The passivity of consumption

Throughout this chapter we have talked of the dynamics of consuming and saving. Now it is important that we recall the main conclusion of our analysis, *the essential passivity of consumption as an economic process.* Consumption spending, we will recall, is a function of income. This means it is a *dependent* variable in the economic process, a factor that is acted *on,* but that does not itself generate spontaneous action.

To be sure, it is well to qualify this assertion. We have earlier paid

---

*For those who are at home in simple algebra, we can generalize our results. We begin with a simple hypothetical formulation of the consumption function as follows:

$C = Y_0 + c(Y - Y_0)$, where
C = consumption
Y_0 = the value of disposable income at the "bottom" (where $Y = C$)
c = long-run ratio of C to Y, and
Y = current value of disposable income

Substituting values for the United States in 1966, we get
Y_0 = $50 billion
c = .943
Y = $509 billion. Thus,
$C = \$50 + .943 (\$509 - 50) = \$483$ billion

special attention to the long-term stability of the savings ratio and pointed out that one cause of this stability was a general movement of all households toward consumption as their incomes grew. This dynamic, although slow-acting, behavioral trend has exerted a strong background force on the trend of the economy. Then, too, there have been occasions, the most famous being the years just following World War II, when consumption seemed to generate its own momentum and—as we have seen—raced out ahead of income. But this was a period when wants were intense, following wartime shortages, and when huge amounts of wartime savings were available to translate those wants into action. During the normal course of things, no matter how intense "wants" may be, consumers ordinarily lack the spendable cash to translate their desires into effective demand.

This highlights an extremely important point. Wants and appetites *alone* do not drive the economy upward; if they did, we should experience a more impelling demand in depressions, when people are hungry, than in booms, when they are well off. Hence the futility of those who urge the cure of depressions by suggesting that consumers should buy more! There is nothing consumers would rather do than buy more, if only they could. Let us not forget, furthermore, that consumers are at all times being cajoled and exhorted to increase their expenditures by the multibillion dollar pressures exerted by the advertising industry.

The trouble is, however, that consumers cannot buy more unless they have more incomes to buy with. It is true, of course, that for short periods they can borrow or they may temporarily sharply reduce their rate of savings; but each household's borrowing capacity or accumulated savings are limited, so that once these bursts are over, the steady habitual ways of saving and spending are apt to reassert themselves.

Thus it is clear that in considering the consumer sector we study a part of the economy that, however ultimately important, is not in itself the source of major changes in activity. Consumption mirrors and, as we shall see, can magnify disturbances elsewhere in the economy, but it does not initiate the greater part of our economic fortunes or misfortunes. For that, we must turn to the two remaining great sectors, where we shall find the driving elements of our economic mechanism.

Summary

1. Consumption is the largest sector of economic activity, and accordingly the largest absolute source of demand within the economy. Nonetheless, *consumption alone will not create enough demand to buy all of the nation's output.*
2. Consumption in absolute amounts is capable of wide fluctuations, but *the relation of consumption to disposable income is relatively stable.*

3. Over the long run (since the mid-1800's), *the fraction of disposable income that has been saved seems to have been more or less unchanged.* This has prevented the economy from facing the problem of a growing proportion of saving. In the short run, the ratio of saving to increases in income is apt to be higher than over the long run.

4. We call the relation between saving and disposable income the *consumption schedule.* This schedule shows us the division of disposable income, at different levels of income, between consumption and saving.

5. The consumption schedule shows that the *amount of consumption rises as income rises, but not by as much as income.* Therefore the amount of saving also rises as income rises.

6. From the consumption schedule we can derive two ratios. One shows us the relation between the *total income* and the *total consumption* of any period. We call this the *average propensity to consume.* The other shows us the relationship between the *change in income* and the *change in consumption* between two periods. This is called the *marginal propensity to consume.*

7. The average propensity to consume shows us how people behave with regard to consumption and saving over the *long run.* The marginal propensity to consume shows us how they behave over the *short run.*

8. The common abbreviations used in economics are: C for consumption, I for investment, S for saving and Y for income (note that I is used only for investment). We also use the symbol f followed by parentheses ( ) to express relationships. It is read "function of."

9. Consumption is generally regarded as a *passive economic force,* rather than an initiating active one. It is acted on by changes in income. Thus we generalize the force of consumption by saying that it is a *function of income: C = f(Y).*

Questions

1. What are the main components of consumption? Why are some of these components more dynamic than others?

2. "The reason we have depressions is that consumption isn't big enough to buy the output of all our factories." What is wrong with this statement?

3. What do you think accounts for the relative stability of the savings ratio over the long run? Would you expect the savings ratio in the short run to be relatively stable? Why or why not?

4. What is meant by the consumption schedule? Could we also speak of a savings schedule? What would be the relation between the two?

5. Suppose that a given family had an income of $8,000 and saved $400. What would be its propensity to consume? Could you tell from this information what its marginal propensity to consume was?

6. Suppose the same family now increased its income to $9,000 and its saving to $500. What is its new propensity to consume? Can you figure out the family's marginal propensity to consume?

7. Draw a scatter diagram to show the following:

Family income	Savings
$4,000	$ 0
5,000	50
6,000	150
7,000	300
8,000	500

From the figures above, calculate the average propensity to consume at each level of income. Can you calculate the marginal propensity to consume for each jump in income?

8. How do you read $S = f(Y)$? From what you know of the propensity to consume, how would you describe the relation of S to Y?

9. Why can't we cure depressions by urging people to go out and spend?

6

The investment sector

Consumption is an activity everyone knows as an experienced economic actor in his own right; investing, on the other hand, is an economy activity foreign to most of us. For investing, in the context of macroeconomic analysis, has very little to do with the kind of "investing" familiar to us in the selection of stocks or bonds as personal assets. Investing, as the economist sees it, is an activity that uses the resources of the community to maintain or add to its stock of capital wealth.

Now this may or may not coincide with the purchase of a security. When we buy an ordinary stock or bond, we usually buy it from someone who has previously owned it, and therefore our personal act of "investment" becomes, in the economic view of things, merely a *transfer* of claims without any direct bearing on the creation of new wealth. A pays B cash and takes his General Manufacturing stock; B takes A's cash and doubtless uses it to buy stock from C; but the transactions between A and B and C in no way alter the actual amount of real capital in the economy. Only when we buy *newly issued* shares or bonds, and then only when their proceeds are directly allocated to new equipment or plant, does our act of personal financial investment result in the addition of wealth to the community. In that case, A buys his stock directly (or through an investment banker) from General Manufacturing itself, and not from B. A's cash can now be spent for new capital goods, as presumably it will be.

Thus investment, as economists see it, is a little-known form of activity for the great majority of us. This is true not only because real investment is not the same as personal financial investment, but because the real investors of the nation usually act on behalf of an institution other than the familiar one of the household. The unit of

73

behavior in the world of investment is typically the business *firm*, just as in the world of consumption it is the household. Boards of directors, chief executives, or small-business proprietors are the persons who decide whether or not to devote business cash to the construction of new facilities or to the addition of inventory; and this decision, as we shall see, is very different in character and motivation from the decisions familiar to us as members of the household sector.

The sector in profile

Before we begin an investigation into the dynamics of investment decisions, however, let us gain a quick acquaintance with the sector as a whole, much as we did with the consumption sector.

Figure 6-1 gives a first general impression of the investment sector in a recent year. Note that the main source of gross private domestic investment expenditure comes from retained earnings of businesses, that is, from profits that have not been distributed to households or paid to the government as taxes. However, as the next bar shows, gross investment *expenditures* are considerably larger than retained earnings. The difference represents funds that business obtains in several ways.

1. It may draw on cash (or securities) accumulated out of retained earnings or depreciation accruals of *previous* years.

2. It may obtain savings from the household sector by direct borrowing, or by sale of new issues of shares of stock, or indirectly via insurance companies, or savings banks, or pension funds, etc.

3. It may borrow from commercial banks.

The last of these sources of funds we will not fully understand until we reach Chapter 9, when we study the money mechanism. But our chart enables us to see that most gross investment is financed by business itself from its *internal* sources—retained earnings plus depreciation accruals—and that external sources play only a secondary role. In particular, this is true of new stock issues which, during the 1960's, raised only some 3 to 8 per cent of the funds spent by the business sector.

The categories of investment

From the total funds at its disposal, the business sector now renews its worn-out capital and adds new capital. Let us say a word concerning some of the main categories of investment expenditure.

1. *Inventories.* At the top of our bar we note an item of $13.4 billion for *additions to inventory*. Note that this figure does not represent total

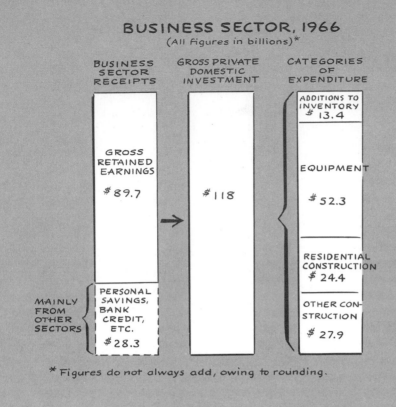

BUSINESS SECTOR, 1966
(All figures in billions)*

BUSINESS SECTOR RECEIPTS	GROSS PRIVATE DOMESTIC INVESTMENT	CATEGORIES OF EXPENDITURE
GROSS RETAINED EARNINGS $89.7	$118	ADDITIONS TO INVENTORY $13.4
		EQUIPMENT $52.3
		RESIDENTIAL CONSTRUCTION $24.4
MAINLY FROM OTHER SECTORS — PERSONAL SAVINGS, BANK CREDIT, ETC. $28.3		OTHER CONSTRUCTION $27.9

* Figures do not always add, owing to rounding.

FIG. 6-1

inventories, but only *changes* in inventories, upwards or downwards. If there had been no change in inventory over the year, the item would have been zero, even if existing inventories were huge. Why? Because those huge inventories would have been included in the investment expenditure flow of *previous* years when they were built up.

Additions to inventories are capital, but they need not be additions to capital *goods*. Indeed, they are likely to include farm stocks, consumers goods, and other items of all kinds. Of course, these are goods held by business, and not by consumers. But that is the very point. We count inventory additions as net investment because they are output that has been produced but that has not been consumed. In another year, if these goods pass from the hands of business into consumers' hands, and inventories decline, we will have a negative figure for net inventory investment. This will mean, just as it appears, that we are consuming goods faster than we are producing them — that we are disinvesting.

Investments in inventory are particularly significant for one reason. Alone among the investment categories, inventories can be *rapidly* used up as well as increased. A positive figure for one year or even one calendar quarter can quickly turn into a negative figure the next. *This means that expenditures for inventory are usually the most volatile element of any in gross national product.* In 1958, for example, net investment in inventories was *minus* $1.5 billion — that is, we drew down

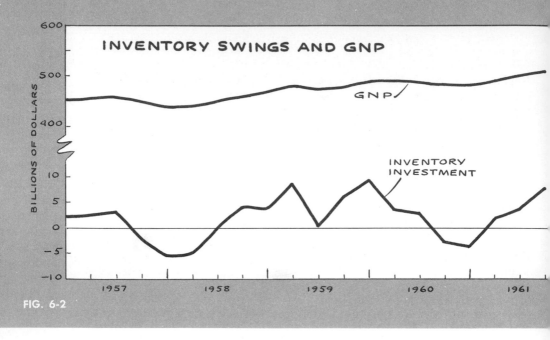

FIG. 6-2

on existing inventories to that amount. The next year, inventory investment was $4.8 billion—a swing of $6.3 billion in twelve months. The close relation between these changes in expenditures and GNP can be seen from Fig. 6-2.

As we shall see more clearly later, this pattern of closely parallel changes has a great deal of significance for business conditions. Note that while inventories are being built up, they serve as an offset to saving—that is, some of the resources released from consumption are used by business firms to build up stocks of inventory capital. But when inventories are being "worked off," this avenue for closing the demand gap is no longer available. As we would expect, this can give rise to serious economic troubles.

2. *Equipment.* The next item in our bar is more familiar: $52.3 billion for *equipment.* Here we find expenditures for goods of a varied sort— lathes, trucks, generators, computers, office typewriters.* The total includes both new equipment and replacement equipment, and we need a word of caution here. Exactly what does it mean to "replace" a given item of equipment? Suppose we have a textile loom that cost $100,000 and that is now on its last legs. Is the loom "replaced" by spending another $100,000, regardless of what kind of machine the money will buy? Suppose loom prices have gone up and $100,000 no longer buys a loom of the same capacity? Or suppose that prices have remained steady; but that owing to technological advance, $100,000 now buys a loom of double the old capacity? Such questions make the definition of

---

*But *not* typewriters bought by consumers. Thus the same good can be classified as a consumption item or an investment item depending on the use to which it is put.

"replacement" an accountant's headache and an economist's nightmare. We need not involve ourselves deeper in the question, but we should note the complexities introduced into a seemingly simple matter once we leave the changeless world of a stationary flow and enter the world of invention and innovation.

3. *Construction.* Our next section on the diagrammatic bar is total *residential construction.* Why do we include this item of $24.4 billion in the investment sector when most of it is represented by new houses that householders buy for their own use?

The answer is that most houses are built by business firms (such as contractors and developers) who put up the houses *before* they are sold. Thus the original expenditures involved in building houses typically come from businessmen, not from households. Later, when the house-holder buys a house, he takes possession of an *existing* asset, and his expenditure does not pump new incomes out into the economy, but only repays the contractor who *did* pump new incomes out.

Actually this is a somewhat arbitrary definition, since, after all, busi-nessmen own all output before consumers buy it. However, in macro-economics, our goal is to understand growth and fluctuation in growth, and we define our terms to serve that purpose. Residential housing "behaves" very much like other items of construction, and it simplifies our understanding of the forces at work in the economy if we classify it as an investment expenditure rather than a consumer expenditure.

The last item on the bar, $27.9 billion of *other construction,* is largely made up of the "plant" in "plant and equipment"—factories and stores and private office buildings and warehouses. (It does not, however, include public construction such as roads, dams, harbors, or public buildings, all of which are picked up under government purchases.) It is interesting to note that the building of structures, as represented by the total of residential construction plus other private construction, accounts for over half of all investment expenditure, and this total would be further swelled if public construction were included herein. This accords with the dominant role of structures in the panorama of national wealth we first encountered in Chapter 2. It tells us, too, that swings in con-struction expenditure can be a major level for economic change.

Investment in historic perspective

With this introduction behind us, let us take a look at the flow of investment, not over a single year, but over many years.

In Fig. 6-3, several things spring to our notice. Clearly, investment is not nearly so smooth an unperturbed flow of spending as consumption. Note that gross investment in the depths of the Depression virtually

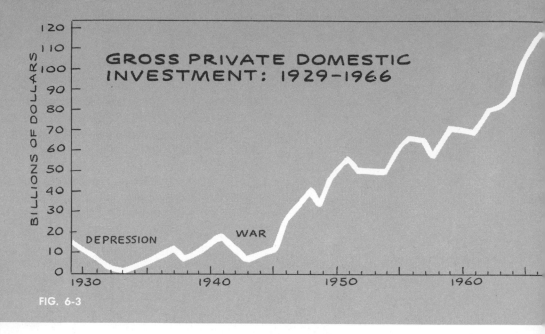

GROSS PRIVATE DOMESTIC INVESTMENT: 1929–1966

BILLIONS OF DOLLARS

120
110
100
90
80
70
60
50
40
30
20
10
0

DEPRESSION   WAR

1930   1940   1950   1960

FIG. 6-3

disappeared—that we almost failed to *maintain*, much less add to, our stock of wealth. (Net investment was, in fact, a negative figure for several years.) Note also how investment was reduced during the war years as private capital formation was deliberately limited through government allocations.

Two important conclusions emerge from this examination of investment spending:

First, as we have already seen, investment spending contains a component—net additions to inventory—that is capable of drastic, sudden shifts. This accounts for much of the wavelike movement of the total flow of investment expenditure.

Second, as can be seen in Fig. 6-3, *investment is also capable of more or less total collapse, to a degree never found in consumption.* During the Great Depression, while consumption fell by 41 per cent, investment fell by *91 per cent.* Similarly, from 1933 to 1940, whereas consumption rose by little more than half, investment increased 9 times.

The instability of investment

At first glance the flow of investment expenditures, especially in the 1960's, seems to be as smooth and relatively unperturbed as the flow of consumption. Yet there are two striking and conspicuous differences between the two streams.

First, as we have seen, investment expenditures contain a component—net additions to inventories—that is capable of drastic sudden shifts, quite unlike any of the constituent flows of consumption.

78

Second, investment spending as a whole is capable of more or less total collapses, of a severity and degree that are never to be found in consumption.

The prime example of such a collapse was, of course, the Great Depression. From 1929 to 1933, while consumption fell by 41 per cent, investment fell by *91 per cent,* as we can see in Fig. 6-3. Similarly, whereas consumption rose by a little more than half from 1933 to 1940, investment in the same period rose by *nine times.*

The importance of investment

This potential for collapse or spectacular boom always makes investment a source of special concern in the economic picture. But even the tendency toward inventory fluctuations, or toward milder declines in other capital expenditures, is sufficient to identify investment as a prime source of economic instability. There is often a tendency among non-economists to equate all buying in the economy with consumer buying. Let us never lose sight of the fact that the maintenance of, and addition to, capital is also a part of GNP spending and that a considerable part of the labor force depends for its livelihood on the making of investment goods. Remember that at the bottom of the Great Depression in 1933, it was estimated that one-third of total unemployment was directly associated with the shrinkage in the capital goods industry.

We shall want to look more closely into the reasons for the sensitivity of investment spending. But first a question must surely have occurred to the reader. For all its susceptibility to change, the investment sector is, after all, a fairly small sector. In 1966, total expenditures for gross private domestic investment came to less than $\frac{1}{6}$ of GNP, and the normal year-to-year variation in investment spending in the 1950's and 1960's was only about $5 billion to $10 billion, or 1 to 2 per cent of GNP. To devote so much time to such small fluctuations seems a disproportionate emphasis. How could so small a tail as investment wag so large a dog as GNP?

The multiplier

The answer — as we may also recall from our historical survey of the Depression era — lies in a relationship of economic activities known as the *multiplier.* The multiplier describes the fact that *additions to spending (or diminutions in spending) have an impact on income that is greater than the original increase or decrease in spending itself.* In other words, even small increments in spending can *multiply* their effects (whence the name).

It is not difficult to understand the general idea of the multiplier. Suppose that we have an island community whose economy is in a perfect circular flow, unchanging from year to year. Next, let us introduce the stimulus of a new investment expenditure in the form of a stranger who arrives from another island (with a supply of acceptable money) and who proceeds to build a house. This immediately increases the islanders' incomes. In our case, we will assume that our stranger spends $1,000 on wages for construction workers, and we will ignore all other expenditures he may make. (We also make the assumption that these workers were previously unemployed, so that our stranger is not merely taking them from some other task.)

Now the construction workers, who have had their incomes increased by $1,000, are very unlikely to sit on this money. As we know from our study of the marginal propensity to consume, they are apt to save some of the increase (and they may have to pay some to the government as income taxes), but the rest they will spend on additional consumption goods. Let us suppose that they save 10 per cent and pay taxes of 20 per cent on the $1,000 they get. They will then have $700 left over to spend for additional consumer goods and services.

But this is not an end to it. The sellers of these goods and services will now have received $700 over and above their former incomes, and they, too, will be certain to spend a considerable amount of their new income. If we assume that their family spending patterns (and their tax brackets) are the same as the construction workers, they will also spend 70 per cent of their new incomes, or $490. And now the wheel takes another turn, as still *another* group receives new income and spends a fraction of it — in turn.

The continuing impact of respending

If our stranger now departed as mysteriously as he came, we would have to describe the economic impact of his investment as constituting a single "bulge" of income that gradually disappeared. The bulge would consist of the original $1,000, the secondary $700, the tertiary $490, and so on. If everyone continued to spend 70 per cent of his new income, after ten rounds all that would remain by way of new spending traceable to the original $1,000 would be about $38. Soon, the impact of the new investment on incomes would have virtually disappeared.

But now let us suppose that after our visitor builds his house and leaves, another visitor arrives to build another house. This time, in other words, we assume that the level of investment spending *continues* at the higher level to which it was raised by the first expenditure for a new house. We can see that the second house will set into motion precisely the same repercussive effects as did the first, and that the new series of respendings will be added to the dwindling echoes of the original injection of incomes.

In Fig. 6-4, we can trace this effect. The succession of white bars at the bottom of the graph stands for the continuing injections of $1,000 as new houses are steadily built. (Note that this means the level of new investment is only being maintained, not that it is rising.) Each of these white bars now generates a series of secondary, tertiary, etc., bars that represent the respending of income after taxes and savings. In our example we have assumed that the respending fraction is 50 per cent.

Our diagram shows us two very important things.

1. *A steady flow of new investment generates an equally steady but larger flow of total incomes.* It is very important to note that the incomes generated by respending are just as permanent as those due to the flow of investment itself.

2. We see, as well, that *the rise in income due to a continuing flow of new investment gradually levels out.* As the successive respending fractions become smaller, the rise in income approaches a plateau.

The marginal propensity to save

We can understand now that *the multiplier is the numerical relation between the initial new investment and the total increase in income.* If the initial investment is $1,000 and the total addition to income due to the respending of that $1,000 is $3,000, we have a multiplier of 3; if the total addition is $2,000, the multiplier is 2.

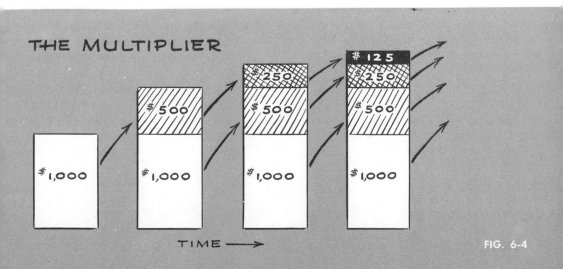

THE MULTIPLIER

$125 $250 $500 $1,000

TIME ⟶

FIG. 6-4

What determines how large the multiplier will be? The answer depends entirely on our marginal consumption (or, if you will, our marginal saving) habits—that is, on how much we consume (or save) out of each dollar of additional income that comes to us. Let us follow two cases below. In the first, we will assume that each recipient spends only one half of any new income that comes to him, saving the rest. In the second case, he spends three-quarters of it and saves one-quarter.

It is very clear that the amount of income that will be passed along from one receiver to the next will be much larger where the marginal propensity to consume is higher. In fact, we can see that the total amount of new incomes (the total amount of the boxes above) must be mathematically related to the proportion that is spent each time.

What is this relationship? The arithmetic is easier to figure if we use not the consumption fraction, but the *saving fraction* (the two are, of course, as intimately related as one slice of cake and the remaining cake). If we use the saving fraction, the *sum of new incomes is obtained by taking the reciprocal of* (i.e., inverting, or turning upside down) *the fraction we save.* Thus, if we save $\frac{1}{2}$ our income, the total amount of new incomes generated by respending will be $\frac{1}{2}$ inverted, or 2—twice the original increase in income. If we save $\frac{1}{4}$, it will be the reciprocal of $\frac{1}{4}$ or 4 times the original change.

The basic multiplier formula

We call the fraction of new income that is saved the *marginal propensity to save* (often abbreviated as mps). As we have just said, this fraction is the complement of an already familiar one, the marginal propensity to consume. If our marginal propensity to consume is 80 per cent,

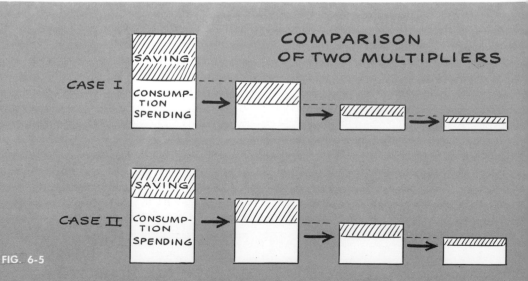

FIG. 6-5

our marginal propensity to save must be 20 per cent; if our mpc is three-quarters, our mps must be one-quarter.

Understanding the relationship between the marginal propensity to save and the size of the resulting respending fractions allows us to state a very simple (but very important) formula for the multiplier:

change in income = multiplier × change in investment

Since we have just learned that the multiplier is determined by the reciprocal of the marginal propensity to save, we can write:

$$\text{multiplier} = \frac{1}{\text{mps}}$$

If we now use the symbols we are familiar with, plus a Greek letter Δ, delta, that means "increase in," we can write the important economic relationship above as follows:

$$\Delta Y = \frac{1}{\text{mps}} \times \Delta I$$

Thus, if our mps is $\frac{1}{4}$ (meaning, let us not forget, that we save a quarter of increases in income and respend the rest), then an increase in investment of $1 billion will lead to a total increase in incomes of $4 billion ($1 billion $\times$ $1/\frac{1}{4}$ = $4 billion). Note that the mps is a complex or *double* fraction—it is $1/\frac{1}{4}$ and *not* $\frac{1}{4}$. If the mps is $\frac{1}{10}$, $1 billion gives rise to incomes of $10 billion; if the mps is 50 per cent, the billion will multiply to $2 billion. And if mps is 1? This means that the entire increase in income is unspent, that our island construction workers tuck away (or find taxed away) their entire newly earned pay. In that case, the multiplier will be 1 also, and the impact of the new investment on the island economy will be no more than the $1,000 earned by the construction workers in the first place.

Leakages

The importance of the size of the marginal savings ratio in determining the effect that additional investment will have on income is thus apparent. Now, however, we must pass from the simple example of our island economy to the more complex behavioral patterns and institutional arrangements of real life. The average propensity to save (the ratio of saving to disposable income) runs around 5 to 6 per cent. In recent years, the *marginal* propensity to save (the ratio of additional saving to increases in income) has not departed very much from this figure. If this is the case, then, following our analysis, the multiplier would be very high. If mps were even as much as 10 per cent of income, a change in investment of $1 billion would bring a $10 billion change in income. If mps were nearer 5 per cent—the approximate level of the average propensity to save—a change of $1 billion would bring a swing of $20 billion. Were this the case, the economy would be subject to the most violent disturbances whenever the level of spending shifted.

In fact, however, the impact of the multiplier is greatly reduced because the successive rounds of spending are damped by factors other than personal saving. One of them we have already introduced in our imaginary island economy. This is the tendency of *government taxation* to "mop up" a fraction of income as it passes from hand to hand. This mopping-up effect of taxation is in actuality much larger than that of saving. For every dollar of change in income, federal taxes will take up to 30 cents, and state and local taxes another 6 cents, compared with less than 5 cents that go into saving.

Another dampener is the tendency of respending to swell *business savings* as well as personal incomes. Of each dollar of new spending, perhaps 10 cents goes into business profits, and this sum is typically saved, at least for a time, rather than immediately respent.

Still another source of damping is the tendency of consumers and businesses to increase purchases from abroad as their incomes rise. These rising *imports* divert 3 to 4 cents of new spending to foreign nations and accordingly reduce the successive impact of each round of expenditure.

All these withdrawals from the respending cycle are called *leakages*, and the total effect of all leakages together (personal savings, business savings, taxes, and imports) is to reduce the over-all impact of the multiplier from an impossibly large figure to a very manageable one. The combined effect of all leakages brings the actual multiplier in the United States in the 1960's to around 2.*

To be sure—and this is very important—all these leakages *can* return to the income stream. Household saving can be turned into capital formation; business profits can be invested; tax receipts can be disbursed in government spending programs; and purchases from foreign sellers can be returned as purchases *by* foreigners. What is at stake here is the regularity and reliability with which these circuits will be closed. In the case of ordinary income going to a household, we can count with considerable assurance on a "return expenditure" of consumption. In the case of the other recipients of funds, the assurance is much less; hence we count their receipts as money that has leaked out of the expenditure flow, for the time being.

---

*In dealing with the multiplier equation ($\Delta Y = \dfrac{1}{\text{mps}} \times \Delta I$), we can interpret mps to mean the total withdrawal from spending due to all leakages. This brings mps to around $\frac{1}{2}$, and gives us a multiplier of 2.

It is interesting to note that the leakages all tend to increase somewhat in boom times and to decline in recessions, which results in a slightly larger multipler in bad times than in good.

The downward multiplier

The multiplier, with its important magnifying action, rests at the very center of our understanding of economic fluctuations. Not only does it explain how relatively small stimuli can exert considerable upward pushes, but it also makes much clearer than before how the failure to offset a small savings gap can snowball into a serious fall in income and employment.

For just as additional income is respent to create still further new income, a loss in income will not stop with the affected households. On the contrary, as families lose income, they cut down on their spending, although the behavior pattern of the propensity to consume schedule suggests that they will not cut their consumption by as much as their loss in income. Yet each reduction in consumption, large or small, lessens to that extent the income or receipts of some other household or firm.

We have already noted that personal savings alone do not determine the full impact of the multiplier. This is even more fortunate on the way down than on the way up. If the size of the multiplier were solely dependent on the marginal propensity to save, an original fall in spending would result in a catastrophic contraction of consumption through the economy. But the leakages that cushion the upward pressure of the multiplier also cushion its downward effect. As spending falls, business savings (profits) fall, tax receipts dwindle, and the flow of imports declines.

All of these leakages now work in the direction of mitigating the repercussions of the original fall in spending. The fall in business profits means that less will be saved by business and thus less withdrawn from respending; the decline in taxes means that more money will be left to consumers; and the drop in imports similarly releases additional spending power for the domestic market. Thus, just as the various leakages pulled money away from consumption on the way up, on the way down they lessen their siphoning effect and in this way restore purchasing power to consumers' hands. As a result, in the downward direction as in the upward, the actual impact of the multiplier is about 2, so that a fall in investment of, say, $5 billion will lower GNP by $10 billion.

The multiplier and investment

Even with a reduced figure, we can now understand how a relatively small change in investment can magnify its impact on GNP. If the typical year-to-year change in investment is around $5 to $10 billion, a multiplier of 2 will produce a change in GNP of $10 to $20 billion, by no means a negligible figure. In addition, as we shall shortly see, the multiplier may set up repercussions that feed back onto investment. But more of that momentarily. First let us make two final points in regard to the multiplier.

1. *Other multipliers.* We have talked of the multiplier in connection with changes in investment spending. *But we must also realize that any change in any spending has a multiplier effect.* An increase in foreigners' purchases of our exports has a multiplier effect, as does an increase in government spending or a decrease in taxes, or a spontaneous increase in consumption itself due to, say, a drop in the propensity to save. Any stimulus to the economy is thus not confined to its original impact, but gives a series of successive pushes to the system until it has finally been absorbed in leakages. We shall come back to this important fact in our next chapter.

2. *Idle resources.* Finally, there is a very important proviso to recognize, although we will not study its full significance until Chap. 10. This is the important difference between an economy with idle resources — unemployed labor or unused machines or land — and one without them.

For *it is only when we have idle resources that the respending impetus of the multiplier is useful.* Then each round of new expenditure can bring idle resources into use, creating not only new money incomes but *new production and employment.* The situation is considerably different when there are no, or few, idle men or machines. Then the expenditure rounds of the multiplier bring higher money incomes, but these are not matched by the increased output.

In both cases, the multiplier exerts its leverage, bringing about an increase in total expenditure larger than the original injection of new spending. In the case without idle resources, however, the results are solely *inflationary,* as the increased spending results in higher incomes and higher prices, but not in higher output. In the case where idle resources exist, we can avoid this mere "money" multiplication and enjoy a rise in output as a result of our increased spending. Indeed, we can even speak of the *employment multiplier* in situations where there is considerable unemployment, meaning by this the total increase in employment brought about by a given increase in spending. We shall return in subsequent chapters to a fuller scrutiny of the difference between the case of idle and of fully employed resources, but we must bear the distinction in mind henceforth.

Summary

1. The investment sector is made up, not of households and their activities, but of *business firms adding to their capital assets.* By and large, these additions to

business capital are financed out of *internal funds* (retained earnings and depreciation accruals) rather than from external sources (borrowing or new equities). The main categories of investment expenditure are additions to inventory, new equipment, residential housing, and other construction.

2. The main characteristic of all investment expenditure is its *potential instability.* In times of serious recession, net investment can virtually cease. Even in ordinary times, inventory investment is capable of drastic changes.

3. Changes in investment (or in any other kind of spending) are given larger economic impact because of the *multiplier effect.* This arises because incomes received from a new investment (or any other source) are *partly respent,* giving rise to additional new incomes which, in turn, are respent.

4. A single "burst" of investment creates a bulge in incomes which disappears over time; but a *continuing level of new investment creates a continuing higher level of new incomes.*

5. The size of the multiplier depends on the fraction of additional income spent for consumption by each new recipient. *The more the spending* (or the less the saving) *the greater will be the multiplier.*

6. *We calculate the multiplier by taking the reciprocal of the marginal propensity to save.* This gives us the important formula:

$$\Delta Y = \frac{1}{mps} \times \Delta I \text{ (change in income} = \text{multiplier} \times \text{change in investment)}$$

7. The *size of mps is determined by leakages.* There are four main leakages:
   - Saving
   - Taxation
   - Business profits
   - Imports
   Total leakages in the U.S. amount to about one-half of increases in income. Therefore the U.S. multiplier is about 2.

8. *Each of these leakages takes money out of the "automatic" respending circuit of consumption.* Money going into leakages *can* return to the economy via additional investment, but it does not do so as reliably as money that stays in the consumption flow.

9. Magnifying the effects on income of a fall in investment, the *multiplier works downward,* as well as upward.

10. The multiplier will have very different economic effects, depending on whether or not the economy is *fully employed.*

Questions

1. If you buy a share of stock on the New York Stock Exchange, does that always create new capital? Why, or why not?

2. Why are additions to inventory so much more liable to rapid fluctuation than other kinds of investment?

3. Why is investment capable of much more complete collapse than consumption?

4. Draw a diagram showing the multiplier effect of $1000 expenditure when the marginal propensity to save is one-tenth. Draw a second diagram, showing the effect when the marginal propensity to consume is nine-tenths. Are the diagrams the same?

5. Compare two multiplier diagrams: one where the marginal propensity to save is one-quarter; the other where it is one-third. The *larger* the saving ratio, the larger or smaller the multiplier?

6. Calculate the impact on income if investment rises by $10 billion and the multiplier is 2. If the multiplier is 3. If it is 1.

7. Income is $500 billion; investment is $50 billion. The multiplier is 2. If inventories decline by $10 billion, what happens to income?

8. Draw a diagram showing what happens to $1 billion of new investment given the following leakages: mps 10 per cent; marginal taxation 20 per cent; marginal propensity to import 5 per cent; marginal addition to business saving 15 per cent. What will be the size of the second round of spending? the third? the final total?

9. If the marginal propensity to consume is three-quarters, what is the size of the marginal propensity to save? If it is five-sixths? If it is 70 per cent?

10. What is the formula for the multiplier?

7

Investment and equilibrium

We have spent some time investigating how variations in investment spending can induce powerful repercussions in the national economy. But we have not yet asked the all-important question of why the flow of capital expenditure should be variable in the first place. Nor have we understood how GNP will settle down after it has been raised or lowered by more or less investment. In this chapter, we must look into these matters — into the motives behind the investment expenditure of the firm, and into the way that changes in investment can shift GNP from one level to another.

The motivation of investment

Consumption spending, let us remember, is essentially directed at the satisfaction of the person. In an increasingly affluent society, we may not be able to say that consumer expenditure is any longer solely geared to necessity, but at least it obeys the fairly constant promptings of the cultural and social environment, with the result that consumer spending, in the aggregate, fluctuates relatively little, except as income fluctuates.

A quite different set of motivations drives the investment impulse. Whether the investment is for replacement of old capital or for the installation of new capital, the ruling consideration is virtually never the personal use or satisfaction that the investment yields to the owners of the firm. Instead, the touchstone of investment decisions is *profit*.

Figure 7-1 shows corporate profits since 1929, as well as their division into retained earnings, dividends, and taxes. What

89

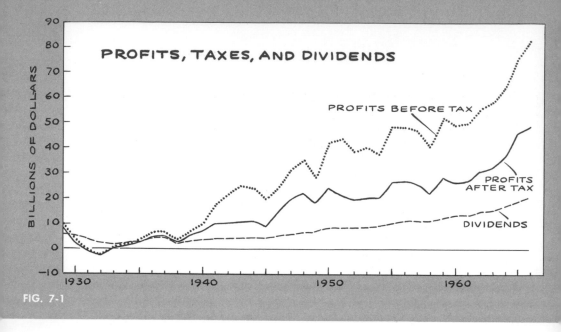

PROFITS, TAXES, AND DIVIDENDS

PROFITS BEFORE TAX

PROFITS AFTER TAX

DIVIDENDS

BILLIONS OF DOLLARS

FIG. 7-1

is strikingly apparent, of course, is the extreme fluctuation of profits between prosperity and recession. Note that corporations as a whole lost money in the depths of the Depression years, but that even in the lush postwar period, the swings from year to year have been considerable (compare 1958 and 1959).*

Expectations

The chart shows us how corporate profits looked to businessmen when the books were tallied at the end of each year. But the results of his last year's operation, although very important, is not the main thing that motivates a businessman to invest. Primarily, he in interested in the profits he expects from *next year's* operations. His view is never backward, but always forward.

Note the important stress on *expectations*. One firm may be enjoying large profits on its existing plant and equipment at the moment; but if it anticipates no profits from the sale of goods that an *additional* investment would make possible, the firm will make no additions to capital. Another firm may be suffering current losses; but if it anticipates a large

*Have corporate profits changed as a per cent of GNP? Surprisingly little. In 1929, corporate profits before tax amounted to about 10 per cent of GNP; in 1965 and 1966, about 11 per cent. Profits *after* taxes fell from some 8 per cent of GNP in 1929 to under 7 per cent in 1965 and 1966. Profits after tax plus depreciation accruals remain unchanged at about 12 per cent. Corporate profits have, of course, increased sharply as a per cent of GNP from their level in the early 1900's, but this is because corporations themselves were not a dominant form of business organization until after World War I.

profit from the production of a new good, it may launch a considerable capital expenditure.

There is a sound reason for this anticipatory quality of investment decisions. Typically, the capital goods bought by investment expenditures are expected to last for years and to pay for themselves only slowly. In addition, they are often highly specialized. If capital expenditures could be recouped in a few weeks or months, or even in a matter of a year or two, or if capital goods were easily transferred from one use to another, they would not be so risky and their dependence on expectations not so great. But it is characteristic of most capital goods that they *are* durable, with life expectancies of ten or more years, and that they tend to be relatively limited in their use.

The decision to invest is thus always forward-looking. Even when the stimulus to build is felt in the present, the calculations that determine whether or not an investment will be made necessarily concern the flow of income to the firm in the future. These expectations are inherently much more volatile than the current drives and desires that guide the consumer. Expectations, whether based on guesses or forecasts, are capable of sudden and sharp reversals of a sort rare in consumption spending. Thus in its orientation to the future we find a main cause for the volatility of investment expenditures.

Induced investment

One kind of profit expectation, and the investment that stems from it, ties in closely with the analysis we have just made of the multiplier. This is an expectation of future profit derived from *an observed rise in current consumption spending.*

Many business firms decide to invest because they must expand their capacity to maintain a given share of a growing market. Real estate developers who build to accommodate an already visible suburban exodus, or supermarkets that build to serve a booming metropolis, or gas stations that must be built to serve a new highway, or additions to manufacturing capacity that must be made because existing facilities cannot keep up with demand — these are all examples of what we call *induced investment.*

The acceleration principle

When rising consumption induces investment, we call the relationship the *acceleration principle* or the *accelerator.* In many ways it resembles the multiplier effect. The multiplier describes the effect that investment has on income via consumption spending; the acceleration principle describes the effect that consumption can have on income via investment spending. When consumption is rising and plant capacity is already tight, investment is likely to be induced, and this induced investment in turn will generate still *additional* incomes through the multiplier effect. Thus the multiplier effect and the acceleration principle can interact to yield even larger "secondary" impacts than either can alone. It is interesting to note that when the Council of Economic Advisers was arguing for the Kennedy tax cut before the Joint Economic Committee of the 88th Congress, it estimated that the pure multiplier effect on GNP was only a little over 2, but that the combined multiplier-accelerator effect was 3 to 4.

A model of the acceleration principle

The acceleration principle thus helps us understand further how small increases in one sector can be magnified and spread throughout the economy. But beyond that, it enlightens us about a surprising thing. Let us discover it by imagining an industry with rising sales and fully utilized equipment and, therefore, induced investment. We will assume that our industry needs a capital equipment twice as large in dollar value as its annual volume of sales, in order to produce effectively. We also assume that 10 per cent of its capital equipment wears out and is replaced each year — that is, the average machine lasts ten years. Table 7-1 gives us a model of such an industry.

In our first view of the industry, we find it in equilibrium with sales of, let us say, 100 units, capital equipment valued at 200 units, and regular replacement demand of twenty units. Now we assume that its sales rise to 120 units. To produce 120 units of goods, the firm will need (accord-

TABLE 7 • 1   A MODEL OF THE ACCELERATION PRINCIPLE

Year	Sales	Existing capital	Needed capital (2 × sales)	Replacement	Induced new investment (2 × addition to sales)	Total investment
1	100	200	200	20	—	20
2	120	200	240	20	40	60
3	130	240	260	20	20	40
4	135	260	270	20	10	30
5	138	270	276	20	6	26
6	140	276	280	20	4	24
7	140	280	280	20	—	20
8	130	280	260	—	—	—

ing to our assumptions) 240 units of capital. This is forty units more than it has, so it must order them. Note that its demand for capital goods now shoots from twenty units to sixty units: twenty units for replacement as before, and forty new ones. Thus investment expenditures *triple*, even though sales have risen but 20 per cent!

Now assume that in the next year sales rise further, to 130 units. How large will our firm's investment demand be? Its replacement demand will not be larger, since its new capital will not wear out for ten years. And the amount of new capital needed to handle its new sales will be only twenty units, not forty as before. Its total investment demand has *fallen* from sixty units to forty.

What is the surprising fact here? It is that *we can have an actual fall in induced investment, though consumption is still rising!* In fact, as soon as the *rate of increase* of consumption begins to fall, *the absolute amount* of induced investment declines. Thus a slowdown in the rate of improvement in sales can cause an absolute decline in the orders sent to capital goods makers. This helps us to explain how weakness can appear in some branches of the economy while prosperity seems still to be reigning in the market at large.

Now look at what happens to our model in the eighth year, when we assume that sales slip back to 130. Our existing capital (280 units) will be greater by twenty units than our needed capital. That year the industry will have no new orders for capital goods and may not even make any replacements, since it can use its new machines in place of the discarded old ones. Its orders to capital goods makers will fall to zero, even though its level of sales is 30 per cent higher than at the beginning. No wonder capital goods industries traditionally experience feast or famine years!

There is, in addition, an extremely important point to bear in mind about the accelerator. *Its upward leverage usually takes effect only when an industry is operating at or near capacity.* When an industry is not near capacity, it is relatively simple for it to satisfy a larger demand for its goods by raising output on its underutilized equipment. Thus, unlike the multiplier, which yields its effects on output only when we have unemployed resources, the accelerator yields its effects only when we do *not* have unemployed capital. That is when induced investment is most likely to follow from increased consumption and when we are also most likely to suffer a decline in total investment, after an initial peak, once the rate of increase in consumption begins to taper off.

Autonomous investment

Not all investment is induced by prior rises in consumption. In fact, perhaps the more significant category of investment is that undertaken in the expectation of a profit to be derived from a *new* good or a *new* way of making a good. This type of investment is usually called *autonomous* investment.

In autonomous investment decisions, prior trends in consumption have little or nothing to do with the decision to invest. This is particularly the case when new technologies provide the stimulus for investment. Then the question in the minds of the managers of the firm is whether the new product will create *new* demand for itself.

Technological advance is not, however, the only cause for autonomous investment, and therefore we cannot statistically separate autonomous from induced investment. With some economic stimuli, such as the opening of a new territory or shifts in population or population growth, the motivations of both autonomous and induced investment are undoubtedly present. Yet there is a meaningful distinction between the two, insofar as induced investment is sensitive and responsive to consumption, whereas autonomous investment is not. This means that induced investment, by its nature, is more foreseeable than autonomous investment.

At the same time, both spontaneous and induced investments are powerfully affected by the over-all investment "climate" — not alone the economic climate of confidence, the level and direction of the stock market, etc., but the political scene, international developments, and so on. Hence it is not surprising that investment becomes by far the most unpredictable of the components of GNP, and thus the key "independent" variable in any model of GNP.

The rate of interest

The profit expectations that guide investment decisions are largely unpredictable. But there exists another guideline for investment decisions that works in a more determinable manner. This is the influence of the *rate of interest* on the investment decisions of business firms.

Typically, the rate of interest offers two guides to the investing firm. If the businessman must borrow capital, a higher rate of interest makes it more expensive to undertake an investment. For huge firms that target a return of 15 to 20 per cent on their investment projects, a change in the interest rate from 5 to 6 per cent may be negligible. But for certain kinds of investment — notably utilities and home construction — interest rates constitute an important component of the cost of investment funds. To these firms, the lower the cost of borrowed capital, the more the stimulus for investment.* The difference in *interest costs* for $1 million

*When interest rates are high, money is called "tight." This means not only that borrowers have to pay higher rates, but that banks are stricter and more selective in judging the credit worthiness of business applications for loans. Conversely, when interest rates decline, money is called "easy," meaning that it is not only cheaper, but literally easier to borrow.

borrowed for twenty years at 3 per cent (instead of 4 per cent) is $200,-000, by no means a negligible sum.

A second guide is offered to those businessmen who are not directly seeking to borrow money for investment, but who are debating whether to invest the savings (retained earnings) of their firms. To them, the interest rate represents a standard of comparison for the returns expected from various investment projects. A businessman, looking ahead to the expected earnings of an investment, sees a series of probable returns (varying, perhaps, from year to year) stretching ahead for a more or less definite number of years into the future. He can reduce this series of expected returns to a single *rate* of return on the cost of the entire investment. This rate, which expresses the expected profitability of the investment, is called the *marginal efficiency of capital* (or the marginal efficiency of investment).

But what is the standard for an "adequate" marginal efficiency of capital? One standard is to compare this rate of expected profitability with the rate of interest.* If the marginal efficiency of capital is not higher than the rate of interest, it will hardly be worth the businessman's while to invest, since he could use his funds with less risk and at the same return by lending them out himself. The fact that his marginal efficiency of capital may be higher than the going rate of interest is no guarantee that he will invest; but if it is not higher, it is a virtual certainty that he will not invest.

The determinants of investment

We have been talking about the determining factors that ultimately affect the rate of investment, the background forces to which we must turn to account for any given level of investment spending (much as we turn to the habits of householders as the background force determining the level of consumption). We have found these background forces for investment are not a single variable, like a propensity to consume income, but a mixture of variables: *increases in consumption that may induce investment; expected levels of profitability of new inventions, techniques, discoveries, etc.; and the marginal efficiency of capital compared with the rate of interest.*

Now we can go a step further. With a general understanding of the

---

*It should be noted that there is no one single thing called *the* rate of interest, but a whole complex of rates, depending on the risk differential among different loans. At any given moment, interest rates may range from 1 or 2 per cent for short-term government notes to 10 to 20 per cent for installment loans, etc. The businessman usually focuses on the range in this spectrum that represents the interest rate for bank loans to business enterprise. These, too, differ from bank to bank and from business to business, but the whole group of these rates tends to move up and down together.

constellation of forces that determines investment, we can begin to understand how a particular level of output is set for the economy as a whole.

An investment model

Let us begin as before, with a simple model; this time, a simple island economy having only two sectors: consumption and investment. We dispense with government and with the export sector for reasons of clarity in exposition. It will be easy enough to reintegrate them into the model, subsequently.

Next we establish schedules for consumption and saving at different levels of income. We have already worked with a hypothetical propensity to consume schedule, so let us merely repeat it here with a new column of figures that will represent the amount of investment spending at various levels of income.

TABLE 7 • 2 SCHEDULES OF SAVING AND INVESTMENT FOR A HYPOTHETICAL ECONOMY (IN BILLIONS OF DOLLARS)

Income	Consumption	Saving	Investment
100	80	20	28
110	87	23	28
120	92	28	28
130	95	35	28
140	97	43	28

From our previous discussion, we have seen that there is no simple functional relation between income and investment, but rather that many forces bear on the investment total. We could, for instance, imagine an investment schedule that rose with income (perhaps due to the accelerator) or one that fell because expectations turned sour. In our model, for the sake of simplicity, we have assumed a schedule of investment expenditures that remains constant. The subsequent analysis would be more difficult but not fundamentally different if we used a variable schedule.

The interplay of saving and investment

If we now look at the last two columns, those for saving and investment, we can see a powerful cross play that will characterize our model economy at different levels of income, for the forces of investment and saving will not be in balance at all levels. At some levels, the propensity to save will outrun the act of purposeful investment; at others, the motivations to save will be less than the investment expenditures made by business firms. In fact, our island model shows that at only one level of income — 120 — will the savings and investment schedules coincide.

What does it mean when intended savings are greater than the flow of intended investment? It means that people are *trying* to save out of their given incomes a larger amount than businessmen are willing to invest. Now if we think back to the exposition of the economy in equilibrium, it will be clear what the result must be. The economy cannot maintain a closed circuit of income and expenditure if savings are larger than investment (or if investment is smaller than savings). This will simply give rise to a demand gap, the dangerous repercussions of which we have already explored.

But a similar lack of equilibrium results if intended savings are less than intended investment expenditure (or if investment spending is greater than the propensity to save). Now businessmen will be pumping out more than enough to offset the savings gap. The additional expenditures, over and above those that compensate for saving, will flow into the economy to create new incomes — and out of those new incomes, new savings.

Income will be stable, in other words, only when the flow of intended investment just compensates for the flow of intended saving. Investment and saving thus conduct a tug of war around this pivot point, driving the economy upward when intended investment exceeds the flow of intended saving; downward when it fails to offset saving.

The careful reader may have noticed that we speak of *intended* savings or of *intended* investments. This is because there is a formal balance between *all* saving and *all* investment in the economy at every instant. After all, saving and investment are only different names for the portion of economic output that is not consumed: from one point of view, this portion is "saved"; from another, it is "invested." But this strict balance between saving and investment is of no more analytic interest than the fact that both sides of a balance sheet always balance, whether a firm is making money or losing it. What matters in the determination of GNP are the *actions* people are taking — actions leading them to try to save, or actions leading them to seek to invest. These are the activities that must be brought into balance and that will drive the economy upward or downward when they are out of balance. Meanwhile, a formal balance of saving and investment will be maintained because there will be temporary *unintended* saving (for instance, unexpected profits) or *unintended* investment (such as inventories that pile up or become depleted, not on purpose, but because business took an unexpected turn). These unintended items can provide our "balance sheet equality" of S and I, but they are important in dynamic analysis only insofar as they affect the powerful currents of our propensity to save and of our willingness to invest.

The idea of equilibrium

We have seen that the forces of intended saving and investment create a tug of war that pushes the economy upward or downward until a point of rest is reached. But where will this point be? At what level of income will the saving and investment schedules converge?

A diagram may once again help to clarify the point. Here is one that resembles the scatter diagram on page 66, but is, in fact, somewhat different. Note first the quantities that we are representing along the two axes. On the vertical axis we measure the total amount of *expenditure* in our simple economy, or $C + I$. Along the horizontal axis, we measure the total amount of *income* and its disposition, or $C + S$. Figure 7-2 shows these two basic categories of measurement. Any point on this diagram will therefore indicate a certain level of spending (the distance from the horizontal axis) and a certain level of income (the distance to the right of the vertical axis).

To our diagram we now add the familiar propensity to consume schedule, marked CC, and on top (28 units higher, as our schedules in Table 7-2 on p. 96 show) the schedule for intended investment. The consumption and the investment schedules added together give us the line marked $C + I$.

Now what will be the pivot point, the *equilibrium income*, given this schedule of investment desires and the propensity to consume? Obviously, it must be at that point *where the amount of income received is just equal to the amount spent*. On our diagram, this is at the point X on the $C + I$ line. Dropping to our income axis, we measure it to be about 150 billion.

Why is this an equilibrium level for income? Well, we know that the

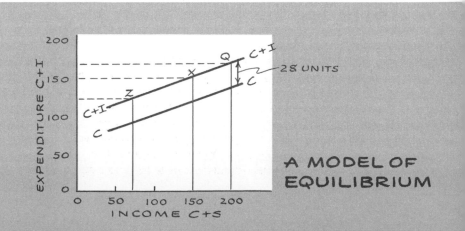

FIG. 7-2

A MODEL OF EQUILIBRIUM

equilibrium level must be at *some* point along the $C + I$ schedule, for income in our model economy is simply the sum of $C + I$. Suppose that we chose point Z, to the left of X, as our pivot point. If we measure the location of point Z on the vertical axis, we can see that it lies at around 125. On the horizontal axis, on the other hand, it measures at less than 75. What this says is that over 125 units of income would have been pumped out by $C + I$ expenditures, but less than 75 units of income have been accounted for as $C + S!$ Something is obviously amiss. The same imbalance would of course be true if we chose a point to the right of X, such as Q. Now we can see that over 200 units of income would have been received (and used for consumption or saving) but that less than 175 units of income would have been expended. Obviously, this cannot be an equilibrium point, either.

There is a quick way of finding where the equilibrium income will be. If the reader will pencil in a line on Fig. 7-2, running upward and to the right at 45° from the meeting point of the two axes, he will find that the equilibrium income lies directly on this line. This is so because the line merely shows us *all* the points on the chart where expenditures $(C + I)$ equal income $(C + S)$.

A new equilibrium

Thus, given our investment schedule and our saving schedule, we see that there is one and only one equilibrium level at which income must settle. But this equilibrium need not be maintained. Suppose investment intentions now increase and that business firms spend *another* $28 billion for investment. Our line $C + I$ changes to $C + I'$, as shown in Fig. 7-3. Now what happens?

By using the short-cut method of the 45° line (which is shown on this diagram), we see that the equilibrium income for the $C + I'$ schedule, shown by the broken line, lies at X'. If we now measure the amount of income represented by this new equilibrium point, we find it to be 200.

Here is a puzzle. We have increased our investment expenditure by 28. But our income has risen by 50. How can this be?

The answer lies in our now familiar multiplier. The increase of 28 in investment spending has brought about a *larger* increase in income because of the respending of the original additional income.

How much larger? That depends, of course, on the marginal propensity to save (or its complement, the marginal propensity to consume). The importance of this crucial pattern of behavior is demonstrated in our next diagram. In Fig. 7-4 we see the effect of the *same* increase in investment with two different marginal propensities to consume—which is to say, two different multipliers. We can imagine the diagram as showing the difference between two nations: both have the same national

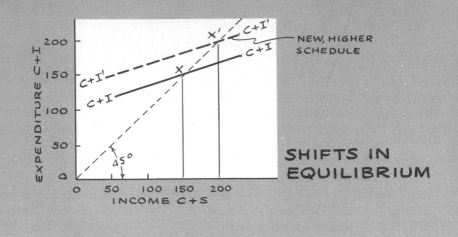

FIG. 7-3

income, but one has a much higher marginal propensity to consume than the other.

We read the diagram by beginning at equilibrium point X. Through this point pass the combined consumption plus investment schedules of the two nations: $C_1 + I$, a country with high marginal propensity to consume, and $C_2 + I$, a country with a low mpc.

Now let us assume that investment in each country increases by the same amount, with the result that the schedules leap from their original position to the higher positions shown by the broken line parallel to each. Note how much further to the right is X'', the new equilibrium income of the high mpc nation, than X', the new equilibrium of the low mpc nation. This should not surprise us, for we already know that a high marginal consumption ratio exerts a stronger multiplier effect than a low ratio. What we see here is only the diagrammatic representation of how different marginal propensities influence the final equilibrium level of income.

Equilibrium: another approach

The idea of equilibrium is never easy to grasp at first, but a second approach to the selfsame problem may clarify things. Suppose that we

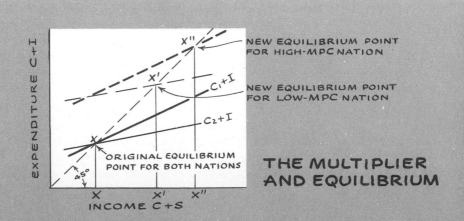

FIG. 7-4

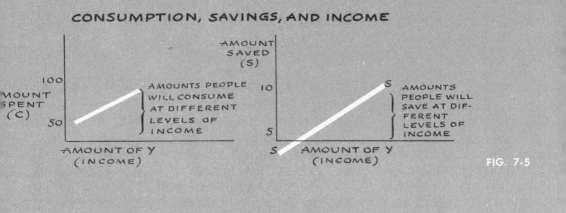

CONSUMPTION, SAVINGS, AND INCOME

AMOUNT
SAVED
(S)

100

MOUNT
SPENT
(C)

50

AMOUNTS PEOPLE
WILL CONSUME
AT DIFFERENT
LEVELS OF
INCOME

AMOUNT OF Y
(INCOME)

10

5

S

S

AMOUNTS
PEOPLE WILL
SAVE AT DIF-
FERENT
LEVELS OF
INCOME

AMOUNT OF Y
(INCOME)

FIG. 7-5

are back on our model island community and are asked by a group of businessmen to predict the island's income for the coming year. We know that income will be the sum of two expenditure streams—consumption and investment (we are still ignoring government)—so we send our two teams of researchers to discover people's intentions concerning their expenditures.

The first team goes to a sample of consumers' houses and asks, "How much will you be consuming next year?" The answer is a bit disconcerting: "It all depends on how large our incomes are," they tell us. What our poll-takers would find, in other words, is that consumption expenditures (or savings plans) could be predicted only in the form of a *schedule*, relating C to Y, or S to Y. In Fig. 7-5, we show the familiar C/Y relationship, and next to it a new (but quite obvious) saving/income relationship.

Now we turn to the poll of business intentions. Here, too, there is an element of "it depends," for some investment, as we know, will be induced by various consumption levels. Yet to a very large extent, businessmen *must* formulate their investment plans on a forward-looking basis, and we will assume that their capital budgets for the coming year are already set at a figure they divulge to us.

In Fig. 7-6, we show those budgets in two ways. In the diagram on

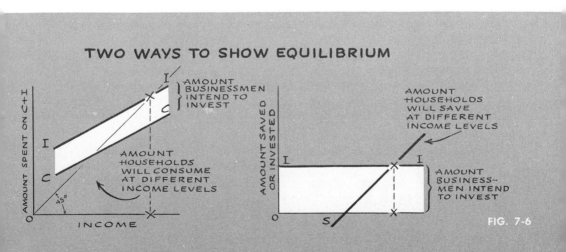

TWO WAYS TO SHOW EQUILIBRIUM

I

AMOUNT
BUSINESSMEN
INTEND TO
INVEST

C

AMOUNT SPENT ON C+I

I

C

45°

INCOME

AMOUNT
HOUSEHOLDS
WILL CONSUME
AT DIFFERENT
INCOME LEVELS

AMOUNT SAVED
OR INVESTED

I

I

S

AMOUNT
HOUSEHOLDS
WILL SAVE
AT DIFFERENT
INCOME LEVELS

AMOUNT
BUSINESS-
MEN INTEND
TO INVEST

FIG. 7-6

the left we add the intended investment expenditures to the schedule of consumption expenditures, bringing us to the familiar equilibrium diagram. In the diagram to the right, we show the investment intentions as a horizontal line on our S/Y chart, indicating that a fixed amount OI will be spent over the income range indicated on the horizontal axis.

Now we are in a position to predict GNP. It must settle at the point where expenditures equal receipts, or at income OX on the familiar diagram. On the savings-investment diagram, we can see that income must settle where the S and I curves intersect. Why? Because if income were to the right of point OX on the income axis, then savings would be larger than investment, since at any point to the right of X, the S curve lies above the I curve. In that event, there would be a demand gap, and income would fall toward the equilibrium level. In the same way, at any point to the left of X, investment is larger than saving, and income would therefore be rising to X.

What if investment expenditures change? We see the effect in Fig. 7-7, where the I curve jumps to $I'I'$.

The new equilibrium point is at x'. Notice that the change in income, between x and x' is larger than the change in investment, I to I'. How much greater? That depends entirely on the slope of the S curve, as you can easily see by penciling in a few different S shapes. In turn, the slope of the S curve depicts the marginal propensity to save, and we are back with our familiar multiplier analysis.

Determinants of the new equilibrium

Thus we have begun to understand how GNP reaches an equilibrium position after a change in investment. Here it is well to remember, however, that the word "equilibrium" does not imply a static, motionless state. We use the word only to denote the fact that *given* certain behavior patterns of consumption and investment, there will be a determinate point to which their interaction will push the level of income; and *so*

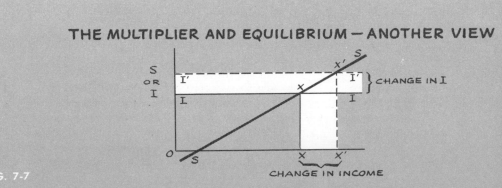

THE MULTIPLIER AND EQUILIBRIUM — ANOTHER VIEW

FIG. 7-7

long as the underlying patterns of consumption and investment remain unchanged, the forces they exert will keep income at this level.

When these forces change, so will the point of equilibrium. The level of the new equilibrium will then be determined by two empirical facts: (1) the size of the given change in investment and (2) the multiplier ratio.

This mechanism applies quite as much on the way down as on the way up. We can, that is, imagine a starting point at a higher income and ask what will be the lower stopping point for an economy in decline. The answer then hinges on (1) the size of the actual drop in investment and (2) the multiplier. The larger the original drop, and the larger its repercussions (this time in successive rounds of *loss* of income), the larger the fall in income that must occur until an equilibrium point is finally reached, where the forces in the economy once again balance.

The paradox of thrift

The fact that income must finally settle at a level where the flows of intended saving and investment are equal leads to one of the most startling—and important—paradoxes of economics. This is the so-called paradox of thrift, a paradox that tells us that the *attempt to save more* may, under certain circumstances, lead to a *fall in actual saving,* whereas an attempt to spend more may lead to an actual rise in saving.

The paradox is not difficult for us to understand at this stage. An attempt to save, *when it is not matched with an equal willingness to invest,* will cause a gap in demand. This means that businessmen will not be getting back enough money to cover their costs. Hence, production will be curtailed or costs will be slashed, with the result that incomes will fall. As incomes fall, savings will also fall, because the ability to save will be reduced. Thus, by a chain of activities working their influence on income and output, the effort to increase savings may end up with an actual reduction of savings.

This frustration of individual desires is perhaps the most striking instance of a common situation in economic life, the incompatibility between some kinds of individual behavior and some collective results. An individual farmer, for instance, may produce a larger crop in order to enjoy a bigger income; but if all farmers produce bigger crops, farm prices are apt to fall so heavily that farmers end up with less income. So too, a single family may wish to save a very large fraction of its income for reasons of financial prudence; but if all families seek to save a great deal of their incomes, the result—unless investment also rises—will be a fall in expenditure and a common failure to realize savings objectives. The paradox of thrift, in other words, teaches us that the freedom of behavior available to a few individuals cannot always be generalized to all individuals.*

A note on the export sector

With an initial understanding of the mechanism of equilibrium and disequilibrium behind us, we have reached a very important stage in our inquiry. The interactions of the macroeconomic variables now begin to come together and the causes and mechanics of prosperity and depression begin to reveal themselves to us.

Before we go on to complete our understanding, however, we must mention, if only in passing, a sector we have largely overlooked in this book. This is the foreign sector, or more properly the sector of net exports.

If we lived in a European, South American, or Asian country, we could not be so casual in our treatment of foreign trade, for this sector constitutes the very lifeline of many, perhaps even most, countries. Our own highly self-sustained economy in which foreign trade plays only a small quantitative (although a much more important qualitative) role, is very much the exception rather than the rule.

In part, it is the relatively marginal role played by foreign trade in the American economy that allows us to treat it so cavalierly. But there is also another problem. The forces that enter into the flows of international trade are much more complex than any we have heretofore discussed. Not alone the reactions of American consumers and firms, but those of foreign consumers and firms must be taken into account. Thus comparisons between international price levels, the availability of foreign or domestic goods, credit and monetary controls, exchange rates – a whole host of "extraneous" considerations – lie at the very heart of foreign trade. To begin to unravel these interrelationships, one must study international trade as a subject in itself. Nevertheless, we should try to understand the main impact of foreign trade on the level of GNP, even if we cannot yet investigate the forces and institutions of foreign trade as thoroughly as we might like.

---

*The paradox of thrift is actually only a subtle instance of a type of faulty reasoning called the fallacy of composition. The fallacy consists of assuming that what is true of the individual case must also be true of all cases combined. The flaw in reasoning lies in our tendency to overlook "side effects" of individual actions (such as the decrease in spending associated with an individual's attempt to save more, or the increase in supply when a farmer markets his larger crop) which may be negligible in isolation but which are very important in the aggregate.

The impact of foreign trade

We must begin by repeating that our initial overview of the economic system, with its twin streams of consumption and investment, was actually incomplete. It portrayed what we call a "closed" system, an economy with no flows of goods or services from within its borders to other nations, or from other nations to itself.

Yet such flows must, of course, be taken into account in computing our national output. Let us therefore look at a chart that shows us the main streams of goods and services that cross our borders, as well as a table of the magnitudes in our bench-mark years.

First a word of explanation. Exports show the total value of all goods and services we sold to foreigners. Imports show the total value of all goods and services we bought from foreigners. Our bottom line shows the net difference between exports and imports, or the difference between the value of the goods we sold abroad and the value we bought from abroad. This difference is called *net exports,* and it constitutes the net contribution of foreign trade to GNP.

If we think of it in terms of expenditures, it is not difficult to see what the net contribution is. When exports are sold to foreigners, their expenditures add to American incomes. Imports, on the contrary, are expenditures that we make to other countries (and hence that we do not make at home). If we add the foreign expenditures made here and subtract the domestic expenditures made abroad, we will have left a net figure that will show the contribution (if any) made by foreigners to GNP.

What is the impact of this net expenditure on GNP? It is much the

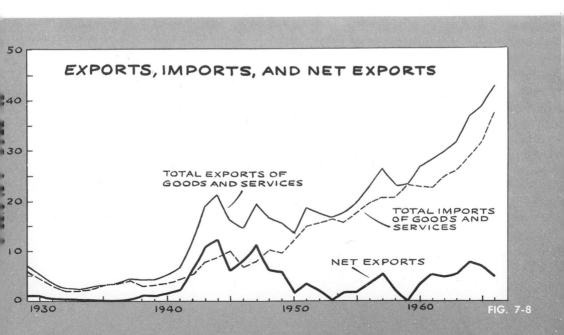

EXPORTS, IMPORTS, AND NET EXPORTS

TOTAL EXPORTS OF GOODS AND SERVICES

TOTAL IMPORTS OF GOODS AND SERVICES

NET EXPORTS

FIG. 7-8

same as net private domestic investment. If we have a rising net foreign trade balance, we will have a net increase in spending in the economy. And this increase in spending, just like that arising from the addition of plant or equipment, will exert a magnified impact on GNP via the multiplier. Conversely, if our imports rise more rapidly than our exports, so that our net foreign trade balance declines or becomes negative, our GNP would decline—not only by the drop in net exports, but by the net fall in spending again magnified by the influence of the marginal propensity to consume.

Leakages and injections

Thus we can consider the effects of the foreign trade sector as if it were a part of the investment sector, even though the underlying forces are extremely different. But as we broaden the model of our economy, from its original simple conception as a society that only consumes and invests, to one that now imports and exports, and in our next chapter to one that has, as well, an active government sector, it becomes convenient to widen our terminology somewhat when we speak of the determinants of GNP.

Now, instead of referring only to "saving" as the cause of a downward pressure on the level of expenditure, or to "investment" as the only cause of upward pressures, we can speak of *leakages in, or withdrawals from, the expenditure flow* and of *injections or additions to that flow*. The word *leakage* is, of course, already familiar to us from our analysis of the multiplier. Here we use it as a general term to describe any activity that diminishes the flow of spending—be it saving or increasing imports, or rising government taxes or growing business profits. Similarly, we speak of injections as any activity—investment, exports, government spending, or a spontaneous rise in consumption—that will increase the flow of spending.

The determination of output can then be generally described as the outcome of the balance between leakages or withdrawals of all kinds and injections or additions of all kinds. So long as injections are outpacing leakages, GNP will rise; when leakages overbalance injections, GNP will fall; and when the two are in a state of balance, GNP will be in stable equilibrium.

Summary

1. The motivation for investment expenditure is not personal use or satisfaction, but *expected profit*. Note that investment is always geared to forward profit *expectations* rather than to past or present results.

2. We distinguish between two kinds of investment motivation. When investments are made to meet an expected demand arising from present or clearly indicated changes in consumption, we speak of *induced investment*. When investment is stimulated by developments (such as inventions) that have little relation to existing trends, we speak of *autonomous* investment.

3. Induced investment is subject to the *acceleration principle* which describes how a given increase in C can give rise to a proportionally larger increase in I. The acceleration principle also shows us that the absolute level of induced investment can fall, even though the level of C is still rising. Thus it helps explain the onset of recessions. Note that the acceleration principle "takes hold" only when an industry is at or near full utilization.

4. The *rate of interest* is, in two ways, an important determinant of investment. It directly affects the *cost of capital*. And it also provides a *standard of comparison* for the returns expected from investment. Unless the expected return from investment (called the marginal efficiency of investment) is higher than the rate of interest, it will not be reasonable to make the investment.

5. The level of income in the economy as a whole is moved upward or downward by the interplay of the schedules of intended saving and investment. *Only where intended S and intended I are equal will income be in equilibrium.*

6. We can show the idea of equilibrium in two kinds of diagrams. In one we ascertain what point on the C + I schedule is equidistant from the expenditure and the income sides of the graph — i.e., lying on a 45° line between the two. In the other diagram, we find the point of intersection between the saving and the investment schedules on a graph that relates saving and investment (on the vertical axis) to income (on the horizontal axis). *Both graphs are only visual ways of showing the point of mutual compatibility between schedules of intended saving and investment behavior at different income levels.*

7. The graphs also show that changes in I lead to larger changes in Y. The reason for this is the slope of the C + I schedule (or in the saving-investment graph, of the S schedule). Since these slopes represent the marginal propensity to consume (or save), *the graphs merely present in visual form the familiar multiplier relationship.*

8. The new level of equilibrium of income, given a change in I, depends on two things: (1) *the size of the actual change in I;* and (2) the *multiplier.*

9. The fact that income must finally settle where the schedules of intended S and I converge leads to the famous *paradox of thrift.* This paradox tells us that the effort to save, unless matched by an equal effort to invest, will lead to an excess of S over I, and thereby drive income lower. At lower levels of income, there will be less S, rather than more. Thus the effort to save more has resulted in the economy's actually saving less! (Note that this occurs only if the effort to save is not matched by more investment.)

10. *Exports and imports* serve as stimuli for, or drags on, the expenditure flow. They act much as investment does in driving the level of income higher or lower. Therefore, we broaden our terminology to include exports and imports and similar stimuli by speaking of *injections* into, or *withdrawals* or *leakages* from, the expenditure flow.

Questions

1. Discuss the difference in the motivation of a consumer buying a car for pleasure and the same person buying a car for his business.

2. Which of the following are induced, and which autonomous, investment decisions: a developer builds homes in a growing community; a city enlarges its water supply after a period of water shortage; a firm builds a laboratory for basic research; an entrepreneur invests in a new gadget.

3. What is the basic idea of the acceleration principle? Describe carefully how the acceleration principle helps explain the instability of investment.

4. Assume that it costs 7 per cent to borrow from a bank. What is the minimum profit that must be expected from an investment before it becomes worthwhile? Could we write that $I = f(r)$ where r stands for the rate of interest? What would be the relation between a change in r and I? Would $I = f(r)$ be a complete description of the motivation for investment?

5. Suppose that an economy turns out to have the following consumption and saving schedule:

Income (billions)	Saving (billions)	Consumption (billions)
$400	$50	$350
450	55	395
500	60	440
550	70	480
600	85	515

Now suppose that firms intend to make investments of $60 billion during the year. What will be the level of income for the economy? If investment rises to $85 billion, then what will be its income? What would be the multiplier in this case?

6. Show the equilibrium income before and after the jump in investment on a $C + I$ graph and on an S and I graph.

7. Exactly what is meant by "equilibrium"? Is a balloon floating in mid-air in equilibrium? Why? If gravity is saving, and the lift of hydrogen is investment, what economic magnitude is represented by the height of the balloon?

8. Is there an opposite to the paradox of thrift? Suppose everyone tried not to save but to spend all his income, and that businessmen did not alter their investment plans. What would happen? (Since there would be no more goods and a good deal more spending, wouldn't someone have to end up holding money and not being able to use it for consumption? Wouldn't the "paradox of spendthrift" lead to more saving, despite the effort not to save?) What does this tell us about the need to coordinate S and I plans to achieve a desired macroeconomic goal?

9. Explain how exports stimulate income and how imports depress it. Does this mean that imports are bad? Are savings bad?

8

The government sector

We turn now to the last of the main sources of GNP
— the government, and as before we shall begin by familiarizing ourselves with the sector in its long historical profile.

Figure 8-2 shows us the emergence of the government
sector as a significant contributor to GNP, a process to which we will
return later in this chapter.

Government in the expenditure flow

Now for a closer look, to help us fit the government
sector, in a recent year, into the flow of national expenditure. Figure
8-1 shows us the familiar bars of our flow diagram. Note that indirect
taxes, totaling some $63 billion in 1966, amounted to some 9 per cent of
the value of GNP. As can be seen, however, income taxes on households and businesses are much more important than indirect taxes in
providing total government revenues. (What the diagram does not show
is that about two-thirds of the indirect taxes are state and local in origin:
property taxes, excise taxes, motor vehicle and gasoline taxes, and
others. Income taxes and Social Security contributions constitute about
nine-tenths of the income of the federal government.)

On the expenditure side, we see that state and local
purchases of goods and services are as important as federal purchases in
providing public demand. Since transfer payments are largely federal in
origin, however, the ratio of all federal *expenditures* (as contrasted with
purchases of goods and services) to all state and local expenditures is
roughly two to one.

109

Finally, it is worth reminding ourselves of the different significance and impact of public purchases and transfers. Public purchases of goods and services, whether they originate with local or federal government, require the use of land, labor, and capital. They are thus *public production,* and constitute a net addition to GNP. Transfer payments, on the other hand, do not increase output. They are simply a reallocation of income, from factors to various groups of the community in the business sector or the household sector. Transfers, therefore, do not require new production and are not a part of GNP.

The government sector in historical perspective

How large does the public sector bulk in the total flow of GNP? Let us again try to put a perspective into our answer by observing the trend of government purchases over our bench-mark years.

The striking change from prewar to postwar years is, of course, immediately visible. The government sector, taken as a whole, has changed from a very small sector to a very large one. In 1929, total government purchases of goods and services were only half of total private investment spending; in 1966, total government purchases were 30 per cent *larger* than private investment. *In terms of its contributions*

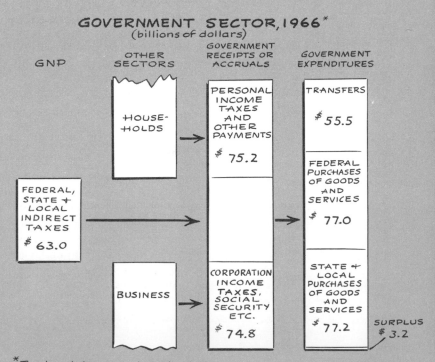

FIG. 8-1   *Tax breakdown partly estimated.

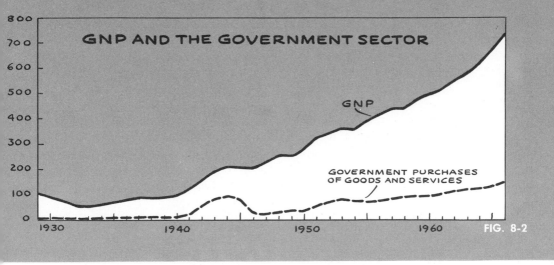

FIG. 8-2

to GNP, government is now second only to consumption.

To make the point even more forcefully, it should be noted that Fig. 8-2 understates the full role of government spending, since it does not include transfer payments, but only purchases of goods and services. If we include the figure for transfer payments, the proportion of all government expenditure to GNP rises from approximately 20 per cent to almost 30 per cent. And since, as we have mentioned, the bulk of these transfers are federal (Social Security, subsidies, and interest), the proportion of all federal spending to GNP rises from 11 per cent to about 20 per cent.

The composition of public spending

Thus, on the face of it, public expenditure is clearly an important source of economic activity. Nevertheless, to emphasize the rise in spending without stressing its causes would be misleading.

First, we should note that much of the growth in public expenditure has been contributed by the *rise of state and local, rather than federal, spending.* What has promoted this rise? The answer lies in the needs and capabilities of a highly urbanized and affluent society. The sheer administrative and housekeeping expenditures of our cities and states have grown enormously as huge populations have crowded into vast megacities. (The supervision of vehicular traffic alone requires the employment of one out of every ten state and local officials.) Equally important, the steadily rising educational reach of the population has vastly increased the need for public expenditure. In 1950 the states and localities spent less than $6 billion for elementary and secondary education; in 1966 it was over $22 billion. In 1950, institutions of higher education cost the states and localities just over $1 billion. In the late 1960's, the cost had risen to over $6 billion.

Second, it is *important to separate the rise in federal defense spending*

111

TABLE   FEDERAL NONDEFENSE PURCHASES
8 • 1   (selected years)

Year	Per cent of GNP
1929	1.0 (est.)
1933	3.0 (est.)
1940	4.0
1944	0.8
1960	1.7
1961	1.8
1962	2.1
1963	2.3
1964	2.4
1965	2.5
1966	2.2

from the rise in its nondefense expenditures. As Table 8-1 shows, the rise of nondefense spending as a percentage of GNP is very small.*

Classifying public expenditure

We could also attempt to divide public expenditures into categories comparable to consumption and investment. The division is not a simple one to make, however. We could have no trouble tagging public construction for roads or airfields or dams as investment. But what are we to make of education expenditures? Economists believe that education is fully as important as capital goods for long-term growth. Shall we then count it as investment? Or what shall we make of spending on recreational facilities or on defense? The line between consumption and investment in the public sector is evidently much harder to draw than in

*This raises the related question of how important armaments or defense spending is within the economy, and of how large a gap in our stream of expenditures would be created, were peace to "break out."

In 1967, our total national defense expenditures (including overseas military aid and the expenses of the Atomic Energy Commission) came to approximately 9 per cent of GNP. It is difficult to know what a peacetime defense budget would be in these days of lingering Cold War suspicions and international unrest, but we might take $20 billion a year (double the 1947 figure) as a realistic, if arbitrary, figure. This would mean that a decline of defense spending to the minimum would entail a reduction in expenditures of $50 billion a year, or some 5 to 6 per cent of GNP. In addition, there would be a decline in private spending as defense industries contracted.

At the same time, however, taxes could be greatly lessened, so that much of this decline in war spending would be offset by a rise in private expenditure, both on the part of consumers and firms. In addition, we would expect a number of federal nondefense programs to rise substantially, once the defense budget was reduced. Hence, the over-all impact would not necessarily be unduly depressive, although the effect on some industries and localities might be very serious indeed. But here, too, vigorous programs of public support could substantially lessen the social cost of disarmament, while providing a stimulus of new expenditure.

the private sector. For reasons that we shall shortly discuss, it might be useful to list separately those items that are unquestionably additions to public capital. But since the distinction between capital and consumption in the public sphere is often unclear, economists take the line of least resistance and lump all kinds of public purchases, however varied, in one undifferentiated public sector.

Characteristics of the public sector

But there is another reason why we differentiate between the private sectors and the public sector. This is the fact that the motivations of the public sector are different in a most important way from those of the private sectors.

We recall that the motivations for the household sector and the business sector are lodged in the free decisions of their respective units. Householders decide to spend or save their incomes as they wish, and we are able to construct a propensity to consume schedule only because there seem to be spending and saving patterns that emerge spontaneously from the householders themselves. Similarly, business firms exercise their own judgments on their capital expenditures, and as a result we have seen the indeterminacy and variability of investment decisions.

But when we turn to the expenditures of the public sector, we enter an entirely new area of motivation. It is no longer fixed habit or profit that determines the rate of spending, but *political decision*—that is, the collective will of the people as it is formulated and expressed through their local, state, and federal legislatures and executives.

As we shall soon see, this does not mean that government is therefore an entirely unpredictable economic force. There are regularities and patterns in the government's economic behavior, as there are in other sectors. Yet the presence of an explicit political will that can direct the income or outgo of the sector *as a whole* (especially its federal component) gives to the public sector a special significance. *This is the only sector whose expenditures and receipts are open to deliberate control.* We can exert (through public action) very important influences on the behavior of households and firms. But we cannot directly alter their economic activity in the manner that is open to us with the public sector.

Fiscal policy

The deliberate use of the government sector as an active economic force is a relatively new conception in economics. Looking back a few years, we see that, like so much of the apparatus of macroeconomic analysis, it stems essentially from the work of John Maynard Keynes during the Great Depression. At that time his proposals were regarded as extremely daring, but they have become increasingly accepted by economists.* Although the bold use of the economic powers of the public sector is far from commanding unanimous assent in the United States today, there is a steadily growing consensus in the use of fiscal policy—that is, the deliberate utilization of the government's taxing and spending powers—to help the stability and growth of the national economy.

The basic idea behind modern fiscal policy is simple enough. We have seen that economic recessions have their roots in a failure of the business sector to offset the savings of the economy through sufficient investment. If savings or leakages are larger than intended investment or injections, there will be a gap in the circuit of incomes and expenditures that can cumulate downward, at first by the effect of the multiplier, thereafter, and even more seriously, by further decreases in investment brought about by falling sales and gloomy expectations.

But if a falling GNP is caused by an inadequacy of expenditures in one sector, our analysis suggests an answer. Could not the insufficiency of spending in the business sector be offset by higher spending in another sector, the public sector? Could not the public sector serve as a supplementary avenue for the "transfer" of savings into investment?

As Fig. 8-3 shows, an expenditure gap can indeed be closed by "transferring" savings to the public sector and spending them.

The diagram shows savings in the household sector partly offset by business investment and partly by government spending. It makes clear that at least so far as the mechanics of the economic flow are concerned, the public sector can serve to offset savings or other leakages equally as well as the private sector.

How is the "transfer" accomplished? It is done much as business does it, by offering bonds that individuals or institutions can buy with their savings. Unlike business, the government cannot offer stock, for it is not run as a profit-making enterprise. However, we must note that the government can also tax incomes to finance its expenditures. This may have complicated results, for the taxes may not cause consumers to cut

*Reviewing a book in 1964 with the word "macroeconomics" in its title, Harold Somers wrote: "The name of Keynes is anathema in some circles. . . . As a result, courses bearing the name of Keynes are very scarce and one publisher . . . even boasts that his elementary economics book contains no mention of Keynes.

"All is not lost. There is available a very competent economist called Macro. This economist, Macro, is most versatile. He . . . encompasses everything that Keynes taught, might have taught, and would have denied teaching. . . ." (*American Economic Review*, March 1964, p. 138.)

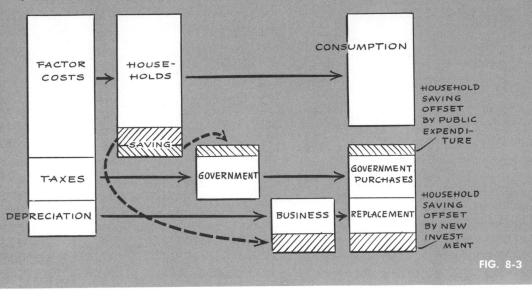

FIG. 8-3

back their spending, but to curtail their saving – or more likely, to cut back some on both consumption and saving.

Taxes, expenditures, and GNP

We will look more carefully into the question of how the government can serve as a kind of counterbalance for the private economy. But first we must discover something about the normal behavior of the public sector; for despite the importance of political decisions in determining the action of the public sector, and despite the multiplicity of government units and activities, we can nonetheless discern "propensities" in government spending and receiving – propensities that play their compensating role in the economy quite independently of any direct political intervention.

The reason for these propensities is that both government income and government outgo are closely tied to private activity. Government receipts are derived in the main from taxes, and taxes – direct or indirect – tend to reflect the trend of business and personal income. In fact, we can generalize about tax payments in much the same fashion as we can about consumption, describing them as a predictable function of GNP. To be sure, this assumes that tax *rates* do not change. But since rates change only infrequently, we can draw up a general schedule that relates tax receipts and the level of GNP. The schedule will show not only that taxes rise as GNP rises, but that they rise *faster* than GNP.

Why faster? Largely because of the progressive structure of the

115

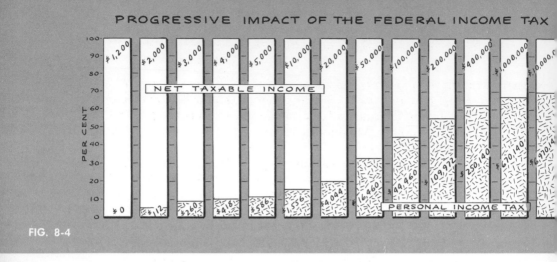

FIG. 8-4

federal income tax. As household and business incomes rise to higher levels, the percentage "bite" of taxes increases, from around 20 per cent on the first dollar of taxable income to much higher percentages for high income brackets. Thus as incomes rise, tax liabilities rise even more. Conversely, the tax bite works downward in the opposite way. As incomes fall, taxes fall even faster, since households or businesses with lowered incomes find themselves in less steep tax brackets.

Government expenditures also show certain "propensities," which is to say, *some government spending is also functionally related to the level of GNP.* A number of government programs are directly correlated to the level of economic activity in such a way that spending *decreases* as GNP *increases,* and vice versa. For instance, unemployment benefits are naturally higher when GNP is low or falling. So are many welfare payments at the state and local level. So, too, are disbursements to farmers under various agricultural programs.

Automatic stabilizers

All these automatic effects taken together are called the *automatic stabilizers* or the *built-in stabilizers* of the economy. What they add up to is an automatic government counterbalance to the private sector. As GNP falls because private spending is insufficient, taxes decline even faster and public expenditures grow, thereby automatically causing the government sector to offset the private sector to some extent. In similar fashion, as GNP rises, taxes tend to rise even faster and public expenditures decline, thereby causing the government sector to act as a brake.

The public sector therefore acts as an automatic compensator, even without direct action to alter tax or expenditure levels, pumping out more public demand when private demand is slow and curbing public demand when private demand is brisk.

How effective are the built-in stabilizers? The evidence of the 1950's suggests that they can be very helpful in preventing declines from snow-balling.* Here is how they work. Suppose that private investment were to fall by $10 billion. Because of the multiplier, household spending might well fall by another $10 billion, causing a total decline of $20 billion in incomes.

The action of the stabilizers will prevent this full fall from taking place. First, the reduction in their incomes will lower the tax liabilities of both households and firms. Let us say that because of the reduced income they owe $6 billion less in taxes. Most of this windfall is likely to be spent: let us estimate that $5 billion of the $6 billion that is no longer owed to the government will be spent by households and firms. Mean-while, as we have seen, some public expenditures will automatically rise, pumping more money into households. Let us arbitrarily place this figure at $3 billion. This gives us a total of $8 billion ($3 billion in direct new expenditures, $5 billion in private spending induced by lower taxes) that will counteract the decline. Instead of a fall of $20 billion as was origi-nally feared, we have a fall of only $12 billion.

This is certainly an improvement over a situation with no stabilizers. Yet if the drop in investment is not to bring about some fall in GNP, it will have to be *fully* compensated by an equivalent increase in govern-ment spending or by a fall in taxes large enough to induce an equivalent amount of private spending. This will require public action more vigor-ous than that brought about automatically. Indeed, it requires that the government take on a task very different from any we have heretofore studied, the task of acting as the *deliberate* balancing mechanism of the economy.

A diagram of government spending

There is nothing in our formal analysis to make us doubt that govern-ment can take on such a task. Government spending is just like private spending so far as its multiplier effects are concerned.† In the same fashion, government taxes serve to constrict private spending, much as additional saving would.

Hence we can draw a new diagram showing an equilibrium for an

*Although we should note that different kinds of private and public spending programs may have different multipliers if they go to different spending groups. A government public works program that uses unskilled labor is not apt to have the same initial repercussions on GNP as a private investment project in computers. *Transfer* expenditures may also have initial multiplier effects different from direct purchases of goods and services. And finally, different tax structures will cause changes in GNP to affect private spending differently.

†We have no evidence before the 1950's. In the prewar period, both tax income and public expenditure were too small a proportion of GNP for their stabilizing propensities to exert much influence.

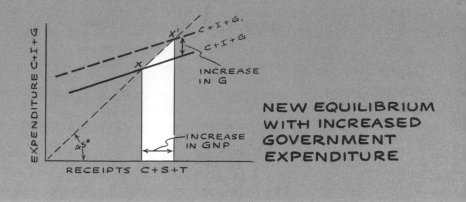

FIG. 8-5

NEW EQUILIBRIUM
WITH INCREASED
GOVERNMENT
EXPENDITURE

economy with various levels of public expenditure. In Fig. 8-5, we enlarge the familiar chart from the last chapter to include a new item on the expenditure axis—government purchases, or G—and a new item on the receipts or income axis—taxes, or T. Once again we draw our 45° slanting line and our schedule of income possibilities, this time as consumption plus investment plus government purchases $(C + I + G)$.* Our new schedule shows an equilibrium point at X, where all receipts, public or private, balance all expenditures, public or private.

Now let us imagine that C and I remain unchanged but that the regular flow of government purchasing increases, raising total outlays from $C + I + G$ to $C + I + G'$, shown by the broken line. Our equilibrium point now shifts to X'. Once again we note that *the change in equilibrium income is greater than the change in initial expenditure.* The reason is, of course, the same as in the case with private investment. All additional injections of expenditure into the economy will exert a multiple income effect as they pass through successive (albeit diminishing) rounds of receipt and re-expenditure.

Another view of equilibrium, again

For clarity, let us go back again to our island community to predict the equilibrium level of GNP for the coming year. Again we send out our teams of pollsters, and as before, we take note of household consuming

---

*Although we do not show it on the diagram, as we add government expenditures and taxation to our model, we must expect the slope of the previous propensity to consume schedule to change. We should picture the impact of taxes as reducing the slope of the curve, since rising income means even faster rising taxes. On the other hand, government expenditure may redistribute income away from savers toward spenders. Hence, one cannot generalize about the way in which the addition of G affects the slope of the propensity to consume schedule. The effect will vary according to the tax and expenditure programs. But it is well to bear this qualification in mind.

118

and saving intentions and of businessmen's investment plans. This time, however, we also study the community's tax schedules and inquire into the island's projected public expenditures.

As a result, our diagram of equilibrium includes more factors than it did formerly. In Fig. 8-6, we show the schedule of savings plans *plus* additional taxes at various levels of income. In the same diagram, the stream of investment is now increased to include projected public expenditures. As a result, the levels and the slopes of the two lines — one now representing leakages and one injections — are different from our former simple model. Yet the intersection of the two lines again tells us what we want to know; that is, given the commitments and propensities of private spending and saving, and public spending and taxing, where the income of our community will settle.

Deficit spending

Thus from an analytic standpoint we can treat the contribution of government very much as if it were investment. Our diagrams of the sectoral flows and equilibrium relationships make it perfectly plain that the government sector can offset saving just as efficiently as the business sector can, from the point of view of maintaining a given level of spending.

Yet the suggestion that the government deliberately exercise compensatory powers opens a new question for us to consider. The use of the government budget as a stabilizing device means that the government must be prepared to spend more than its normal tax receipts. It must purposefully plan a budget in which outgo exceeds income, leaving a negative figure called a *deficit*.

Like a business, however, a government cannot spend money it does not have in a bank account. Therefore it must *borrow* from individuals, firms, or banks in order to cover its planned deficit. Deficit spending, in other words, means the spending of borrowed money, money derived from the sale of government bonds.

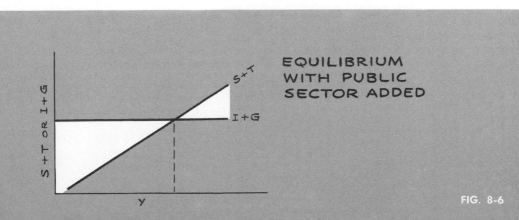

EQUILIBRIUM WITH PUBLIC SECTOR ADDED

FIG. 8-6

Deficits and losses

Can the government safely run up a deficit? Let us begin to unravel this important but perplexing question by asking another: can a private business afford to run up a deficit?

There is one kind of deficit that a private business *cannot* afford: a deficit that comes from spending more money on current production than it will realize from its sale. This kind of deficit is called a *business loss;* and if losses are severe enough, a business firm will be forced to discontinue its operations.

But there is another kind of deficit, although it is not called by that name, in the operations of a private firm. This is an excess of expenditures over receipts brought about by spending money on *capital assets.* When the American Telephone and Telegraph Company or the Consolidated Edison Company use their own savings or those of the public to build a new power plant, they do not show a "loss" on their annual statement to their stockholders, even though their total expenditures on current costs and on capital may have been greater than their sales. Instead, expenditures are divided into two kinds, one relating current costs to current income, and the other relegating expenditures on capital goods to an entirely separate "capital account." Instead of calling the excess of expenditures a "deficit," they call it "investment."*

Debts and assets

Can A.T.&T. or Consolidated Edison afford to run deficits of the latter kind indefinitely? Let us answer the question by imagining ourselves in an economic landscape with no disturbing changes in technology or in consumers' tastes, so that entrepreneurs can plan ahead with great safety. Now let us assume that in this comfortable economy, Consolidated Edison decides to build a new plant, perhaps to take care of the growing population. To finance the plant, it issues new bonds, so that its new asset is matched by a new debt.

Now what about this debt? How long can Consolidated Edison afford to have its bonds outstanding?

The answer is—forever!

Remember that we have assumed an economy remaining changeless in tastes and techniques, so that each year the new factory can turn out a quota of output, perfectly confident that it will be sold; and each year it

*Investment does not *require* a "deficit," since it can be financed out of current profits. But many expanding companies do spend more money on current and capital account than they take in through sales and thereby incur a "deficit" for at least a part of their investment.

can set aside a reserve for wear and tear, perfectly confident that the factory is being properly depreciated. As a result, each year the debt must be as good as the year before—no better and no worse. The bond-holder is sure of getting his interest, steadily earned, and he knows that the underlying asset is being fully maintained.

Admittedly, after a certain number of years the new factory will be worn out. But if our imaginary economy remains unchanged and if depreciation accruals have been properly set aside, when the old plant gives out, an identical new one will be built from these depreciation reserves. Meanwhile, the old debt, like the old plant, will also come to an end, for debts usually run for a fixed term of years. Consolidated Edison must now pay back its debtholders in full. But how? The firm has accumulated a reserve to buy a new plant, but it has not accumulated a second reserve to repay its bondholders.

Nevertheless, the answer is simple enough. When the bonds come due in our imaginary situation, Consolidated Edison issues *new* bonds equal in value to the old ones. It then sells the new bonds and uses the new money it raises to pay off the old bondholders. When the transaction is done, a whole cycle is complete: both a new factory and a new issue of bonds exist in place of the old. Everything is exactly as it was in the first place. Furthermore, as long as this cycle can be repeated, such a debt could safely exist in perpetuity! And why not? Its underlying asset also exists, eternally renewed, in perpetuity.

Real corporate debts

To be sure, not many businesses are run this way, for the obvious reason that tastes and techniques in the real world are anything but changeless. Indeed, there is every reason to believe that when a factory wears out it will *not* be replaced by another costing exactly as much and producing just the same commodity. Yet, highly stable businesses such as Consolidated Edison or A.T.&T. do, in fact, continuously "refund" their bond issues, paying off old bonds with new ones, and never "paying back" their indebtedness as a whole. A.T.&T., for instance, actually did increase its total indebtedness from $1.1 billion in 1929 to $10.3 billion in 1967. Consolidated Edison Company actually did run up its debt from $240 million in 1929 to $1.8 billion in 1967. And the credit rating of both companies today is as good as, or better than, it was in 1929.

Thus some individual enterprises that face conditions of stability similar to our imaginary situations do actually issue bonds "in perpetuity," paying back each issue when it is due, only to replace it with another (and, as we have seen, *bigger*) issue.

Total business debts

Only a few very strong individual businesses can carry their debts indefinitely, but the business sector *as a whole* can easily do so. For although most individual businesses must prudently seek to retire their debts, as we look over the whole economy we can see that as one business extinguishes its debt, another is borrowing an even larger sum. Why larger? Because the *assets* of the total business sector are also steadily rising.

Table 8-2 shows this trend in the growth of corporate debt.*

**TABLE
8 • 2**   CORPORATE NET DEBT

Year	Billions of dollars
1929	88.9
1933	76.9
1940	75.6
1944	94.1
1960	302.7
1961	324.5
1962	348.4
1963	376.2
1964	401.7

Note that from 1929 through 1940, corporate debt *declined.* The shrinkage coincided with the years of depression and slow recovery, when additions to capital plant were small. But beginning with the onset of the war, we see a very rapid increase in business indebtedness, an increase that continues down to our present day.

If we think of this creation of debt (and equity) as part of the savings-investment process, the relationship between debts and assets should be clear. Debts are claims, and we remember how claims can arise as the financial counterpart of the process of real capital formation. Thus, rising debts on capital account are a sign that assets are also increasing.† Debts (on capital account) and assets go very much hand in hand; and when we see that corporate debts are rising, we can take for granted that assets are probably rising as well. The same is true, incidentally, for the ever-rising total of consumer debts that mirror a corresponding increase in consumers' assets. As our stock of houses grows,

*We do not show the parallel rise in new equities (shares of stock), since changes in stock market prices play so large a role here. We might, however, add a mental note to the effect that business issues new stock each year, as well as new bonds. In the 1960's, net new stock issues have ranged from about $1 to $5 billion per annum.

†It is important to emphasize the *capital account.* Debts incurred to buy capital assets are very different from those incurred to pay current expenses.

so does our total mortgage debt; as our personal inventories of cars, washing machines, and other appliances grow, so does our outstanding consumer indebtedness.

Government deficits

Can government, like business, borrow "indefinitely"? The question is important enough to warrant a careful answer. Hence, let us begin by comparing government borrowing and business borrowing.

One difference that springs quickly to mind is that businesses borrow in order to acquire productive assets. That is, matching the new claims on the business sector is additional real wealth that will provide for larger output. From this additional wealth, business will also receive the income to pay interest on its debt or dividends on its stock. But what of the government? Where are its productive assets?

We have already noted that the government budget includes dams, roads, housing projects, and many other items that might be classified as assets. During the 1960's, federal expenditures for such civil construction projects averaged about $5 billion a year. Thus the total addition to the gross public debt during the 1960's (it rose from roughly $285 billion in 1959 to $327 billion by mid-1967) could be construed as merely the financial counterpart of the creation of public assets.

Why is it not so considered? Mainly because, as we have seen, the peculiar character of public expenditures leads us to lump together all public spending, regardless of kind. In many European countries, however, public capital expenditures are sharply differentiated from public current expenditures. If we had such a system, the government's deficit on capital account could then be viewed as the public equivalent of business's deficit on capital account. Such a change might considerably improve the rationality of much discussion concerning the government's deficit.

Sales vs. taxes

But there is still a difference. Private capital enhances the earning capacity of a private business, whereas most public capital, save for such assets as toll roads, does not "make money" for the public sector. Does this constitute a meaningful distinction?

We can understand, of course, why an individual business insists that its investment must be profitable. The actual money that the business will pay out in the course of making an investment will almost surely not return to the business that spent it. A shirt manufacturer, for instance, who invests in a new factory cannot hope that the men who build that factory will spend all their wages on his shirts. He knows that the money he spends through investment will soon be dissipated throughout the economy, and that it can be recaptured only through strenuous selling efforts.

Not quite so with a national government, however. Its income does not come from sales but from taxes, and those taxes reflect the general level of income of the country. Thus *any* investment money that government lays out, just because it enters the general stream of incomes, redounds to the taxing capacity or, we might say, the "earning capacity" of government.

How much will come back to the government in taxes? That depends on two main factors: the impact of government spending on income via the multiplier, and the incidence and progressivity of the tax structure. Under today's normal conditions, the government will recover about half or a little more of its expenditure.* But in any event, note that the government does not "lose" its money in the way that a business does. Whatever goes into the income stream is always *available* to the government as a source of taxes; but whatever goes into the income stream is not necessarily available to any single business as a source of sales.

This reasoning helps us understand why federal finance is different from state and local government finance. An expenditure made by New York City or New York State is apt to be respent in many other areas of the country. Thus taxable incomes in New York will not, in all probability, rise to match local spending. As a result, *state and local governments must look on their finances much as an individual business does*. The power of full fiscal recapture belongs solely to the federal government.

Internal and external debts

This difference between the limited powers of recoupment of a single firm and the relatively limitless powers of a national government lies at the heart of the basic difference between business and government deficit spending. It helps us understand why the government has a capacity for financial operation that is inherently of a far higher order of magnitude from that of business. We can sum up this fundamental difference in the contrast between the *externality of business debts* and the *internality of national government debts*.

*We can make a rough estimate of the multiplier effect of additional public expenditure as 2 and of the share of an additional dollar of GNP going to federal taxes as 30 per cent (see page 84). Thus $1 of public spending will create $2 of GNP, of which 60¢ will go back to the federal government.

What do we mean by the externality of business debts? We simply mean that business firms owe their debts to someone distinct from themselves, whether this be bondholders or the bank from which they borrowed. Thus, to service or to pay back its debts, business must transfer funds from its own possession into the possession of outsiders. If this transfer cannot be made, if a business does not have the funds to pay its bondholders or its bank, it will go bankrupt.

The government is in a radically different position. Its bondholders, banks, and other people or institutions to whom it owes its debts belong to the same community as that whence it extracts its receipts. In other words, the government does not have to transfer its funds to an "outside" group to pay its bonds. It transfers them, instead, from some members of the national community (taxpayers) to other members of the *same* community (bondholders). The contrast is much the same as that between a family that owes a debt to another family, and a family in which the husband has borrowed money from his wife; or again between a firm that owes money to another, and a firm in which one branch has borrowed money from another. *Internal debts do not drain the resources of one community into another, but merely redistribute the claims among members of the same community.*

Problems of a national debt

A government cannot always borrow without trouble, however. Important and difficult problems of money management are inseparable from a large debt. More important, the people or institutions from whom taxes are collected are not always exactly the same people and institutions to whom interest is paid, so that servicing a government debt often poses problems of *redistribution of income.* For instance, if all government bonds were owned by rich people and if all government taxation were regressive (i.e., proportionately heavier on low incomes), then servicing a government debt would mean transferring income from the poor to the rich. Considerations of equity aside, this would also probably involve distributing income from spenders to savers, and would thereby intensify the problem of closing the savings gap.

In addition, a debt that a government owes to foreign citizens is *not* an internal debt. It is exactly like a debt that a corporation owes to an "outside" public, and it can involve payments that can cripple a firm.* Do not forget that the internality of debts applies only to *national* debts held as bonds by members of the same community of people whose incomes contribute to government revenues.

*About 5 per cent of the U.S. debt is held by foreigners.

Expenditures vs. tax cuts

Finally, we must not overlook the practical difficulties of government spending. The problem is that there is usually a long lag between the time of recognition, when the need for more public spending is first admitted, and the actual expenditure of the money itself. The time lag may, in fact, be so long—eighteen to twenty-four months—that by the time the public expenditures take effect, the condition they were supposed to remedy may have disappeared or worsened. In either case, the original government program is no longer the proper one. To counteract this difficulty, many economists have urged that the government keep a "stockpile" of approved public works, to be rapidly put into effect when needed. Numerous political and technical difficulties surround this proposal, however.

Because of the time-lag problem, interest has recently focused on another method of achieving a government deficit: a deliberate tax cut (while holding expenditures steady). The purpose of such a tax cut is also to create a deficit in the government sector—but a deficit which is brought about not by increased government spending, but by encouraging increased *consumer* spending.

This is the method of stimulating the economy used in the now famous Kennedy tax cut of early 1964, and it is a method likely to be employed again when the need for government stimulus arises. It need hardly be said that cutting taxes is always politically popular and that tax cuts therefore have a somewhat easier time than increased spending programs have in getting through Congress. Yet even tax cuts take time to get through, and some economists have therefore suggested that we should have *flexible tax rates* that could be adjusted upward or downward, within limits, by presidential action to create quickly a budgetary deficit or surplus.*

Despite their speedy impact, tax cuts still present some problems. One problem is that some of the tax cut will undoubtedly result in higher consumer saving, so that the net effect on demand of a tax cut of

---

*An interesting problem in the offing is that of "fiscal drag." Because of its progressive tax schedules, the tax income of the federal government rises faster than GNP, as we have already seen. It is now estimated that a normally growing GNP will yield increased revenues of about $6 billion a year to the federal government. Unless these revenues are spent, they will cause a demand gap, just as any uncompensated savings would. Some economists, led by Walter Heller, Chairman of the Council of Economic Advisers under President Kennedy, are suggesting that the government should get rid of this "drag" by automatically distributing all or part of this surplus to the states where it would be used to bolster weak state finances and to help with their pressing expenditure needs. Thereafter, if there is still a surplus at the federal level, taxes can be trimmed or expenditures of various kinds increased. If the economy is in need of a brake, perhaps we can even pay back some of the national debt, that is, deliberately create a public demand gap. All this, needless to say, assumes the absence of armed conflict such as the Vietnam war.

$1 billion will be less than the net effect of increased expenditures of $1 billion. The other difficulty is that tax cuts are not likely to stimulate demand among those portions of the population who are most in need of help during a recession, because their incomes are so low that they pay no income taxes. On the contrary, the increased flow of private purchasing activity may well bypass the most afflicted portion of the community.

There is no reason, however, why both tax cuts and increased expenditures cannot be used jointly, the one for speedy effect and the other for purposeful social action. We should recognize, nevertheless, that increasing demand by public action is not a simple matter, but one that poses very substantial problems of its own.

Perpetual public debts

These important caveats notwithstanding, can a national government have a perpetual debt even in a dynamic and changeful economy? We have seen that it can. To be sure, the debt must be constantly refunded, much as business refunds its debts, with new issues of bonds replacing the old. But like the business sector, we can expect the government debt in this way to be maintained indefinitely.

Will our public debt grow forever? That depends largely on what happens to our business debts and equities. If business debts and equities grow fast enough—that is, if we are creating enough assets through investment—there is no reason why government debts should grow. Government deficits, after all, are designed as *supplements* to private deficits. The rationale behind public borrowing is that it will be used only when the private sector is not providing enough expenditure to give us the GNP we need.

Nonetheless, the prospect of a rising national debt bothers many people. Some day, they say, it will have to be repaid. Is this true? It may aid us to think about the problem if we try to answer the following questions:

1. *Will public assets continue to increase?* If so, we can understand why debts grow with them, just as is the case with private debts and private assets. Conversely, if we imagine that at some future date we will have enough public assets, then public debts should cease rising, just as one day when we have enough private capital, private debts and equities will cease growing. The reason will be simple enough: we will no longer need any more net saving or net investment. All our output will go for consumption and replacement.

2. *Can we afford to pay interest on a rising debt?* The capacity to expand debts, both public and private, depends largely on the willingness of people to lend money, and this willingness in turn reflects their confi-

dence that they will be paid interest regularly and will have their money returned to them when their bond is due.

We have seen how refunding can take care of the repayment problem. But what about interest? With a private firm, this requires that interest costs be kept to a modest fraction of sales, so that they can easily be covered. With government, similar financial prudence requires that interest costs stay well within the taxable capacity of government. The figures in Table 8-3 give us some perspective on this problem today.

TABLE

8 • 3   DEBT AND INTEREST COSTS, 1966

	Net interest $ billions	Interest as proportionate cost
All corporations (1962)	18.4	2.0 per cent of receipts
Federal government	9.5	⎰4.4 per cent of receipts ⎱1.3 per cent of GNP

It can be seen that interest is a much higher percentage of federal revenues than of corporate revenues. But there is a reason for this. Corporations are supposed to maximize their sales; the government is not supposed to maximize its tax income. Hence we must also judge the size of the federal interest cost in comparison with the size of GNP, the total tax base from which the government can draw. Finally, we should know that interest as a percentage of all federal expenditures has remained very steady in recent years, and it is actually much lower than in the 1920's, when interest costs amounted to about 20 to 30 per cent of all federal outlays.

3. *Can we afford the burden of a rising debt?* What is the "burden" of a debt? For a firm, the question is easy to answer. It is the *cost* that must be borne by those who owe the debt. Here, of course, we are back to the externality of debts. *The burden of a debt is the obligation it imposes to pay funds from one firm or community to another.*

But we have seen that there is no such cost for an internal debt, such as that of a nation. The *cost* of the debt—that is, the taxes that must be levied to pay interest—becomes *income* to the very same community, as checks sent to bondholders for their interest income. Every penny that the debt costs our economy in taxes returns to our economy as income.

The same is also true of the principal of the debt. The debts we owe inside the nation we also *own* inside the nation—just as the I.O.U. a husband owes his wife is also an I.O.U. owned by the family; or, again, just as an amount borrowed by Branch A of a multibranch firm is owed to Branch B of the same firm.

There is a further point here. Internal debts are debts that are considered as financial *assets* within the "family." Nobody within A.T.&T.

considers its debts to be part of the assets of the firm, but many thousands of people in the U.S. consider the country's debts to be their assets. Indeed, everyone who owns a government bond considers it an asset. Thus in contrast to external debts, paying back an internal debt does not "lift a burden" from a community, because no burden existed in the first place! When a corporation pays off a debt to a bank, it is rid of an obligation to an outside claimant on its property. But when a husband pays back a wife, the *family* is no richer, any more than the *firm* is better off if one branch reimburses another. So, too, with a nation. If a national debt is repaid, the national economy is not rid of an obligation to an outside claimant. We would be rid only of obligations owed to one another.

Real burdens

This is not to say—and the point is important—that government spending is costless. Consider for a moment the main cause of government spending over the past fifty years: the prosecution of three wars. There was surely a terrific cost to these wars in lives, health, and (in economic terms) in the use of factors of production to produce guns instead of butter. But note also that all of this cost is irrevocably and unbudgeably situated in the past. The cost of all wars is borne during the years when the wars are fought and must be measured in the destruction that was then caused and the opportunities for making civilian goods that were then missed. The debt inherited from these wars is no longer a "cost." Today it is only an instrument for the transfer of incomes within the American community.

So, too, with debts incurred to fight unemployment. The cost of unemployment is also borne once and for all at the time it occurs, and the benefits of the government spending to combat unemployment will be enjoyed (or if the spending is ill-advised, the wastes of spending will be suffered) when that spending takes place. Afterward, the debt persists as a continuing means of transferring incomes, but the debt no longer has any connection to the "cost" for which it was made.

Costs, in other words, are *missed opportunities*, potential well-being not achieved. Debts, on the other hand (when they are held within a country) only transfer purchasing power and do not involve the nation in giving up its output to anyone else.

Indirect effects

Does this mean that there are no disadvantages whatsoever in a large national debt?

We have talked of one possible disadvantage, that of transferring incomes from spenders to savers, or possibly of transferring purchasing power from productive groups to unproductive groups. But we must pay heed to one other problem. This is the problem a rising debt may cause indirectly, but nonetheless painfully, *if it discourages private investment.*

If government spending serves to turn business expectations downward, then for each dollar of government spending, we may find that we must allow for a dollar *less* of private investment spending. Were such to be the case, the real burden of government deficits would be the new productive resources that might have been laid down in the country but were not.

This could be a very serious, real cost of government debts, were such a reaction to be widespread and long-lasting. It may well be (we are not sure) that the long drawn-out and never entirely successful recovery from the Great Depression was caused, to a considerable extent, by the adverse psychological impact of government deficit spending on business investment intentions. Business did not understand deficit spending and interpreted it either as the entering wedge of socialism (instead of a crash program to save capitalism), or as a wastrel and a hare-brained economic scheme. To make matters worse, the amount of the government deficit (at its peak $4 billion) while large enough to frighten the business community, was not big enough to begin to exert an effective leverage on total demand, particularly under conditions of widespread unemployment and financial catastrophe.

Today, however, it is much less likely that deficit spending would be attended by a drop in private spending. A great deal that was new and frightening in thought and practice in the 1930's is today well-understood and tested. The war itself was, after all, an immense laboratory demonstration of what public spending could do for GNP. The experience of 1954, 1958, and above all, of 1964 gives good reason to believe that deficit spending in the future will not cause a significant slowdown in private investment expenditure.

Personal debts and public debts

In view of the fact that our national debt today figures out to approximately $1,600 for every man, woman, and child, it is not surprising that we frequently hear appeals to "common sense," telling us how much better we would be without this debt, and how our grandchildren will groan under its weight.

Is this true? We have already discussed the fact that internal debts are different from external debts, but let us press the point home from a different vantage point. Suppose we decided that we would "pay off" the debt. This would mean that our government bonds would be redeemed for cash. To get the cash, we would have to tax ourselves (unless we wanted to roll the printing presses), so that what we would really be doing would be transferring money from taxpayers to bond-holders.

Would that be a net gain for the nation? Consider the typical holder of a government bond — a family, a bank, or a corporation. It now holds the world's safest and most readily sold paper asset from which a regular income is obtained. After our debt is redeemed, our families, banks, and corporations will have two choices: (1) they can hold cash and get *no* income, or (2) they can invest in other securities that are slightly *less* safe. Are these investors better off? As for our grandchildren, it is true that if we pay off the debt they will not have to "carry" its weight. But to offset that, neither will they be carried by the comfortable government bonds they would otherwise have inherited. They will also be relieved from paying taxes to meet the interest on the debt. Alas, they will be relieved as well of the pleasure of depositing the green Treasury checks for interest payments that used to arrive twice a year.

The public sector again in perspective

We have spent enough time on the question of the debt. Now we must ask what is it that close examination of the problems of government finance reveals, making them look so different from what we expect. The answer is largely that we think of the government as if it were a firm or a household, when it is actually something else. *The government is a sector;* and if we want to think clearly about it, we must compare it, not to the maxims and activities of a household or a firm, but to those of the entire consumer sector or the entire business sector.

Then we can see that the government sector plays a role not too dis-similar from that of the business sector. We have seen how businesses, through their individual decisions to add to plant and equipment, act in concert to offset the savings of consumers. The government, we now see, acts in precisely the same way, except that its decisions, rather than reflecting the behavior of innumerable entrepreneurs in a search for profit, reflect the deliberate political will of the community itself.

Persons who do not understand the intersectoral relationships of the economy like to say that business must "live within its income" and that government acts irresponsibly in failing to do so. These critics fail to see that business does *not* live within its income, but borrows the savings of other sectors, and thus typically and normally spends more than it takes in from its sales alone. By doing so, of course, it serves the invaluable function of providing an offset for saving that would otherwise create a demand gap and thereby precipitate a downward movement in economic activity.

Once this offsetting function is understood, it is not difficult to see that government, as well as business, can serve as a "spender" to offset savings, and that in the course of doing so, both government and business typically create new assets for the community.

Public and private assets

Finally, we have seen something else that gives us a last insight into government spending. We have seen that the creation of earning assets is indispensable for business, because each asset constitutes the means by which an individual business seeks to recoup its own investment spending. But with the government, the definition of an "earning asset" can properly be much larger than with a business firm. The government does not need its assets to make money for itself directly, for the government's economic capability arises from its capacity to tax *all* incomes. So far as the government is concerned, then, all that matters is that savings be turned into expenditures, and thereby into taxable incomes.

As a result, government can and should be motivated—even in a self-interested way—by a much wider view of the economic process than would be possible or proper for a single firm. Whereas a firm's assets are largely its capital goods, the assets of a nation are not only capital wealth but the whole productive capacity of its people. Thus government expenditures that redound to the health or well-being or education of its citizens are just as properly considered asset-building expenditures as are its expenditures on dams and roads.

Political problems

One last thought remains. We have seen that the government can undertake fiscal operations far beyond those of any single firm. What we have not considered are the *political dangers* that may result from such a course. Is the use of the public sector compatible with the freedom of action on which a market society is based?

Much ink has been spilled on the problem of the "mixed economy" —the economy in which the public sector undertakes some responsibilities formerly entrusted to the private sector. Unquestionably, a mixed economy produces problems of many kinds, and in our next chapters we shall have something to say about various criteria that bear on the use of the government's powers. Yet few economists today would advocate returning to an economy without a strong fiscal policy. We have come to understand that the operation of the economy depends on the interplay of the sectors, and that the public sector is the *only* one inherently and legitimately under our collective control.

We should understand as well that the idea of compensatory public finance is based on a *minimal interference* into the operations of the market economy. For what are the alternatives? One would be not to intervene at all and to allow the savings-investment balance to work itself out as the propensity to consume and the inducement to invest might dictate. The risk here is that an imbalance could well precipitate a severe and cumulative depression with unforeseeable social and political consequences. The other alternative is to penetrate directly into the decision-making activities of the economy, to enforce household or business spending in conformance with a central plan. Here the cost is plain: the severe infringement of personal economic freedom. As a means of correcting the gross mistakes of the economy without running the risks of these extremes, the compensatory use of the public spending power would seem to have much to recommend it.

Political vs. economic considerations

In the end, an important distinction must be made between two kinds of judgments to be passed on government spending, one valid and one not. The valid judgments have to do with *how large the public sector should be, for what purposes it should be employed, or what techniques — such as tax cuts — are appropriate at a given time.* The public sector is rightfully subject to these judgments, where reasonable men may well differ.

The other kind of judgment concerns the "soundness" of fiscal policy itself, including in particular, deficit spending, as a means of offsetting the savings gap. Here the issue is not the size of the public sector or the purpose for which it is used, for one can have a large deficit even with a small public sector. The issue in the second case concerns only the validity of the economic principles of sectoral analysis. Here political judgments must be laid aside, and the logic of government spending as a demand-creating device must be considered on its own merits, in the light of an understanding of the macroeconomic process as a whole. Reasonable men may still differ as to the relative worth of different government measures, but on the propriety of the basic economics of public finance there should be a large area of agreement.

Summary

1. The *public sector* derives its income from three main sources: indirect taxes (mainly for state and local governments), personal income and other taxes, and

corporate taxes. Expenditures for goods and services are roughly equally divided between federal government and state and local government, but the Federal government is the main source of transfer expenditures.

2. Comparing the 1960's with the 1920's, we find that the public sector has grown considerably as a proportion of GNP. During the 1960's, the level remains roughly unchanged. Federal purchases have grown largely for defense purposes.

3. The critical differentiating factor between the public and the private sectors is that the public sector can be deliberately employed as an instrument of *national economic policy*.

4. The use of government spending and taxing to achieve national growth or stability is called *fiscal policy*. There are two main instruments of fiscal policy: *expenditures* can be increased or decreased, and *taxes* can be raised or cut. The former acts much as an increase or decrease in private investment; the latter is mainly used to induce or to discourage consumer spending.

5. *Automatic stabilizers* help implement fiscal policy by lessening the momentum of booms and cushioning the impact of recessions. The stabilizers arise from the progressive incidence of income taxation, from expenditure programs geared to unemployment, and so on.

6. The use of the government budget as a deliberate antirecession instrument leads to *deficits*. These deficits are financed by *government borrowing* and hence lead to government debt.

7. The government debt can be thought of in the same way as much private debt: as the *financial counterpart of assets*.

8. *All debts, as long as their underlying assets are economically productive, can be maintained indefinitely* by being refunded when they come due.

9. In a *progressive and growing economy, debts increase* as assets rise. Debts are only a way of financing the growth in assets.

10. National governments have the power of fiscal recapture of any money spent by them — a power not available to state governments or even to the largest businesses. Hence national governments are in a fundamentally different position regarding the safety of their domestically-held debts. This difference is expressed in the concept of *internal debts* versus *external* ones.

11. Domestically-held national debts do not lead to bankruptcy. They do present important and difficult problems of *monetary management,* and they can also result in the *redistribution of income*. These are *real burdens* of the debt.

12. *Repaying the debt would not lift a burden from the economy.* Taxes would decrease (because the debt need no longer be serviced), but income would also decrease (because interest would no longer be paid). Former government bondholders would have to find another acceptable financial asset.

13. The confusion with which the public debt is often viewed arises from a failure to understand that the *government is not a "household" but a sector,* fully comparable to the business sector in its intersectoral operations.

14. Deficits can be incurred by *tax cuts* or by *increased expenditures.* Both present problems. *Tax cuts may not put income where it is needed.* Also, tax cuts will probably not be wholly spent, but will result in some additional saving. On the other hand, *increased expenditures may take much too long* to combat a turn-down efficiently.

15. The true problem with regard to the public sector lies in the *uses to which its*

activities are put, and *the skill with which its policies are managed.* These can be very important problems, but they do not involve the propriety of fiscal policy, as such.

Questions

1. What are the main differences between the public and the private sectors? Are these differences economic or political?
2. Show in a diagram how increased government expenditure can offset a demand gap. Show also how decreased government taxation can do the same.
3. Show diagrammatically how equilibrium is the result of the interplay of two sets of forces: on the one hand, investment and public spending; on the other hand, saving and taxation.
4. What is meant by the automatic stabilizers? Give an example of how they might work if we had an increase in investment of $20 billion and the multiplier were 2; and if the increase in taxes and the decrease in public expenditure associated with the boom in investment were each $5 billion.
5. In what ways is a government deficit comparable to business spending for investment purposes? In what way is it not?
6. What is meant by the internality of debts? Is the debt of New York State internal? The debt of a country like Israel or Egypt?
7. What relation do debts generally have to assets? Can business debts increase indefinitely? Can a family's? Can the debt of all consumers?
8. What do you consider a better way of combating a mild recession—tax cuts or higher expenditures? Why? Suppose we had a deep recession, then what would you do?
9. In what sorts of economic conditions should the government run a surplus?
10. Suppose the government cuts taxes by $10 billion and also cuts its expenditures by the same amount. Will this stimulate the economy? Suppose it raises its expenditures and also raises taxes? Would this be a good antirecession policy?
11. What are the real burdens of a national debt?
12. Trace out carefully the consequences of paying back all the national debt.
13. How would you explain to someone who is adamantly opposed to all deficit financing that it is perfectly sound policy in certain circumstances?
14. What do you think are the principal dangers to be guarded against in public expenditure?

9

Money

We have almost completed our study of the determinants of gross national product, and soon we can combine the separate sectoral analyses into an over-all view of the economy. But first there is a matter that we must integrate into our discussion. This is the role that money plays in fixing or changing the level of GNP, along with the other forces that we have come to know.

Actually, we have been talking about money throughout our exposition. After all, one cannot discuss "expenditure" without assuming the existence of money. But now we must look behind this unexamined assumption and find out exactly what we mean when we speak of money. This will entail two tasks. In this chapter we shall investigate the perplexing question of what money *is*—for as we shall see, money is surely one of the most sophisticated and curious inventions of human society. Then in our next chapter, once we have come to understand what currency and gold and bank deposits are and how they come into being, we will look into the effect that money has on our economic operations.

The supply of money

Let us begin, then, by asking—"What is money?" The question is by no means as simple to answer as it would appear. Coin and currency are certainly money. But are checks money? Are the deposits from which we draw checks money? Are savings accounts money? Stamps? Government bonds?

The answer is a somewhat arbitrary one. From the spectrum of possible candidates, we reserve the term *money* for those items used to make *payments*. This means that we include cash in the public's possession and checking accounts, because we pay for most things by cash or check. Surprisingly, it means that we do not count savings accounts, since we have to draw "money" *out* of our savings accounts, in the form of cash or a check, if we want to use our savings account to make an expenditure. So, too, we have to sell government bonds to get money. Stamps can sometimes be used to make small payments, but they are too insignificant to matter.

Currency

Money, then, is mainly currency and checking accounts; and of these, currency is the form most familiar to us. Yet there is a considerable mystery even about currency. Who determines how much currency there is? How is the supply of coins or bills regulated?

We often assume that the supply of currency is "set" by the government that "issues" it. Yet when we think about it, we realize that the government does not just hand out money, and certainly not coin or bills. When the government pays people, it is nearly always by check.

Then who does "fix" the amount of currency in circulation? You can answer the question by asking how you yourself determine how much currency you will carry. If you think about it, the answer is that you "cash" a check when you need more currency than you have, and you put the currency back into your checking account when you have more than you need.

What you do, everyone does. The amount of cash that the public holds at any time is no more and no less than the amount that it *wants* to hold. When it needs more — at Christmas, for instance — the public draws currency by "cashing" checks on its own checking accounts; and when Christmas is past, shopkeepers (who have received the public's currency) return it to their checking accounts.

Thus the amount of currency we have bears an obvious, important relation to the size of our bank accounts, for we can't write checks for cash if our accounts will not cover them.

Does this mean, then, that the banks have as much currency in their vaults as the total of our checking accounts? No, it does not. But to understand that, let us follow the course of some currency that we deposit in our bank for credit to our account.

Bookkeeping money

When you put money into a commercial bank,* the bank does not hold that money for you as a pile of specially earmarked bills or as a bundle of checks made out to you from some payer. The bank takes notice of your deposit simply by crediting your "account," a bookkeeping page recording your present "balance." After the amount of the currency or check has been credited to you, the currency is put away with the bank's general store of vault cash and the checks are sent to the banks from which they came, where, of course, they will be charged against the accounts of the people who wrote them.

There is probably no misconception in economics harder to dispel than the idea that banks are warehouses stuffed with money. In point of fact, however, you might search as hard as you pleased in your bank, but you would find no other kind of money that was yours but a bookkeeping account in your name. This seems like a very unreal form of money, and yet, the fact that you can present a check at the teller's window and convert your bookkeeping account into cash proves that your account must nonetheless be "real."

But suppose that you and all the other depositors tried to convert your accounts into cash on the same day. You would then find something shocking. There would not be nearly enough cash in the bank's till to cover your total withdrawals. In 1966, for instance, total demand deposits in the United States amounted to about $132 billion. But the total amount of coin and currency held by the banks was only $5 billion!

At first blush, this seems like a highly dangerous state of affairs. But second thoughts are more reassuring. After all, most of us put money into a bank because we do *not* need it immediately, or because making payments in cash is a nuisance compared with making them by check. Yet, there is always the chance—more than that, the certainty—that some depositors *will* want their money in currency. How much currency will the banks need then? What will be a proper "reserve" for them to hold?

The Federal Reserve System

For many years, the banks themselves decided what "reserve ratio" constituted a safe proportion of currency to hold against their demand

---

*A commercial bank is a bank that is empowered by law to offer checking services. It may also have savings accounts. A savings bank has only savings accounts and may not offer checking services.

deposits (the technical name for checking accounts). Today, however, most large banks are members of the Federal Reserve, a central banking system established in 1913 to strengthen the banking activities of the nation. Under the Federal Reserve System, the nation is divided into twelve districts, in each of which there is a Federal Reserve Bank owned (but not really controlled) by the member banks of its district. In turn, the twelve Reserve Banks are themselves coordinated by a seven-man Federal Reserve Board in Washington. Since the members of the board are appointed for fourteen-year terms, they constitute a body that has been purposely established as an independent, nonpolitical monetary authority.*

One of the most important functions of the Federal Reserve Board is to establish reserve ratios for different categories of banks, within limits set by Congress. Historically these reserve ratios have ranged between 13 and 26 per cent of demand deposits for city banks, with a somewhat smaller reserve ratio for country banks. Today, the reserve city ratio is 17 per cent; the country ratio 12.5 per cent. The Federal Reserve Board also sets reserve requirements for "time" (savings) deposits. These are only 3 per cent. Do not forget, however, that time deposits do not count — or directly serve — as "money."

The banks' bank

Yet here is something odd! We noticed that in 1966 the total amount of deposits was $132 billion and that banks' holdings of coin and currency were only $5 billion. This is much less than the 17 per cent — or even 12.5 per cent — reserve against deposits established by the Federal Reserve Board. How can this be?

The answer is that cash is not the only reserve a bank holds against deposits. It also holds as its reserve *claims on other banks.*

What are these claims? Suppose you deposit a check from someone who has an account in Bank B into your account in Bank A. Bank A credits your account and then presents the check to Bank B for "payment." By "payment" Bank A does not mean coin and currency, however. Instead, Bank A and Bank B settle their transaction at still *another*

---

*This has resulted, on occasion, in sharp clashes of viewpoint with the Treasury Department or the Bureau of the Budget where fiscal and economic policy is formulated by each administration. There is some disagreement over whether the nation is better served by a Federal Reserve that can impede an economic policy it disagrees with or one that is bound to assist the economic aims of each incumbent administration. Generally speaking, however, there has been a harmony of views between the monetary and the fiscal authorities.

bank where both Bank A and Bank B have their own accounts. These are the twelve Federal Reserve Banks of the country, where all banks who are members of the Federal Reserve System (and this accounts for banks holding most of the deposits in our banking system) *must* open accounts. Thus at the Federal Reserve Bank, Bank A's account will be credited and Bank B's account will be debited, in this way moving reserves from one bank to the other.*

In other words, *the Federal Reserve Banks serve their member banks in exactly the same way as the member banks serve the public.* Member banks automatically deposit in their Federal Reserve accounts all checks they get from other banks. As a result, banks are constantly "clearing" their checks with one another through the Federal Reserve System, because their depositors are constantly writing checks on their own banks payable to someone who banks elsewhere. Meanwhile, *the balance that each bank maintains at the Federal Reserve—that is, the claim it has on other banks—counts, equally as much as any currency, as part of its reserve against deposits.*

In 1966, therefore, when demand deposits were $132 billion and cash in the banks only $5 billion, we would expect the member banks to have had heavy accounts with the Federal Reserve banks. And so they did—$19 billion in all. Thus, total reserves of the banks were $24 billion ($5 billion in cash plus $19 billion in Federal Reserve accounts), enough for legal backing of all deposits.

Fractional reserves

Thus we see that our banks operate on what is called *a fractional reserve system.* The size of the minimum fraction is determined by the Federal Reserve, for reasons of control that we shall shortly learn about. It is *not* determined, as we might be tempted to think, to provide a "safe" backing for our bank deposits. For under *any* fractional system if *all* depositors decided to draw out their accounts in currency and coin from all banks at the same time, the banks would be unable to meet the demand for cash and would have to close. We call this a "run" on the banking system. Needless to say, runs can be terrifying and destructive economic phenomena.†

*When a bank account is credited, money is put into it; when it is debited, money is taken out.

†A run on a *single* bank can be met by other banks lending cash. But a run on all banks far exceeds the cash resources of the community. Do not forget, however, that nowadays most accounts are insured up to $15,000 by the Federal Deposit Insurance Corporation, an agency of the federal government. This makes a run highly improbable; and even if a run should occur, it assures most depositors that they will eventually get their money back.

Why, then, do we court the risk of runs, however small this risk may be? What is the benefit of a fractional banking system? To answer that, let us look into our bank again.

Loans and investments

Suppose its customers have given our bank $1 million in deposits and that the Federal Reserve Board requirements are 20 per cent, a simpler figure to work with than the actual one. Then we know that our bank must at all times keep $200,000, either in currency in its own till or in its checking account with the Federal Reserve Bank.

But having taken care of that requirement, what does the bank do with the remaining deposits? If it simply lets them sit, either as vault cash or as a deposit at the Federal Reserve, our bank will be very "liquid," but it will have no way of making an income. Unless it charges a great deal for its checking services, it will have to go out of business.

And yet there is an obvious way for the bank to make an income, while performing a valuable service. The bank can use all the cash and check claims it does not need for its reserve to make *loans* to businessmen or families or to make financial *investments* in corporate or government bonds. It will thereby not only earn an income, but it will assist the process of business investment and government borrowing. Thus the mechanics of the banking system lead us back to the concerns at the very center of our previous analysis.

Increasing the supply of money

Fractional reserves allow banks to lend or to invest in securities part of the funds that have been deposited with them. But that is not the only usefulness of the fractional reserve system. It works as well to help enlarge or diminish the supply of investable or loanable funds, as the occasion demands. Let us follow how this process works.

We start again with our bank with its $1,000,000 in deposits and its $200,000 of required reserves. All the rest, we now agree, has been lent out or put into safe bonds. Now let us assume that our bank suddenly acquires *new* deposits of $100,000 (perhaps the public simply decides to carry that much less cash and deposits it to its accounts). Our bank now has deposits of $1,100,000, but its reserves have risen to $300,000 — $200,000 of former reserves plus the $100,000 of newly deposited currency. Since this is more currency than it needs, it will send most of it to its Federal Reserve Bank, where the currency will be credited to its account there, just as your bank credits your account when you deposit currency.

Our bank officers immediately realize that they have *excess* reserves. To back their deposits of $1,100,000, all they need by law is $220,000, which is $80,000 less than they actually have. The rest, the $80,000 of excess reserve, they are free to put to use in loans or investments.

And so they do. If the officers decide to use the excess reserve to buy more government bonds for the bank, they will simply write a check for $80,000 on their Federal Reserve bank account to pay the seller of the bond, and thereby acquire interest-bearing securities. More interesting, the bank officers may decide to increase their loans. When the next attractive borrower comes around, they will make use of the excess reserves to lend him up to $80,000. This time, however, they will not write a check on their Federal Reserve account. Much easier. The bank will simply open a checking account in the borrower's name for the amount of the loan it makes to him. With the stroke of a bank officer's pen, it *creates a deposit account that never existed before,* an account secured by the loan agreement signed by the businessman and "backed" to the same extent as every other account, thanks to the excess reserves the bank had previously gained.

New money

All this seems perfectly safe and sound. As our bank president would be the first to tell us, the bank has not lent out a penny more than it has every right to. It has not lent out money belonging to anyone else. It has not lent out so much money that its reserves dip below the legal line. The $80,000 new account it opened was, in fact, "backed" not by a 20 per cent reserve but *by a 100 per cent reserve,* the excess reserve stemming from the original increase in deposits.

Yet, if we look again, we can see that the bank, for all its caution, has done something very unusual. *It has created new money!* As we know, money in our system consists largely of bank deposits.* Originally there were $1 million in deposits. Then the bank gained $100,000 in new cash deposits. This was new money for the bank, but not new money for the economy. It was simply a swap; the public gave up currency and took checking accounts instead.

But thereafter our bank opened a new account in the amount of $80,000, the amount it was entitled to lend because of its excess reserve. *This was new money.* It was a new deposit that came from no one's else deposit. It was nothing less than the creation of new spending power.

*The currency *in* the banks is counted as a reserve against those deposits and is not part of our money supply. Only the cash *outside* the banks, in the pockets of the public, counts as part of the money supply. Note that our earlier definition counted as "money" demand deposits and currency outside the banks.

The expansion of deposits

Nor is this an end to it. The businessman in whose name the new account was opened will probably soon use his money. Businessmen do not borrow to let funds sit idle. But notice that as he spends his money, it will become the basis for still more new money, for his checks will be deposited in *other* banks that will send them to the Federal Reserve Bank for clearance. *Thereby they will gain new reserves for themselves from the banks against which the checks were drawn.* In turn, these new reserves will make it possible to open still more new deposit accounts as banks put their enhanced lending or investing power to work. Note that the process of multiple deposit creation does not create more reserves for the system as a whole. It merely spreads the original addition to reserves among banks until it is used to its maximum effectiveness.

As Fig. 9-1 shows, much as additional spending creates additional incomes via the multiplier, so additional deposits create still more deposits via the fractional reserve system. And just as the existence of a savings fraction made each multiplier round smaller than the previous, so the existence of a reserve ratio makes each additional creation of new demand deposits smaller than before.

In fact we can say, just as with the multiplier, that the cumulative effect of an increase in deposits will be determined by the reciprocal of the reserve ratio. If each bank must keep one-fifth of its increased deposits as reserves, then the cumulative effect of a net increase in deposits, when it has been expanded through this system, is five times the original increase. If reserves are one-fourth, the expansion is limited to four times the original increase, and so on.

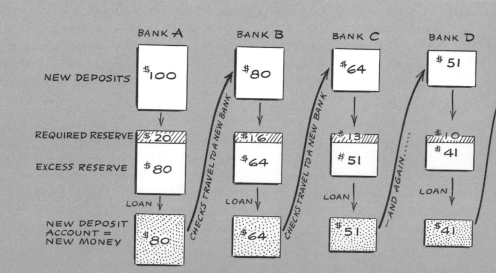

FIG. 9-1   EXPANSION OF THE MONEY SUPPLY

Why banks must work together

There is an interesting problem concealed behind this crisscrossing of deposits that leads to a slowly rising level of the money supply. Suppose that an imaginary island economy was served by a single bank (and let us forget about all complications of international trade, etc.), and suppose that this bank, which worked on a 20 per cent reserve ratio, was suddenly presented with an extra million dollars worth of reserves—let us say newly mined pure gold. Our bank could, of course, increase its loans to customers. By how much? *By five million dollars!*

Our island bank, all by itself, could use an increase in its reserves to create a much larger money supply. It is not difficult to understand why. Any borrower of the new five million, no matter where he spent his money on the island, would only be giving his checks to someone who also banked at the single and solitary bank. The whole five million, in other words, would stay *within* the bank as its deposits, although the identity of those depositors would, of course, shift. Indeed, there is no reason why such a bank should limit its expansion of the money supply to five million. As long as the "soundness" of the currency was unquestioned, such a bank could create as much money as it wanted through new deposits, since all of those deposits would remain in its own keeping.

The imaginary bank makes it plain why ordinary commercial banks *cannot* expand deposits beyond their excess reserves. Unlike the monopoly bank, they must expect to *lose* their deposits to other banks when their borrowers write checks on their new accounts. As a result they will also lose their reserves, and this can lead to trouble.

Take our original bank in this chapter with its $1 million of deposits, $200,000 of reserves, and its increase in deposits of $100,000. We saw how such a bank, working on a 20 per cent reserve ratio, could lend an amount equal to its excess reserves, or $80,000. (Remember that its reserves jump to $300,000, of which only $220,000 is needed for its deposits of $1,100,000.) Now suppose such a bank foolishly lent not $80,000 but $100,000.

At first its position would look sound enough. Its deposits would rise to $1,200,000 ($1,000,000 plus the original $100,000 increase, and now plus a new account it would open in the name of the borrower), and its reserves of $300,000 would more than cover the necessary 20 per cent reserve requirement of $240,000. But now let us suppose—very realistically—that the borrower draws down his entire newly-created deposit via checks made out to people who bank elsewhere. Suddenly our bank finds itself in trouble. As the $100,000 account is drawn upon, its deposits fall back to $1,100,000. But as these same checks reach other banks, its reserve account at the Fed will be reduced from $300,000 to $200,000. This is no longer enough to provide the $220,000 of reserves required by law. The erring bank must now borrow reserves from the Fed (for which it must pay interest charges) until by selling bonds or by failing to renew other loans, it re-establishes its legal reserve requirements. If our bank had lent $300,000, rather than $100,000, it would lose *all* its reserves and would be unable to meet its commitments: it would fail.

Thus we can see that a bank is safe in lending only an amount that it can afford to lose to another bank. But of course one bank's loss is another's gain. That is why, by the exchange of checks, the banking system can accomplish the same result as the island monopoly bank, whereas no individual bank can hope to do so.

Investments and interest

If a bank uses its excess reserves to buy securities, does that lead to the same multiplication effect as a bank loan?

It can. When a bank buys government securities, it usually does so from a securities dealer, a professional trader in bonds. Its check (for $80,000 in our example) drawn on its account at the Federal Reserve will be made out to a dealer, who will deposit it in his bank. As a result, his bank suddenly finds itself with $80,000 in new deposits. It must keep 20 per cent of this as required reserve, but the remainder is excess reserve that it can lend or invest as it wishes. Is there a new deposit, corresponding to that of the businessman borrower? There is—the deposit of the securities dealer.

It is possible for new deposits, albeit diminishing each time, to remain in this financial circuit for some time, moving from bank to bank as an active business is done in buying government bonds. But the very activity in bidding for government bonds is likely to raise their price, and thereby lower their rate of interest.* A lower rate of interest on bonds makes higher yielding loans to business look more attractive. Thus, sooner or later, excess reserves are apt to be channeled to new loans as well as new investments. Thereafter the deposit-building process follows it familiar course.

---

*A bond has a *fixed* rate of return and a stated face value. If it is a 4 per cent, $1,000 bond, this means it will pay $40 of interest yearly. If the bond now sells on the market-place for $1,100, the $40 yearly interest will be less than a 4 per cent return. If the price should fall to $900 the $40 return will be more than 4 per cent. Thus the *yield* of a bond varies inversely—in the other direction—from its market price.

Creating reserves

We have seen how a banking system can create money through the successive creation of excess reserves.* But the key to the process is the creation of the *original* excess reserves, for without them, the cumulative process will not be set in motion. Where do these extra reserves come from—or go to? That is the question we must turn to next.

In our example we have already met one source of changes in reserves. When the public needs less currency, and deposits its extra holdings in the banks, reserves rise, as we have seen. Contrariwise, when the public wants more currency, it depletes the banks' holdings of currency and thereby lowers their reserves. In the latter case, the banks may find that they have insufficient reserves behind their deposits. To get more currency or claims on other banks, they will have to sell securities or reduce their loans. This might put a very severe crimp in the economy. Hence, to allow bank reserves to be regulated by the public's fluctuating demand for cash would seem to be an impossible way to run our monetary system.

But we remember that bank reserves are not mainly currency; in fact, currency is a relatively minor item. Most reserves are the accounts that member banks hold at the Federal Reserve. Hence, if these accounts could somehow be increased or decreased, we could regulate the amount of reserves—and thus the permissible total of deposits—without regard to the public's changing need for cash.

This is precisely what the Federal Reserve System is designed to do. Essentially, the system is set up to regulate the supply of money by raising or lowering the reserves of its member banks. When these reserves are raised, member banks find themselves with excess reserves and are thus in a position to make loans and investments by which the

---

*What *is* money, really? We said before it was whatever we used to make payments with. But what do we use? The answer is a surprising one. We use *debts*—specifically, the debts of commercial banks. Deposits are, after all, nothing but the liabilities which banks owe their customers. Furthermore, we can see that one purpose of the banking system is to buy debts from other units in the economy, such as businesses or governments, in exchange for its own debts (which *are* money). For what else does a bank do, when it opens an account for a business to whom it has granted a loan or when it buys a government bond, but accept a debt that is *not* usable as money, in exchange for its deposit liabilities which *are* usable as money? And why is it that banks create money when they make loans, but you or I do not, when we lend money? Because we all accept bank liabilities (deposits) as money, but we do not accept personal or business I.O.U.'s to make payments with. Someone who would like to probe deeper into the curious (and very important) problem of money and how it affects our economy could do no better than to read the lucid and sparkling analysis by Peter L. Bernstein, *A Primer on Money, Banking and Gold* (New York: Random House, 1965).

supply of money will increase further. Conversely, when the Federal Reserve lowers the reserves of its member banks, they will no longer be able to make loans and investments, or may even have to reduce loans or get rid of investments, thereby extinguishing deposit accounts and contracting the supply of money.

Monetary control mechanisms

How does the Federal Reserve operate? There are three ways.

1. *Changing reserve requirements.* It was the Federal Reserve, itself, we will remember, that originally determined how much in reserves its member banks should hold against their deposits. Hence by changing that reserve requirement, from a given level of reserves, it can give its member banks excess reserves or can create a shortage of reserves.

In our imaginary bank we have assumed that reserves were set at 20 per cent of deposits. Suppose now that the Federal Reserve determined to lower reserve requirements to 15 per cent. It would thereby automatically create extra lending or investing power for our *existing* reserves. Our bank with $1 million in deposits and $200,000 in reserves could now lend or invest an additional $50,000 without any new funds coming in from depositors. On the other hand, if requirements were raised to, say, 30 per cent, we would find that our original $200,000 of reserves was $100,000 short of requirements, and we would have to curtail lending or investing until we were again in line with requirements.

Changing reserve ratios is a very effective way of freeing or contracting bank credit. But it is a massive instrument that sweeps across the entire banking system in an undiscriminating fashion. It is therefore used only rarely, when the Federal Reserve Board feels that countrywide reserves are seriously short or dangerously excessive.

2. *Changing discount rates.* A second means of control uses interest rates as the money-controlling device. Member banks that are short on reserves have a special privilege, if they wish to exercise it. They can *borrow* reserve balances from the Federal Reserve Bank itself, adding them of course, to their regular reserve account at the bank. The way member banks borrow is to take the government bonds they have bought and to use these as collateral, or to take the signed loan agreements they have received from their own customers and to "re-discount" these loans—that is, to borrow on them—from their Federal Reserve Bank.

The Federal Reserve Bank, of course, charges interest for lending reserves, and this interest is called the discount rate. By raising or lowering this rate, the Federal Reserve can make it attractive or unattractive for member banks to borrow to augment reserves. Thus in contrast with changing the reserve ratio itself, changing the discount rate is a mild device that allows each bank to decide for itself whether it wishes to increase its reserves or not. In addition, changes in the discount rate tend to influence the whole structure of interest rates — either tightening or loosening money in general.

3. *Open-market operations.* Most frequently used, however, is a third technique called open-market operations. This technique permits the Federal Reserve Banks to change the supply of reserves by buying or selling U.S. government bonds on the open market.

How does this work? Let us suppose that the Federal Reserve authorities wish to increase the reserves of member banks. They will begin to buy government securities from dealers in the bond market; and to pay for these bonds, they will send Federal Reserve Bank checks in the amount of their purchases to dealers.

But notice something about these checks: *they are not drawn on any commercial bank!* They are drawn on the Federal Reserve Bank itself. The security dealer who sells the bond will, of course, deposit the Fed's check, as if it were any other check, in his own commercial bank; and his bank will send the Fed's check through for credit to its own account, as if it were any other check. *As a result, the dealer's bank will have gained reserves, although no other commercial bank has lost reserves.* On balance, then, the system has more lending and investing capacity than it had before. In fact, it now has *excess* reserves, and these, as we have seen, will spread out through the system. *Thus by buying bonds, the Federal Reserve has, in fact, deposited money in the accounts of its members, thereby giving them the extra reserves that it set out to create.*

Conversely, if the authorities decide that the member banks have too many reserves, they will sell securities. Now the process works in reverse. Security dealers or other buyers of bonds will send their own checks on their own regular commercial banks to the Federal Reserve in payment for these bonds. This time the Fed will take the checks of its member banks and charge them against their accounts, thereby reducing their reserves. *Since these checks will not find their way into another commercial bank, the system as a whole will have suffered a diminution of its reserves.* By selling securities, in other words, the Federal Reserve authorities lower the Federal Reserve accounts of member banks, thereby diminishing their reserves.

Federal Reserve notes

Is there any limit to this reserve-creating or reserve-destroying power of the Federal Reserve System? There used to be very strict limits in a requirement that 25 per cent of the liabilities of the system be backed by gold certificates—special paper currency issued by the U.S. Treasury and backed 100 per cent by gold bullion in Fort Knox. Since one of the main liabilities of the Federal Reserve System was its member bank deposits (just as the main liability of a commercial bank is *its* customers' deposits), the 25 per cent gold limitation prevented the Federal Reserve from accepting deposits (that is, from creating reserves) beyond this ceiling.

We shall revert in a moment to the question of the present limitations on the Fed's reserve-creating power. But here is a good place to clear up one last mystery of the monetary system—the mystery of where currency (coin and bills) actually comes from and where it goes. For if we examine most of our paper currency, we will find that it says *Federal Reserve Note* on it. That is, it is paper money issued by the Federal Reserve System. As such, it is also a liability of the system, against which the gold limitation applies.

Let us see how this limitation works. We understand, by now, how the public gets cash; it simply draws it from its checking accounts. When it does so, the commercial banks, finding their supplies of vault cash low, ask their Federal Reserve district banks to ship them as much new cash as they need.

And what does the Federal Reserve Bank do? It takes packets of $1's and $5's and $10's out of its vaults, *where these stacks of printed paper have no monetary significance at all,* charges the requisite amount against its member banks' balances, and ships the cash out by armored truck. So long as these new stacks of bills remain in the member banks' possession, they are still not money! But soon they will pass out to the public, where they will be money. Do not forget, of course, that as a result, the public will have that much *less* money left in its checking accounts.

Could this currency-issuing process go on forever? Could the Federal Reserve ship out as much money as it wanted to? Suppose that the authorities at the Fed decided to order a trillion dollars worth of bills from the Treasury mints. What would happen when those bills arrived at the Federal Reserve Banks? The answer is that they would simply gather dust in their vaults. *There would be no way for the Fed to "issue" its money unless the public wanted cash.* And the amount of cash the public could want is always limited by the amount of money it has in its checking accounts.*

---

*What about wild inflations such as the German post-World War I or the Hungarian post-World War II debacles? Inflations such as these are not orderly price changes that can be discussed in terms of the supply of money, but reflect complete collapses of monetary systems where the public loses all faith in the monetary unit. There is no cure for such panics other than the constitution of a new monetary unit in which public faith will again reside.

The gold cover

As we have mentioned, there is also a legal limit placed on the ability of the Federal Reserve to issue notes when its member banks request them. This lies in a requirement that the Fed's holdings of gold certificates amount to at least 25 per cent of the value of all outstanding Federal Reserve notes. In mid-1967, the total value of these notes was over $39 billion, whereas our total gold certificate reserves came to less than $13 billion*, so that our margin was extremely thin.

Now suppose — as is likely — that the demand for Federal Reserve notes rises (it has been growing steadily throughout the 1960's), or that our gold stock continues to shrink, for reasons of international finance. Will we not then reach a point where there will be too little gold to permit the Federal Reserve Banks to issue any more notes? What then?

There would be two possible ways out of such a difficulty. One would be to *change the official ratio of gold "cover"* for Federal Reserve notes from the present 25 per cent to, say, 10 per cent. Thereupon our gold stock would immediately be more than adequate. The second way out is really only a continuation of the first to its limits. It is to *eliminate the requirements for gold cover* entirely.

Actually we have already taken the second course in regard to member bank reserves. Formerly, as we mentioned, the 25 per cent gold cover applied to member bank reserves as well as to Federal Reserve notes. But the situation we imagined above actually came to pass. The total of our needed reserves grew each year as our economy expanded, and the size of our gold stock shrank because of developments in the international monetary sphere. The result was that by late 1964 we were in clear danger of running out of enough gold to "back" both the currency issue and the member bank deposits of the Fed. With very little fuss, the decision was thereupon made to remove the gold cover from reserves, entirely.†

Gold and money

Does the presence or absence of a gold cover make any difference? From the economist's point of view it does not. Gold is a metal with a long and rich history of hypnotic influence, so there is undeniably a

---

*Not all of the gold held by the United States is matched by a certificate in the Fed. Some is held in a Stabilization Fund for international purposes and is not available for cover of Federal Reserve liabilities.

†A decision to remove the gold cover must be made by Congress.

psychological usefulness in having gold "behind" a currency. But unless that currency is 100 per cent convertible into gold, *any* money demands an act of faith on the part of its users. If that faith is destroyed, the money becomes valueless; so long as it is unquestioned, the money is "as good as gold."

Thus the presence or absence of a gold backing for currency is purely a psychological problem, so far as the value of a domestic currency is concerned.* Gold is, however, the accepted medium of settling accounts in international exchanges (where again, of course, its "value" is essentially psychological), so that the possession of a substantial gold stock has very real benefits in foreign relations.

But the point is worth pursuing a little further. Suppose our currency *were* 100 per cent convertible into gold—suppose, in fact, that we only used gold coins as currency. Would that improve the operation of our economy?

A moment's reflection should reveal that it would not. We would still have to cope with a very difficult problem that our bank deposit money handles rather easily. This is the problem of how we could increase the supply of money or diminish it, as the needs of the economy changed. With gold coins as money we would either have a frozen stock of money (with consequences that we shall trace in the next chapter), or our supply of money would be at the mercy of our luck in gold-mining or the currents of international trade that funneled gold into our hands or took it away. And incidentally, a gold currency would not obviate inflation, as many countries have discovered when the vagaries of international trade or a fortuitous discovery of gold mines increased their holdings of gold faster than their actual output.

Money and belief

As we cautioned at the outset, money is a highly sophisticated and curious invention. At one time or another nearly everything imaginable has served as the magic symbol of money: whales' teeth, shells, feathers,

---

*Some years ago a patriotic women's organization, alarmed lest the Communists had tunneled under the Atlantic, forced an inspection of the gold stock buried at Fort Knox. It proved to be all there. An interesting question arises as to the repercussions of having found the great vault to be bare. Perhaps we might have followed the famous anthropological example of the island of Yap in the South Seas, where heavy stone cartwheels are the symbol of wealth for the leading families. One such family was particularly remarkable insofar as its cartwheel lay at the bottom of a lagoon, where it had fallen from a canoe. Although it was absolutely irretrievable and even invisible, the family's wealth was considered unimpaired, since everyone knew the stone was there. A patriotic declaration by the ladies that the gold really *was* in Fort Knox might have saved the day for the United States.

bark, furs, blankets, butter, tobacco, leather, copper, silver, gold, and (in the most advanced nations) pieces of paper with pictures on them or simply numbers on a ledger page. In fact, anything is usable as money, provided that there is a natural or enforceable scarcity of it, so that men can usually come into its possession only through carefully designated ways. Behind all the symbols, however, rests the central requirement of faith. Money serves its indispensable purposes as long as we believe in it. It ceases to the moment we do not. Money has well been called "the promises men live by."

But the creation of money and the control over its supply is still only half the question. We have yet to trace how our money supply influences the flow of output itself — or to put it differently, how the elaborate institutions through which men promise to honor one another's work and property affect the amount of work they do and the amount of new wealth they accumulate. This is the subject to which our next chapter will be devoted.

Summary

1. Money is defined as whatever we use to make *payments*. As such, in modern economies, the most important constituents of money are *currency outside the banking system* and *demand deposits* (checking accounts).

2. Currency flows into, and is drawn out of, checking accounts. There is, however, much less currency in banks than the total amount of checking accounts.

3. Banks are forced, by law, to hold *reserves* against stated fractions of their demand deposits. For most banks these reserves can be either in *vault cash* or in *accounts* at a *Federal Reserve Bank*.

4. There are *twelve Federal Reserve Banks* that service their member banks exactly as the member banks service the public. The Reserve Banks are coordinated by a policy-making Board of Governors (Federal Reserve Board) in Washington. The Board is empowered to change reserve ratios for city or country banks, within legally established limits, and to take other actions to control the supply of money.

5. The function of the reserves established by the Federal Reserve Board is not to ensure the "safety" of the currency, but to provide a means of *controlling the supply of money*.

6. Any reserves of a commercial bank over and above those imposed by the Federal Reserve are called *excess reserves*. Commercial banks make money by lending or investing amounts equal to their excess reserves.

7. When a bank makes a loan, it opens an account in the name of the borrower. This account is a *net addition to total deposits and is therefore new money*. Thus bank lending can increase the supply of money. Investing in government bonds is also likely to lead to new demand deposits.

8. New deposits created by loans are typically drawn on by checks that go into other banks. Here they also give rise to excess reserves and to the possibility of *further deposit creation through more loans or investments*.

9. The total amount of new money that the banking system can create depends on the *reserve ratio*. The size of credit expression is determined by the reciprocal of the reserve ratio.

10. It is only the *banking system* that can expand the money supply up to the limit imposed by the reciprocal of the reserve ratio. A single bank can lend only up to the amount that it is prepared to "lose." *Hence each individual bank lends only an amount that is fully covered by its excess reserves.*

11. The Federal Reserve System controls the ability of the banking system to expand the supply of money by *controlling the amount of its reserves.* It can do so in three ways:
    - By changing *reserve ratios*
    - By changing the *discount rate*
    - By *open-market operations*

12. The most commonly used method is open-market operations. This is a means of controlling the size of reserves by *purchases and sales of government bonds on the open market.* When the Federal Reserve System buys bonds, it issues in payment its own checks, which enter the commercial banks and are added to their reserves. This gives the commercial banks excess reserves and enables them to make additional loans or investments. Selling bonds brings checks from commercial bank accounts to the Federal Reserve Banks, and thereby lowers the reserve accounts of member banks. This reduces their ability to make loans or investments.

13. The Federal Reserve System is *limited in its ability to issue paper money* (Federal Reserve notes) to the member banks, by the requirement that 25 per cent of the value of these notes be "backed" by gold certificates (representing gold bullion held by the U.S. Treasury). There is no longer any gold backing required behind member bank reserves.

14. The amount or percentage of gold cover is essentially arbitrary. *Gold plays only a symbolic role in a national monetary system.* The true value of money ultimately reposes in the faith men have in it.

Questions

1. Why do we not count cash in the tills of commercial banks in the money supply? Why don't we include savings accounts?

2. When you deposit currency in a commercial bank, what happens to it? Can you ask for your particular bills again? If you demanded to see "your" account, what would it be?

3. What determines how much vault cash a bank must hold against its deposits? Would you expect this proportion to change in some seasons, such as Christmas? Do you think it would be the same in worried times as in placid ones? In new countries as in old ones?

4. Is currency the main reserve of a bank? Do reserves ensure the safety of a currency? What function do they have?

5. What are excess reserves? Suppose a bank has $500,000 in deposits and that there is a reserve ratio of 30 per cent imposed by law. What is its required reserve? Suppose it happens to hold $200,000 in vault cash or at its account at the Fed. What, if any, is its excess reserve?

6. If the bank above wanted to make loans or investments, how much would it be entitled to lend or invest?

7. Suppose its deposits increased by another $50,000. Could it lend or invest this entire amount? Any of it? How much?

8. If a bank lends money, it opens an account in the name of the borrower. Now suppose the borrower draws down his new account. What happens to the reserves of the lending bank?

9. Suppose the borrower sends his check for $1,000 to someone who banks at another bank. Describe what happens to the deposits of the second bank. If the reserve ratio is 20 per cent, how much new lending or investing can it do?

10. If the reserve ratio is 20 per cent, and the original addition to reserves is $1,000, what will be the total potential amount of new money that can be created by the banking system? If the ratio is 25 per cent?

11. What is the difference between a banking system and a single competitive bank? Can a single bank create new money? Can it create more new money than an amount equal to its excess reserves? Can a banking system create more money than its excess reserves?

12. Suppose that a bank has $1 million in deposits and $100,000 in reserves, and is fully loaned up. Now suppose the Federal Reserve System lowers reserve requirements from 10 per cent to 8 per cent. What happens to the lending capacity of the bank?

13. If the discount rate rises from 5 per cent to 6 per cent, does that affect the willingness of banks to lend? How?

14. The Federal Reserve Banks buy $100 million in U.S. Treasury notes. How do they pay for these notes? What happens to the checks? Do they affect the reserves of member banks? Will buying bonds increase or decrease the money supply?

15. Now explain what happens when the Fed sells Treasury notes. Who buys them? How do they pay for them? Where do the checks go? How does payment affect the accounts of the member banks at the Federal Reserve Banks?

16. Suppose that our gold stock dropped dangerously close to the present legal requirement. What would you advise a congressional committee to do?

17. Why do you think gold has held such a place of prestige in the minds of men?

10

Money and the macro system

In our preceding chapter, we found out something about what money is and how it comes into being. Now we must turn to the much more complicated question of how money works — of what effect changes in the supply of money have on the level of output. What happens when the banks create or destroy deposits? Can we directly raise or lower incomes by altering the quantity of money? Can we control inflation or recession by using the monetary management powers of the Federal Reserve System? These extremely important questions will be the focus of discussion in this chapter.

The quantity equation

One relation between money and economic activity must already have occurred to us. It is that the quantity of money must have something to do with *prices*. Does it not stand to reason that if we increase the supply of money, prices will go up, and that if we decrease the amount of money, prices will fall?

Something very much like this belief lies behind one of the most famous equations in economics. The equation looks like this:

$$MV = PT$$

where

M = *quantity of money* (currency outside banks plus demand deposits)
V = *velocity of circulation*, or the number of times per period or per year that an average dollar changes hands
P = *the general level of prices*, or a price index
T = *the number of transactions made in the economy* in a year, or a measure of physical output

If we think about this equation, its meaning is not hard to grasp. What the quantity equation says is that *the amount of expenditure* (*M* times *V*, or the quantity of money times the frequency of its use) equals the amount of receipts (*P* times *T*, or the price of an average sale times the number of sales). What the quantity equation *seems* to say, however, is that there is a direct *causal* connection between money and prices—that if you increase the amount of money, you will increase prices, or if you decrease the supply of money you will cause prices to fall.

The quantity theory

Is this causal relation true? Can we directly manipulate the price level by changing the size of our stock of money?

The original inventors of the quantity equation, over half a century ago, thought this was indeed the case. And of course it would be the case, if everything else in the equation held steady while we moved the quantity of money up or down. In other words, if the velocity of circulation, *V*, and the number of transactions, *T*, were assumed to be fixed, changes in *M* would have to operate directly on *P*.

Can we test the validity of this assumption? There is an easy way to do so. Figure 10-1 shows us changes in the supply of money compared with changes in the level of prices.

A glance at Fig. 10-1 answers our question. Between 1929 and 1966, the supply of money in the United States increased over *sixfold*, while prices rose only *twofold*. Clearly, something *must* have happened to *V* or to *T* to prevent the sixfold increase in *M* from bringing about a similar increase in *P*. Let us see what those changes were.

Changes in V

Figure 10-2 gives us a first clue as to what is wrong with a purely mechanical interpretation of the quantity theory. In it we show how

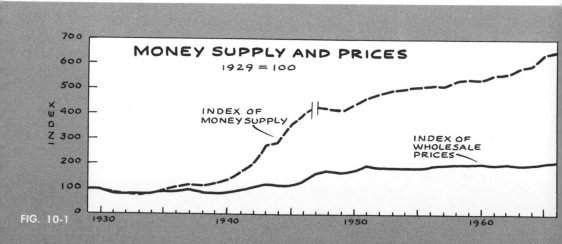

FIG. 10-1

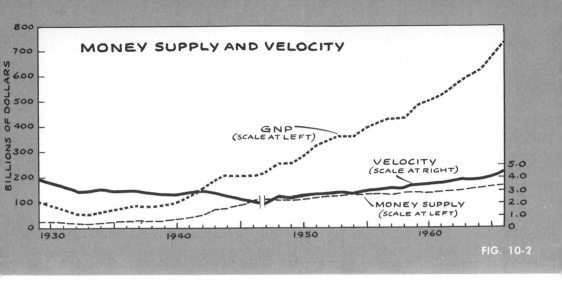

MONEY SUPPLY AND VELOCITY

FIG. 10-2

many times an average dollar was used to help pay for each year's output.* We derive this number by dividing the total expenditure for each year's output (which is, of course, the familiar figure for GNP) by the actual supply of money — currency plus checking accounts — for each year. As the chart shows, there was a very marked fall in V from 1929 through the war period, followed by a slow gradual rise since then.

How do we account for this change? Why does the rate at which we spend money vary? Proponents of the quantity theory in the 1920's argued that velocity was essentially determined by people's normal spending habits and that these were not subject to radical shifts. They thought of V as an essentially *stabilizing* economic influence.

Perhaps in a larger sense the quantity theorists were correct — people do not vary their expenditure habits wildly, except in periods of economic crisis. Yet it is also clear from an inspection of the chart that V is certainly not a rigidly fixed variable. Indeed when we think about it, it would be most surprising if it were.

Why is this? We can understand the reason more easily by turning the idea of velocity upside down. If I spend my salary more quickly than usual, what other financial magnitude will change? The answer is the size of my average bank balance. (Clearly, if I get rid of the money more quickly, it can hardly be in my bank account.)

People vary the size of their average bank balances very considerably depending on what they think of the future. Businessmen, for example, will alter their cash balances (or, we might say, their rate of spending) depending on their expectations as to the prices of goods and the level of

---

*Note that final output is not quite the same as T, which embraces *all* transactions, including those for intermediate goods. But if we define T so that it includes only *transactions that enter into final output*, PT becomes a measure of gross national product. In the same way, we can count only those expenditures that enter into GNP when we calculate MV. It does no violence to the idea of the quantity theory to apply it only to final output, and it makes statistical computation a good deal simpler.

159

demand for their product. If they are optimistic, they will draw down their balances to finance new expenditures. If they are pessimistic, they will shelve investment plans with the result that money will tend to pile up.

So, too, if investors expect security prices to fall, they will be motivated to increase the amount of money they hold, in order to buy securities when they become cheaper. Conversely, if they expect stocks or bonds to go up, they will get rid of their extra cash by putting it into the securities from which they hope to profit.

The point is, then, that velocity, whether we think of it as a rate of spending or a tendency to hold larger or smaller balances, is not an unchanging characteristic of behavior. Swings of expectation will bring swings in V — perhaps not wild swings, but changes large enough to affect appreciably the amount of expenditure that a given supply of money can support.

The rate at which we spend money can change — a fact that has significance beyond explaining why the quantity theory of money cannot be applied mechanically. The variability of the velocity of circulation reveals, more clearly than we have yet seen, why money itself can be a destabilizing influence on the flow of production: it is because money enables us to do two things that would be impossible in a pure barter economy.

1. *We can delay between receiving our rewards for economic effort and expending them.*
2. *We can spend more than, or less than, our receipts, by drawing on, or adding to, our savings.*

Thus the use of money, indispensable as it is for the facilitation of complex transactions, introduces an element of uncertainty into the circular flow.*

Changes in T

Now we must turn to a last and perhaps most important reason why we cannot use this mechanical way to relate the supply of money to the price level. This reason lies in the role played by T; that is, by the volume of output.

Just as the early quantity theorists thought of V as essentially unvarying, so they thought of T as a relatively fixed term in the quantity equation. In the minds of nearly all economic theorists before the Depres-

---

*Technically, the standard economic definition of money is that it is both a means of exchange and a store of value. It is the latter characteristic that makes money a potentially disturbing influence.

sion, output was always assumed to be as large as the available resources and the willingness of the factors of production would permit. While everyone was aware that there might be minor variations from this state of full output, virtually no one thought they would be of sufficient importance to matter. *Hence the quantity theory implicitly assumed full employment or full output as the normal condition of the economy.* With such an assumption, it was easy to picture *T* as an unimportant term in the equation and to focus the full effect of changes in money or in money spending (*MV*) on *P*.

The trauma of the Great Depression effectively removed the comfortable assumption that the economy "naturally" tended to full employment and output. At the bottom of the Depression, real output had fallen by 25 per cent in real terms — that is, after adjustment for changing price levels — and one-quarter of the labor force was unable to find work. Quite aside from what the Depression taught us in other ways, it made unmistakably clear that changes in the volume of output (and employment) were of crucial importance in the over-all economic picture.

Output and prices

How does our modern emphasis on the variability of output and employment fit into the over-all question of money and prices? The answer is very simple, but very important. We have come to see that *the effect of more money on prices cannot be determined unless we also take into account its effect on the volume of transactions or output.*

It is not difficult to grasp the point. Let us picture an increase in spending, perhaps initiated by businessmen launching a new investment program, or by the government inaugurating a new public works project. These new expenditures will be received by many other entrepreneurs, as the multiplier mechanism spreads the new spending through the economy. But now we come to the key question. What will these entrepreneurs do with their new receipts?

It is at this point that the question of **output** enters. For if businessmen are operating factories or stores *at less than full capacity,* and if there is an *employable supply of labor available,* the result of their new receipts is almost certain to be an increase in output. That is, employers will take advantage of the rise in demand to produce and sell more goods and services. They may also try to raise prices and increase their profits further, but if their industries are reasonably competitive, it is doubtful that prices can be raised very much; other businessmen with idle plants will simply undercut them and take their business away. An example is provided by the period 1934 through 1940, when output increased by 50 per cent while prices rose by less than 5 per cent. The reason, of course, lay in the great amount of unemployed resources, making it easy to expand output without price increases.

Thus we reach a general conclusion of the greatest importance. *An increase in spending of any kind tends to result in more output and employment whenever there are considerable amounts of unemployed resources.* But this is no longer true when we reach a level of high employment or very full plant utilization. Now an increase in spending *cannot* quickly lead to an increase in output, simply because the resources for more production are lacking. The result, instead, will be a rise in prices, for no firm can lose business to competitors when competitors are unable to fill additional orders. Thus the corollary of our general conclusion is that *additional spending* — from any source — *is inflationary when it is difficult to raise output.*

Inflation and public finance

This conclusion puts a capstone on our previous discussion of deficit spending. For now we can see that a hitherto undiscussed but major consideration attends the question of whether or not to use the public sector as a supplement to the private sector. This is the question of whether substantially "full" employment has been reached.*

If the economy is operating at or near the point of full employment, additional net public spending will only add more MV to a situation in which T is already at capacity and where, therefore, P will rise. But note that this conclusion attaches to more than additional *public* spending. When full employment is reached, additional spending of any kind — public or private, consumption or investment — will increase MV and, given the ceiling on T, affect P.

A different conclusion is reached when there is large-scale unemployment. Now additional public (or private) spending will result not in higher prices, but in larger output and higher employment. Thus we cannot say that public spending in itself is "inflationary." Rather, we must see that *any kind of additional spending can be inflationary in a fully employed economy, and will not be inflationary in an underemployed one.*

Full employment vs. underemployment

So we must distinguish between two fundamentally different situations in macroeconomics: the situation of full employment and that of under-

*The definition of employment, as we shall see in Chapter 11, is far from simple, and "full" employment accordingly is a complex idea. Economists usually call employment "full" when about 96 per cent of all job seekers are at work.

employment. Policies that make sense when one situation obtains make no sense at all in the other. To spend more in the public or the private sector is clearly a main objective for economic well-being in an underemployed economy, for more spending will lead to more output and employment. But to spend more in a fully employed economy is only to cause economic mischief, for now more spending will lead only to higher prices and not to more goods or jobs. Similarly, to balance budgets or to run a budget surplus in the public sector makes little sense when an economy is underutilized, but it is the course of wisdom when there are no idle resources to absorb additional expenditures.

It is impossible to overstress the importance of this major finding of macroeconomics. One of the main differences between contemporary economic thought and that of the past is precisely this sharp division between policies that make sense in full employment and those that make sense in conditions of underemployment. It was not that the economists of the past did not understand the tragedy of unemployment or did not wish to remedy it. It was rather that they did not see how an economy could be in *equilibrium* even though there was heavy unemployment.

The dragging years of the Great Depression taught us not only that output could fall far below the levels of full utilization, but—and perhaps this was its most intellectually unsettling feature—that an economy could be plagued with unemployed men and machines for almost a decade and yet not spontaneously generate the momentum to reabsorb them. Today we understand this condition of unemployment equilibrium, and we have devised various remedial measures to raise the equilibrium point to a satisfactory level, including, not least, additional public expenditure. But this new understanding must be balanced with a keen appreciation of its relevance to the underlying situation of employment. Remedies for an underemployed economy can be ills for a fully employed one.

Bottlenecks

This brings us to a caution worth remarking on. The economy does not move sharply from unemployment to full employment over a clear-cut line of demarcation. On the contrary, as spending increases, general unemployment gives way at first to "tight" areas of labor in a few localities or industries, or to shortages of plant capacity in a few places. Thus "bottlenecks" are typically the first sign that we are crossing over from a condition of general, to one of only partial, unemployment.

These bottlenecks may, however, begin to exert their constricting effect before the economy as a whole can be considered in a state of healthy over-all employment. This is especially the case if the bottleneck is in a strategic industry, where a price rise may lead to increases in the costs of many other industries. Bottlenecks may thus cause the beginnings of inflationary trouble *before* the economy as a whole has absorbed its unemployed.

Inflation vs. unemployment

This poses the serious problem of choosing between a degree of price rise *or* a degree of unemployment. For the experience of the 1950's and early 1960's makes it appear that a small degree of inflation, through bottlenecks, is probably unavoidable if we wish the economy to operate at high levels of output and employment. Whether this mildly rising price level is an acceptable price for high employment is not a question that can be answered unequivocally. There is always the risk that a mild *continuous* inflation may gain dangerous momentum and take on speculative tendencies. On the other hand, there is the very great damage done to the social fabric by the failure to offer jobs to all who want them.

It is now thought likely that the price creep becomes serious at about 4 per cent unemployment. Since this includes the rock-bottom "unemployables" (who are really a welfare problem rather than an economic one) as well as a considerable amount of voluntary unemployment as workers quit jobs to look for better ones, a policy that maintained a 4 per cent unemployment level would probably be considered an over-all success. To tread this line, however, requires a sensitive and strong fiscal and monetary policy; the likelihood is that we are apt to swing from one side of the line to the other, with alternations of tight labor markets and slow inflation, and loose markets with stable or even declining prices.*

Money and sticky prices

There is only one last point to be made, but it is an important one. All along in our discussion we have taken for granted that we need a larger supply of money in order to expand output. But why should we? Why could we not grow just as well if the quantity of money were fixed?

Theoretically, of course, we could. If we cut prices as we increased output, a given amount of money (or a given amount of expenditure) could cover an indefinitely large real output. Furthermore, as prices fell,

*It is worth noting that all Western European nations have experienced this problem of "choosing" between unemployment and inflation. In Europe, where the percentage of unemployment since World War II has been considerably below ours, the year-to-year inflation of prices has been roughly twice as great as ours.

workers would be content not to ask for higher wages (or would even accept lower wages), since in real terms they would be just as well or better off.

It is not difficult to spot the flaw in this argument. In the real world, prices of many goods cannot be cut easily. If the price of steel rose and fell as quickly and easily as prices on the stock exchange, or if wages went down without a murmur of resistance, or if rents and other contractual items could be quickly adjusted, then prices would be flexible and we would not require any enlargement of our money supply to cover a growing real output.

In fact, as we know, prices are extremely "sticky" in the downward direction. Union leaders do not look with approval on wage cuts, even when living costs fall. Contractual prices cannot be quickly adjusted. Many of this country's largest firms administer their prices and carefully avoid price competition: note, for example, that the prices of many consumer items are printed on the package months before the item will be sold.

Thus we can see that a fixed supply of money would put the economy into something of a straitjacket. As output tended to increase, businessmen would need more money to finance production, and consumers would need more money to make their larger expenditures. If businessmen could get more money from the banks, all would be well. But suppose they could not. Then the only way a businessman could get his hands on a larger supply of cash would be to persuade someone to lend it to him, and his persuasion would be in the form of a higher rate of interest. But this rising interest rate would discourage other businessmen from going ahead with their plans. Hence the would-be boom would be stopped dead in its tracks by a sheer shortage of spending power.

A flexible money supply obviates this economic suffocation. The fact that banks can create money (provided that they have excess reserves) enables them to take care of businesses that wish to make additional expenditures. The expenditures themselves put additional money into the hands of consumers. And the spending of consumers in turn sends the enlarged volume of purchasing power back to business firms to complete the great flow of expenditure and receipt.

Money and interest rates

Our discussion has brought to a conclusion our first line of inquiry. We began by asking whether the mechanical relation of the quantity theory — more money = higher prices — was in fact valid. What we have learned is that we cannot make such a mechanical linkage, for two reasons. One is that velocity is itself subject to changes as economic conditions and expectations change. And the second is that the level of employment and output is an all-important consideration in determining what effect, if any, a change in money supply will have on prices.

But now let us advance our inquiry another step. We know that the quantity of money has no simple effect on prices. But does it directly affect velocity and output? In other words, by changing the supply of money, can we change people's rate of spending (or the size of their average balances), and in this manner bring about a change in the level of output itself?

Most economists believe that this is in fact the way that changes in the stock of money work their effect on the economy. For what happens when the Federal Reserve buys bonds on the open market, or in some other way expands member bank reserves, is that banks now find themselves with extra funds that can be put to use. If they use them to buy bonds, they will be bidding bond prices up, and as we have seen, lowering interest rates as a consequence. This should lead, under normal conditions, to an increase in expenditure. It may be, of course, that banks will use their increased reserves directly to make additional loans. This will result in an immediate increase in expenditure as businessmen put their loans to use.

As we shall see in a moment, the relationship between the supply of money and velocity and output is not a simple one. It is no more mechanical than that between *M* and *P*. But the *route of influence of changes in the supply of money is now generally agreed to lie in changes in the rate of interest or in the availability of bank credit to would-be borrowers—both of these affecting the rate of expenditure*. In turn, as we have seen, a changed rate of expenditure can alter the level of prices.

The financial demand for money

Thus the answer to the problem of money and output appears quite simple. The monetary authorities need only to increase the reserves of member banks (perhaps by making open-market purchases) just enough so that the banks can take care of the needs of the growing economy. But unfortunately, the world is more complicated than that. For not all the demand for money comes from businessmen who want to invest in capital goods or inventory, or from consumers who want to make purchases of goods and services. There is also a powerful source of demand for money from investors who want to hold more or less cash as part of their *financial assets*.

We have so far disregarded the world of finance—of stocks and bonds and idle bank balances—while we concentrated on the world of production. But at this point the world of production and that of finance come together. When we study the impact of money on the economy we must realize that not all money is used for transactions purposes—that is, to pay for the regular production and sale of goods.

A substantial part of our money supply is used for financial purposes—not to buy materials or factors but to buy securities, or simply to serve as a liquid reserve. These financial balances are much more variable than our transactions balances. At certain times, for safety's sake or to be in a position to make advantageous purchases on the securities markets, people wish to be very "liquid"—to hold large balances in cash. At other periods, for different precautionary or speculative motives, people will be content with much smaller financial balances.

The existence of a separate financial demand for money complicates the task of money management; for holders of financial balances, whether prudence or speculation dominates their behavior, are much more prone to rapid changes in their demand for money than holders of transactions balances who must go on paying many bills, good times or bad. For instance, when interest rates are high, many holders of financial balances will seek to put their money into bonds that are selling at low prices and pay a large return. When interest rates are low, these people may prefer to enjoy the safety and potential advantageousness of liquidity, and their desire to hold cash will, therefore, rise.

Liquidity preference

We call this relationship between the rate of interest and the amount of money people wish to hold in cash *liquidity preference*. Liquidity preference is simply a way of saying that people will be content to hold more cash when interest rates are low (and therefore the pecuniary advantage of being in securities is not so great), and less cash when interest rates are high (and therefore the pecuniary advantage of being an interest-receiver is greater).

Exactly how much cash will the public wish to hold if interest rates are, say, 4 per cent? That depends on their expectations as to the future, their level of well-being, and many other things. At some times, more than at other times, the public will be willing to buy bonds (i.e., to give up liquidity) at 4 per cent. But whatever its state of mind, it will always prefer to give up liquidity when interest rates go up rather than when they go down.

Liquidity preference and interest rates

Now, how does the existence of liquidity preference affect the influence of money on the economy? We have already seen that money works its effect mainly through changes in the availability of credit, or in the rate of interest which can tempt businessmen to expand or contract their investment expenditures. Now we must see that it is liquidity preference—that is, the variable desire of the public to hold cash—that is a main factor in determining the rate of interest itself. For the banks cannot force any rate of interest on the public, any more than the seller of a good or service can charge whatever price he desires. Prices must balance the forces of demand and those of supply; and if a price is arbitrarily "set" too high or too low, the forces of the marketplace will push it to a point where supply and demand are in balance.

The rate of interest is also a price—the price of money—and it, too, must abide by the laws of supply and demand. The supply of money, as we now know, is mainly influenced by the monetary authorities who have the power of easing or restricting excess reserves, and thereby of influencing the size of bank deposits. But whereas the banking authorities have considerable control over the supply of money, they have nothing to say about the demand for it. That depends, in the final analysis, on the public itself, and on its desire to hold money both for transactions purposes and for financial purposes.

It is here that the liquidity preferences of millions of money holders play their critical part. For in the end, the price of money must be one that nicely accords with the public's demands and desires. If the going rate of interest is too low, for example, the public will refuse to buy bonds or will sell the bonds it owns. This preference for cash will drive down the price of bonds (and thereby drive up the rate of interest) until the public *will be* content to hold bonds, and will no longer seek more liquidity.

Similarly, if the interest rate is higher than warranted by the public's attitudes and expectations, the opposite train of events will take place. People will be so attracted by the high interest rates that they will all scramble to turn their cash balances into bonds. This will drive bond prices up (and interest rates down) until again a rate is reached at which the public's desire to be liquid is just balanced by the attractions of whatever interest rate prevails.

Liquidity preference and money management

Thus the public's desire for liquidity, together with its need for money for transactions, provides the force of demand that interacts with the money supply to determine what the rate of interest will be. But this introduces a new difficulty into the art of money management. Suppose, for example, that the Federal Reserve creates excess reserves in the expectation that money will be pumped by bank loans into transactions balances. If liquidity preferences are rising, the money may go instead into financial holdings. Thus an attempt by the monetary authorities to drive down the rate of interest in order to encourage investment may be frustrated if the public uses all the additional funds for liquidity and not for expenditure. At the depressed bottom of the Great Depression, for example, banks had huge excess reserves because businessmen would not risk expenditure for new capital projects. People had an insatiable desire for liquidity, and no attempted reductions of the rate of interest could persuade them to transfer money held for "security" into active expenditures. In the same way, an attempt to raise interest rates and to halt price inflation by making credit tight may come to naught if the public reacts to higher interest rates by giving up its liquidity, thereby making funds available to others to finance increased transactions expenditure.

Fiscal policy and monetary policy

We can see, then, that it is not always easy to bring about a change in *expenditure* through a change in money supply. Policies of easy money may fail in their purpose of stimulating capital growth, and policies of tight money may not provide the check on inflation that is desired.

For these reasons, few economists today would rely on monetary measures as the sole remedy for either recession or inflation. Rather, monetary policy is seen as the necessary accompaniment of fiscal policy, the two together acting as much more powerful influences than either separately. When the economy is sluggish and capital expenditures lag, the appropriate remedy is a combination of a strong fiscal push—through higher government expenditures or tax cuts—and the monetary stimulant provided by Federal Reserve actions that raise excess reserves. Conversely, when the economy is "overheated"—when prices are rising beyond the rate of a "normal" full-employment creep of perhaps 1 per cent a year—we need the restraint provided not only by a tightening of monetary supplies, but also by the braking action of a budget surplus brought about by tax increases or expenditure cuts or both.

Note, however, that fiscal policy will work much less effectively without a strong supporting monetary policy—just as monetary policy will be less effective without fiscal support. A deliberate government deficit, for example, will not cure a recession if the Federal Reserve has not loosened money supplies. In that case, the government would have to borrow its needed dollars from individuals and commercial banks that have no surplus investible funds. If the government is then to tempt money into its bond issues, it will have to make them more attractive than existing issues by offering a higher rate of interest. But this would serve to *discourage* private investment, which is exactly the opposite of what the government is seeking to do. So, too, a government surplus designed to slow down a boom will hardly prove effective if the banks are flush with unused reserves and in a position to expand their loans to business as fast as the government cuts back its own expenditures.*

Monetary policy in perspective

All these difficulties make it clear that it is no easy task to adjust the supply of money to the flow of production, in order to encourage output and maintain stable prices. Mistakes in timing, premature alarms, and delayed rescues are virtually inescapable. For a monetary authority to act in such a way that subsequent economic historians will wholeheartedly approve of its decisions is to expect superhuman intelligence.

Yet it is well to reflect that some of the monetary problems we will undoubtedly encounter in the future should not necessarily be charged against the money mechanism as such. As long as there remain striking divergences in economic performance between region and region — say between Cumberland and California — or as long as there exist vast discrepancies in the ability of various parts of the economic world to gather funds or to withstand adversity — as the difference between huge and tiny businesses or between powerful unions and the ragged fringes of the labor force — or as long as the economic tides lift and drop such differently situated groups as corporate executives or farmers or industrial unions or Social Security retirees, then *any* turn of monetary events is bound to penalize some and reward others, often with cruel indifference. When these failures occur, however, they should remind us not only of the inadequacies of monetary or fiscal policies, but of the weaknesses of the environment that they reveal. It is the environment that then often needs to be strengthened or changed rather than the policy.

Summary

1. *The quantity equation,* $MV = PT$, is actually a truism, saying that expenditure (*MV*) equals receipts (*PT*). It was originally intended as a causal statement saying that an increase in the supply of money leads to higher prices.

*There *are* times when fiscal and monetary policies are properly used in opposite directions. These instances usually have to do with balance of payments problems or with situations in which economic growth and economic stability pose almost contrary requirements. Such problems are important for students of advanced monetary and fiscal policy, but they are better relegated to a footnote in this introduction to the subject.

2. This statement would be true only if V and T were fixed. In fact, V *is capable of considerable change* as businessmen and investors revise their attitudes about spending or holding cash balances.

3. Even more important, we find that *changes in the level of output are very marked* over the long run. This is contrary to the expectations of the early quantity theorists that the economy would always operate at full employment.

4. When a competitive economy is operating at less than full employment, an increase in the quantity of money (really in the volume of expenditure) leads to a rise in output rather than prices. *This distinction between the effects of additional expenditure, private or public, at full employment and underemployment, is one of the central conceptions of modern macroeconomics.*

5. The distinction is blurred in practice because of *bottlenecks that bring rising prices before full employment is reached.* The choice between high employment and a rising price level is one of the most difficult that monetary and fiscal authorities must face.

6. We need a growing money supply to permit economic expansion in a world of *sticky prices*. The problem of adjusting the money supply is, however, complicated by the existence of a *financial demand* for money as well as a demand for money for transactions purposes.

7. Increases or decreases in the supply of money exert their effect through changes in the *rate of interest*, which stimulate or deter investment. The rate of interest, in turn, is a price that balances the desire for liquidity on the part of money holders with the opportunities for earning interest.

8. *Liquidity preferences* can complicate the job of monetary management by absorbing into financial balances cash that was intended to find its way into the transactions balances of the economy, or by supplying cash for transactions when the authorities wish to contract the availability of credit.

9. *Fiscal and monetary policy usually work side by side, each requiring the other.* Fiscal policy needs easy money to be effective in combating recessions, and tight monetary policies directed against inflation require fiscal stringency if they are to be effective.

Questions

1. Why is the quantity equation a truism? Why is the interpretation of the quantity equation that M affects P not a truism?

2. Suppose you are paid $100 a week and you put it in the bank. On each of the seven days of the week, you spend one-seventh of this sum. What is your average balance? Now suppose that you spend the whole sum on the first day of the week. Will your average balance be the same? What is the relation between velocity of circulation and size of average balances?

3. What considerations might lead you, as a businessman, to carry higher cash balances? Could these considerations change rapidly?

4. The basic reason why the original quantity theorists thought that M affected P was their belief that V and T were fixed. Discuss the validity of this belief.

5. Why is the level of employment the critical determinant of fiscal policy?

6. If employment is "full," what will be the effects of an increase in private investment, supposing that everything else stays the same?

7. In what way can an increase in excess reserves affect V or T? Is there any certainty that an increase in reserves will lead to an increase in V and T?

8. Suppose that you had $1,000 in the bank. Would you be more willing to invest it if you could earn 2 per cent or 5 per cent? What factors could make you change your mind about investing all or any part at, say, 5 per cent? Could you imagine conditions that would make you unwilling to invest even at 7 per cent? Other conditions that would lead you to invest your whole cash balance at, say, 3 per cent?

9. Suppose that everyone is eager to buy bonds that pay 4 per cent. Suppose that the monetary authorities want to establish an interest rate that is higher than this — say 5 per cent. What would happen? Would you be quick to snap up bonds at 5 per cent? What would this do to their price? What would thereupon happen to the rate of interest?

10. Suppose that the monetary and fiscal authorities want to encourage economic expansion. What are the general measures that each should take? What problems might liquidity preference interpose?

11. If bottlenecks brought a price creep at 5 per cent unemployment, what would you counsel as a proper economic policy?

11

Employment and output

We have reached a point in our investigations where we can now understand the forces that give rise to the flow of production. To that extent we have completed one long stage of our journey into macroeconomics. But all our journey is not yet complete. We have concerned ourselves heretofore almost entirely with output in real or money terms, but we have somewhat thoroughly disregarded one crucial aspect of the real world: employment. In other words, we may now be able to give a general answer to the question of how GNP is determined, but we cannot as yet answer the equally important query: how is employment determined? How many people will be employed if GNP is of such-and-such a size? What are the forces that work for more or for less employment? Until we can come to grips with these problems, we have not fully answered the very questions that impelled us originally on our investigation.

Employment in perspective

As before, let us begin by acquainting ourselves with the historical dimensions of the problem. In Figure 11-1, we see the main variables of the employment process—the total labor force and the total *civilian* labor force (members of the armed forces constituting the difference), total employment and its complement, unemployment.

Our attention is naturally drawn at first to the hatched area that depicts the profile of unemployment. But we cannot discuss this aspect of the employment problem until we have looked into a more fundamental question. This is what determines the size of the total labor force itself—that is, the size of the fraction of the population that is

173

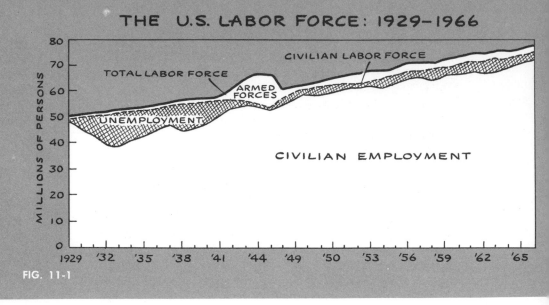

THE U.S. LABOR FORCE: 1929–1966

FIG. 11-1

actively looking for work. For clearly, the volume of unemployment will depend, at least in part, on how many of a given population *want* to work.

Participation in the labor force

What per cent of the American population does want to work? The answer, in round numbers, is about 57 out of every 100 persons over the age of 14. In itself, this fact does not mean very much. But suppose we now ask: is this fraction of the population growing or shrinking? Do more people or fewer people seek work today than, say, in 1890 or 1900? What is the outlook for the year 2000?

Here the answer is surprising. One would expect, perhaps, that as a society grows richer and more affluent, fewer people would seek employment. But that is not the case. Looking back to 1890 or 1900, we find that only 52 out of every 100 persons over 14 sought work. Looking forward is more uncertain; but if we can extrapolate (extend) the trend of the past several decades to the year 2000, we can expect perhaps as many as 60 persons out of 100 to be in the labor market by that date.

How can we explain this curious upward drift of the labor force itself? The answer is to be found in an examination of the different labor participation trends of different ages and different sexes. Figure 11-2 shows this very clearly.

Note that the over-all trend toward a larger participation rate for the entire population masks a number of significant trends.

1. *Younger males enter the labor force later than they did in the past,* and they will undoubtedly continue to do so. The reason is, of course,

174

that a larger number of young men remain in high school now or go on to college. This trend will certainly increase; only a third of elementary school pupils now go on to college, but the ratio is steadily growing.

2. *Older males show a dramatic withdrawal from the labor force.* The reason is the advent of Social Security and private pension plans. It is probable that the proportion of older males in the labor force will continue to fall as the retirement age is slowly reduced and as some still unprotected occupations come under Social Security or private pension arrangements.

3. *Counterbalancing this fall in male participation is a spectacular rise in total female participation. Indeed, the over-all trend toward an increasing search for work within the population at large is entirely the result of the mass entrance of women into the labor force.*

This surge of women onto the labor market reflects several changing factors in the American scene (many of which, incidentally, can be found abroad as well). One of these is the growth of nonmanual, as contrasted with manual, jobs. Another is the widening cultural approval of working women and working wives—it is the amazing fact that the average American girl who marries today in her early twenties and goes on to raise a family will nevertheless spend twenty-five years of her life in paid employment after her children are grown. Yet another reason for the influx of women is that technology has released them from household work. And not least is the pressure to raise living standards by having two incomes within the household.

Actually, we must view the growing number of females in the labor force as part of a very old economic phenomenon whose roots we traced back to the Middle Ages—the monetization of work. For the upward trend of female participation does not imply an increasing amount of

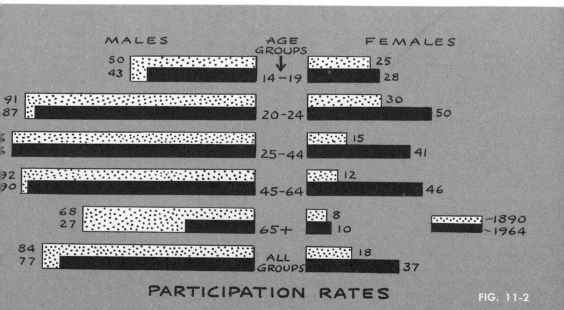

PARTICIPATION RATES

FIG. 11-2

labor performed within society. Rather, it measures a larger amount of *paid* labor. In the 1890's, many persons worked long and hard hours on a family farm or in a family enterprise, and above all within a household, *without getting paid* and, therefore, were not counted as members of the "labor force." To a very considerable extent, the rising numbers of female participants in the labor force mirror the transfer of these unpaid jobs onto the marketplace where the same labor is now performed in an economically visible way. There is every likelihood this process will continue.

These are not, of course, the only factors that bear on the fundamental question of how many persons will seek work out of a given population. The drift from country to city, the decline in the number of hours of labor per day expected of a jobholder, the general lengthening of life, the growth of general well-being—all these changes bear on the decision to work or not. Over all, what the complex trends seem to show is that we are moving in the direction of a society where employment absorbs a larger fraction of the life (but not of the day) of an average woman, and a diminishing fraction of the life and of the day of an average man.

Short-run changes

These trends indicate the direction of persistent, albeit slow-moving, main currents within the total fraction of the population that seeks work. But when we concern ourselves with employment or unemployment on a year-to-year basis, we must also take heed of short-run shifts in and out of the active labor force. That is, while the decade-to-decade percentages reveal the gradual changes we have discussed, from one year to the next, the proportion of the population actively seeking work—particularly among young people or women—may vary sharply.

If we look into the years of the 1960's, we can see how the labor force evidences these short-run expansions and contractions.

TABLE 11•1   SHORT-RUN CHANGES IN THE LABOR FORCE, 1960–1965 (IN MILLIONS)

	1960	1961	1962	1963	1964	1965	1966
Number in civilian labor force	70.6	71.6	70.6	71.8	73.1	74.5	75.8
Civilian employment	66.7	66.8	66.7	67.8	69.3	71.1	72.9
Unemployment	3.9	4.8	3.9	4.1	3.8	3.4	2.9

Notice that between 1960 and 1961, employment and unemployment *both* rose. One would think that as employment rose, unemployment would fall! Yet the same phenomenon appears between 1962 and 1963. How can this be?

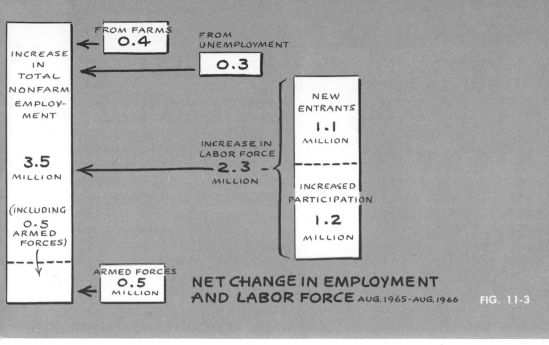

FIG. 11-3

NET CHANGE IN EMPLOYMENT AND LABOR FORCE AUG.1965-AUG.1966

The answer to the apparent paradox lies in the short-run responsiveness or *income-elasticity*, of the labor supply. In good times when jobs are plentiful, more youths and women will seek work. The whole labor force will then temporarily expand; and since not all of it may find work, both employment and unemployment may show increases. The reverse is true in a year of recession. What happens then is that many will be discouraged by bad times and "withdraw" from the labor force, remaining in school or in the household. As a result, the number of unemployed will then be smaller than if the larger labor force of a boom year had continued actively looking for work.

In Figure 11-3, we see how important increased participation can be in augmenting the work force.

The meaning of unemployment

The concept of a variable participation rate (or an elastic supply) for labor in the short run helps to elucidate for us a term with which we shall be much involved in this chapter: unemployment.

Clearly, unemployment is not a static condition, but one that varies with the participation rate itself. Technically, the measure of unemployment is determined by a household-to-household survey conducted each month by the Bureau of the Census among a carefully selected sample. An "unemployed" person is thereupon defined not merely as a person without a job—for perhaps such a person does not *want* a job—but as someone who is "actively" seeking work but is "unable" to find it. Since, however, the number of people who will be seeking work will rise in good times and fall in bad times, figures for any given period must be viewed with caution. A relatively low unemployment rate *may* mean only that general discouragement has driven many job seekers from the search for work. Similarly, a tendency for the unemployment rate to remain relatively steady as employment rises may testify only to an increased number of persons who have been attracted into the labor force.

These cautions by no means invalidate the concept of unemployment; but they warn us against assuming that in measuring unemployment over time, we are measuring variations in a fixed quantity. An economist first looks at the labor participation figures and then at the unemployment rates before he judges the seriousness of the situation.

Shifting demands for labor

What we have studied thus far are the forces that determine the supply of labor—that is, the number of persons who will be looking for a job at any time. But the problem of employment and unemployment is not decided just from the supply side. Now we must add the demand side of the equation.

From the first circular flow diagram, nine chapters ago, up to the beginning of this one, we have constantly been concerned with demand, mainly *aggregate demand* or the total demand generated by the sum of all spending in the economy. Historically, most of the social ills of unemployment can be put on the doorstep of an inadequate aggregate demand—that is, of a level of expenditure not high enough to give jobs to all who want them.

Shortly, we will discuss the relation of aggregate demand to employment. But first we must put the force of "total spending" into perspective by viewing it in the context of an economy whose pursuits are constantly changing and which therefore constantly alters the structure within which spending is generated. Industrialization of the economy gradually but profoundly affects employment, changing the location of work from country to city and the nature of work from manual to mechanical.

A glance at Table 11-2 gives added meaning to this shift in the job structure, for it is apparent that a pervasive transformation has occurred in the composition of the aggregate demand of society. An economy principally concerned with wresting goods from nature and then transforming them, or transporting them, has become increasingly a society concerned with selling or administering the activities of the relatively dwindling proportion who obtain, or fashion, or carry material wealth.

TABLE   DISTRIBUTION OF EMPLOYMENT*
11 • 2   (PER CENT DISTRIBUTION OF ALL EMPLOYED WORKERS)

	Agriculture, forests, and fisheries	Manufacturing, mining, transportation, construction, utilities	Trade, government, finance, professional and personal services
1900	38.1	37.7	24.2
1966	5.5	40.1	54.5

Source: Calculated from *Historical Statistics*, p. 74; also from *Hearings*, Joint Economic Committee, 88th Congress; Part I, p. 193.

*It is customary to include transportation and utilities among the third, or service, area of activities. In this analysis, however, we group them with goods-producing or goods-handling activities, to highlight the drift into "purely" service occupations. Since domestic servants, proprietors, and the self-employed are omitted (owing to inadequate statistics), the table under-represents the labor force in the service and trade sector.

What accounts for this enormous change in the nature of the productive activity of society? Mainly, we can account for it by the interaction of two factors: technology and the changing demand for goods and services.

The impact of technology

Underlying the great migration from "primary" occupations (farming, fishing, etc.) through "secondary" ones (manufacturing, etc.) into the "tertiary" service trades lies the impelling force of technology. Without the productive capacity given us by a technology that has developed in a certain sequence and form, this migration could not have taken place. In both the agricultural and the manufacturing–mining–transporting –power fields, we have experienced a startling increase in productivity, so that a dwindling manpower base can adequately provide the products required of them by society.

Agriculture presents, of course, the most extreme example of the power of technology to enhance productivity. Between 1880 and today, for instance, the time required to harvest one acre of wheat on the Great Plains has fallen from twenty hours to two. Meanwhile, the man-hours needed to raise 100 bushels of corn has dropped from 147 to 1910 to four or five. Not quite so dramatic but also far-reaching in their effect have been technological improvements in other areas. Table 11-3 shows the increase in productivity in various mining, transportation, and manufacturing activities during the past two decades.

Finally, by way of contrast to the very great degree of technological advance in the primary and secondary occupation sectors, we must note the laggard advance in productivity in the tertiary sector of activity.

TABLE   INDEX OF OUTPUT PER MAN-HOUR
11 • 3   FOR PRODUCTION WORKERS

Industry	1940	1962
Coal mining	100	277
Railroad transportation	100	243
Basic steel (1959)	100	188
Paper and pulp	100	160
Petroleum refining	100	230

Source: Calculated from *Statistical Abstract,* 1965, p. 236.

Output per man-hour in trade, for instance, or in education or in the service professions such as law or medicine or, again, in domestic or personal services such as barbering or repair work or in government has not increased nearly so much as in the primary and secondary sectors.*

Thus we find the *uneven entry* of technology to be one main cause behind the over-all migration of employment that we have discovered. Had we not enjoyed the enormous technical improvements in agriculture or mass production, but instead discovered vastly superior techniques of government services (in the sense of increasing the man-hour output of, say, policemen or firemen or teachers), the distribution of employment might look very different. We shall return to this point when we discuss the question of automation. At the moment, we need only accept the unequal efficiencies of technology in the various sectors of economic activity as constituting one main cause for the change in employment patterns.

The influence of demand

The differential rates of progress of technology are not, however, by themselves enough to explain the shift in employment. The fact that each farmer has become enormously more productive than his grandfather does not explain the decline of farm employment, nor does the enhancement of manufacturing and goods-handling productivity explain the stability of the employment ratios of these sectors. To account for the impact of technology on employment we must link the changes in productivity with the nature of the demand for the products emanating from these various industries and activities.

---

*It is only proper to note that we cannot measure productivity of output in the service sector nearly so unambiguously as in the goods sector, and there is no doubt that the *quality* of many services has increased substantially. Compare, for example, the "productivity" of a surgeon operating for appendicitis in 1900, 1930, and 1960. On the other hand, insofar as we are interested in the effect of technology in increasing the saleable output of work, there seems little doubt of its considerable superiority in the goods-producing branches of the economy.

We can see this shift in demand in Table 11-4, showing the division of national income among the three main sectors and their components.*

What we see here is a shift working in a direction different from the impetus of technology. Note that as productivity has increased in agriculture, demand for the products of agriculture has *fallen* as a per cent of total national expenditure. In technical language, the demand for food products was not "income-elastic"; that is, it did not rise proportionately with the rise in income. The result of this confrontation of a high-powered technology by a low-powered demand was a squeeze on employment. If the existing labor force in agriculture were equipped with the more productive techniques, the consequence would be a torrent of output that would far surpass the demand of the market. Instead, the new technology was utilized to permit a smaller labor force to fulfill demand, while the now redundant farm labor was forced to look elsewhere for employment.

TABLE 11 • 4   PERCENTAGE DISTRIBUTION OF DEMAND FOR OUTPUT (NATIONAL INCOME)

	1899 – 1908*		1963 – 1966	
Primary sector (Agriculture)	16.7		3.7	
Secondary sector	36.7		44.9	
Mining		3.1		1.0
Manufacturing		18.4		30.4
Construction		4.5		5.5
Transportation, communication, and public utilities		10.7		8.0
Tertiary sector	46.5		51.4	
Trade		15.3		15.0
Misc. services		9.6		11.2
Government		5.6		13.6
Finance and other		16.0		11.6

*Source: *Historical Statistics*, Series F34 – 43.

Where did it go? In part, it was directed by the shift of both technology and demand to the secondary sector. Farmers, moving to factory towns, produced trucks and tractors, thereby transferring some agricultural tasks to manufacturing. Meanwhile, as incomes rose, purchasing power that was not required for food products turned to the purchase of manufactured goods, homes, power, communication, and other things.

*The figures actually show the *income originating in these sectors*. But we know from our macroeconomic studies that this income must have been produced by the expenditures—the demand—of society as it was distributed among the sectors.

The result was that employment rose in this sector, as Table 11-2 shows. Equally important, however, by way of its employment-offering effects, was the rise of the "tertiary" occupations. Here an elastic demand for services of various kinds and an absence of revolutionary labor-saving techniques permitted employment to increase very rapidly.

The evolution of demand

What we seem to be witnessing, in these shifts, is a natural "evolution" of demand in an increasingly affluent and industrialized society. Demand appears to pass from an initial concentration on the products of the earth, to and through a focus on the products of manufacture, toward a "highest" stage, where it fastens on the enjoyment of the personal services made possible by a highly productive society and on the increased need to administer the internal affairs of a complex industrial mechanism. Thus we should note that the shift in employment visible in Table 11-2, already striking enough, would be made even more so, were we to transfer the growing "service" (i.e., administration and nonproduction) component in the secondary sector to the tertiary sector. In manufacturing alone, between 1950 and 1964, the nonproduction work force grew from 18 to 26 per cent of total employees.

Employment, demand, and leisure

What light does this discussion of the demand for labor shed on our original inquiry into the problem of over-all employment? The conclusion points up the *importance of the shift in demand from less labor-requiring tasks to more labor-requiring tasks.* Had consumers not evinced a desire for the relatively more labor-using manufactures and highly labor-intensive services, the total labor time required to provision society would have been considerably less. We would then have become an economy that mainly produced agricultural goods very efficiently — that is, with relatively little labor input — and one that had but few "demands" for labor in other occupations.

Such a society would not necessarily suffer high unemployment. It could use its agricultural productivity, in the absence of other wants, to reduce the workweek drastically; and by distributing the remaining quota of necessary work among its population, it could still give employment to all who sought it. Its standard of living, would of course, be no higher than the amount of agricultural produce it would then bring forth, but this would be a voluntarily chosen standard that accorded leisure a higher value than the nonagricultural goods and services that might have been produced.

It need hardly be said that the United States is not such a society. As our productivity in primary products has confronted the stone wall of our inelastic demand for primary products, we have shifted both our wants and our labor power into the secondary and tertiary sectors. Nonetheless, so great has been the rise in productivity in primary and secondary sectors that we have also been able to cut back our work-week from sixty to forty hours. In other words, we have absorbed the employment-displacing effect of technology not only by shifting our demands, but *by substituting leisure for work.*

Importance of the tertiary sector

The conclusion, then, is that the demand for labor reflects the inter-play of technology (which exerts differing leverages on different indus-tries and occupations at different times) and of the changing demand for goods and services. Typically, the entrance of technology into industry has a twofold effect. The first is to raise the *potential* output of the industry, with its present labor force. The second is to enable the costs of the industry to decline, or its quality to improve, so that actual de-mand for the product will increase. But normally, the rise in demand is not great enough to enable the existing labor force to be retained along with the new techniques. Instead, some labor is displaced and must now find its employment elsewhere.

There are exceptions, of course. A great new industry, such as the automobile industry in the 1920's, will keep on expanding its labor force despite improved technology, for in such cases demand *is* sufficiently strong to absorb the output of the new technology, even with a growing labor force. Then too, there is the exception of capital-saving technol-ogy, making it possible for an industry to turn out the same product with a cheaper capital equipment, thereby making it attractive to expand production and to hire more labor.

But taking all industries and all technological changes together, the net result is unambiguous. As Table 11-5 reveals, technology has steadily increased our ability to create goods, both on the farm and on the fac-

TABLE 11 • 5	INDICES OF OUTPUT AND EMPLOYMENT IN AGRICULTURE AND MANUFACTURING: 1950 = 100	
	1950	*1965*
Manufacturing output	100	182
Manufacturing employment (production workers only)	100	102
Agricultural output	100	129
Agricultural employment	100	61

tory floor, more rapidly than we have wished to consume them, with the result that employment in these areas has lagged behind output.

Note how agricultural output has increased by over a fourth in this period, in part because of the needs of a rapidly growing population, while agricultural employment has shrunk by over a third; and notice that whereas manufacturing output has risen by over three-quarters, employment on the factory floor has increased by only 2 per cent.

During this same period, however, our total civilian labor force increased by over 13 million. Where did these millions find employment? As we would expect, largely in the service sector.* Actual totals for employment in various parts of the economy appear in Table 11-6.

TABLE 11 • 6 NONAGRICULTURAL EMPLOYMENT: 1950 AND 1966* (IN MILLIONS)

Year	Secondary Sector (mining, construction, mfg., trans., utilities, etc.)	Trade	Tertiary Sector Finance, etc.	Personal services	Government	Total, Tertiary Sector
1950	22.4	9.4	1.9	5.4	6.0	22.7
1966	27.1	13.2	3.1	9.6	10.9	36.8
Increase, 1950–1966						
	4.7	3.8	1.2	4.2	4.9	14.1

*Omits household and self-employed workers.

EMPLOYMENT AND GNP

We have seen how the long-run employment trends reflect slow-moving changes in the supply and demand for labor, and we have had a glimpse of some of the problems these forces may create. Yet all this has seemed somehow at a considerable remove from the problems of saving

*Note that the employment shift from agriculture "through" manufacturing is by no means limited to the United States. As Table 11-7 shows, it seems to be visible in all industrialized nations.

TABLE 11 • 7 PERCENTAGE DISTRIBUTION OF EMPLOYMENT

	Farms	Manufacturing	Services
France, 1950	35.0	45.0	20.0
France, 1962	20.7	45.8	33.5
West Germany, 1950	24.2	48.2	27.6
West Germany, 1962	13.9	53.7	32.4
Britain, 1950	5.6	55.7	38.7
Britain, 1962	4.0	54.9	41.1

Source: OECD.

and investment and credit creation that have absorbed us in the earlier chapters of this book. How can we now connect the supply and demand for labor with the fluctuations in aggregate expenditure and output that have served as our focus of attention heretofore?

Let us begin, as so often before, at the simplest possible starting point, an imaginary economy uncluttered by many of the complicating factors of real life, such as changing technology or tastes. Then it is easy to trace the cause of changes in employment. They must be the result of changes in GNP—that is, of changes in expenditure. In turn, we can trace these changes to our familiar basic motive forces: fluctuations in investment spending or in government spending (or on rare occasions to spontaneous changes in consumer spending).

In point of fact, even with technology and all other complexities added back in, the volume of spending is *still* the single most important determinant of employment. With the exception of only the war years, with their special demands on manpower, in every year from 1929 to the present, when GNP has risen, employment has also risen; and in every year that GNP has declined, employment has followed suit.

But the impact of spending on *unemployment* is not quite so simple as this over-all correlation of employment might suggest. We have already seen that short-run changes in GNP will bring about short-run changes in the labor participation rate, so that rising GNP can produce both more jobs *and* more unemployment. In the same way, a declining GNP will discourage participation and thereby "abolish" some unemployment by causing people to withdraw from the job market. During the 1960's, as we have seen, *unemployment and employment and GNP* all rose from 1960 to 1961, and again from 1962 to 1963.

Irregularities in the population's age distribution

Another reason why changes in spending may not be mirrored by changes in unemployment is that the age groupings of the population are not always the same. In some years there will be relatively more job seekers than in other years, with the result that a given increase in spending will leave more unemployed at some times than at others.

This has particular relevance for the years now ahead of us. If we compare the age distribution in 1960 with that for 1975, we can see a very marked increase in the number of young job seekers for whom additional spending will have to provide jobs.

Note that the ranks of *youthful* job seekers will be disproportionately enlarged during the years ahead. Young people will, for a time, be coming onto the labor market faster than older workers are leaving it, with the result that the proportion of the entire population seeking work

TABLE   DISTRIBUTION OF THE LABOR FORCE
11 • 8   BY AGE: 1960 AND 1975

Age group	1960 (millions)	1975 (millions)	Per cent Increase
14 – 19	4.9	9.2	88
20 – 34	21.7	33.4	54
35 – 64	33.9	46.7	38
over 65	3.1	3.7	19

Source: *Hearings,* Joint Economic Committee, 88th Congress, 1st Session I, p. 203.

will temporarily rise. If the level of unemployment is also to be prevented from rising, there will have to be an unusually large increase in total national expenditure.

Technological change

Our discussion of the supply side of employment allows us to understand why an increase in spending may not always be met by a proportional decrease in unemployment. But now we must consider an even more important reason on the demand side: technological change.

Why is technological change relevant to the demand for labor? One reason is that the introduction of new technology is usually achieved through the means of new capital investment. Hence, the steady process of investment, indispensable for the maintenance of an even flow of GNP, is a vehicle for the steady introduction of new technology into the economy. To be sure, not all investment incorporates technological change—some investment merely expands or duplicates existing facilities with very little, if any, changes in design or end use. Yet historically, investment and technology have gone hand in hand, the technology stimulating the new investment and the investment incorporating the new technology. In addition, much so-called replacement investment is actually the source of a steady upgrading of the quality of capital assets, as old and obsolete plants and parts are replaced by new and modern ones.

Thus technological change is closely allied with the ongoing flow of investment spending. But how does technological change affect the demand for labor? To answer the question, it will help us to differentiate between two kinds: demand-creating technology and cost-reducing technology.

Demand-creating technology

Let us suppose that an inventor patents a new product—let us say an electronic stove that automatically cooks things to perfection. Will such an invention create employment?

We will suppose that our inventor assembles his original models himself and peddles them in local stores, and we will ignore the small increase in spending (and perhaps in employment) due to his orders for raw materials. Instead, let us fasten our attention on the consumer who first decides to buy the new product in a store, because it has stimulated his demand.

Will the consumer's purchase result in a *net* increase in consumer spending in the economy? If this is so — and if the new product is generally liked — it is easy to see how the new product could result in sizeable additional employment.

But will it be true? Our consumer has, to be sure, bought a new item. *But unless his income has increased, there is no reason to believe that this is a net addition to his consumption expenditures.* The chances are, rather, that this unforeseen expenditure will be balanced by lessened spending for some other item. Almost surely he will not buy a regular stove. (When consumers first began buying television sets, they stopped buying as many radios and going to the movies as often.) But even where there is no direct competition, where the product is quite "new," everything that we know about the stability of the propensity to consume schedule leads us to believe that *total* consumer spending will not rise.

Thus we reach the important conclusion that new products do not automatically create *additional* spending, even though they may mobilize consumer demand for themselves. Indeed, many new products emerge onto the market every year and merely shoulder old products off. Must we then conclude that demand-creating inventions do not affect employment?

Employment and investment

We are by no means ready to jump to that conclusion. Rather, what we have seen enables us to understand that if a new product is to create employment, it must give rise to new *investment* (and to the consumption it induces in turn). If the electronic stove is successful, it may induce the inventor to borrow money from a bank and to build a plant to mass-produce the item. If consumer demand for it continues to rise, a very large factory may have to be built to accommodate demand. As a result of the investment expenditures on the new plant, consumers' incomes *will* rise, and more employment will be created as they spend their incomes on various consumer items.*

*To be sure, investment will decline in those areas that are now selling less to consumers. At most, however, this decline can affect only their replacement expenditures, which probably averaged 5 to 10 per cent of the value of their capital equipment. Meanwhile, in the new industry, an entire capital structure must be built from scratch. We can expect the total amount of investment spending to increase substantially, with its usual repercussive effects.

When we think of a new product not in terms of a household gadget but in terms of the automobile, airplane, or perhaps the transistor, we can understand how large the employment-creating potential of certain kinds of inventions can be. Originally the automobile merely resulted in consumer spending being diverted from buggies; the airplane merely cut into railroad income; the transistor, into vacuum tubes. But each of these inventions became in time the source of enormous investment expenditures. The automobile not only gave us the huge auto plants in Detroit, but indirectly brought into being multibillion dollar investment in highways, gasoline refineries, service stations, and industries whose impact on employment has been gigantic. On a smaller, but still very large, scale, the airplane gave rise not alone to huge aircraft-building plants, but to airfields, radio and beacon equipment industries, and others, whose employment totals are substantial. In turn, the transistor offered entirely new design possibilities for miniaturization and thus gave many businesses an impetus for expansion.

Industry-building inventions

What sorts of inventions have this industry-building capacity? We can perhaps generalize by describing them as inventions that are of sufficient importance to become "indispensable" to the consumer or the manufacturer, and of sufficient mechanical or physical variance from the existing technical environment to necessitate the creation of a large amount of supporting capital equipment to integrate them into economic life.

Demand-creating inventions, then, can indeed create employment. *They do so indirectly, however—not by inducing new consumer spending, but by generating new investment spending.**

Unfortunately, there is no guarantee that these highly employment-generative inventions will come along precisely when they are needed. There have been long periods when the economy has not been adequately stimulated by this type of invention and when employment has lagged as a result. We shall return to these dynamic inventions when we discuss growth, in our last chapter. But first let us consider another kind of invention that affects employment.

---

*We should mention one effect of demand-creating inventions on consumption. It is probable that without the steady emergence of new products, the long-run propensity to consume would decline instead of remaining constant, as we have seen in Chapter 5. In this way, demand-creating technology is directly responsible for the creation of employment, by helping to keep consumer spending higher than it would be without a flow of new products.

Cost-reducing inventions

By a cost-reducing invention, we generally mean an invention or an innovation that enables a manufacturer to turn out the *same* end product with less factor input. The factor that is saved may be, and often is, land or capital. But the type of cost-cutting invention that interests us here is probably the most common and surely the most important. These are *labor-saving* inventions or innovations, changes in technique or technology that enable an entrepreneur to turn out the same output as before, with less labor, or a larger output than before, with the same amount of labor.

Do such inventions "permanently" displace labor? Let us trace an imaginary instance and find out.

We assume in this case that an inventor has perfected a technique that makes it possible for a local shoe factory to reduce its production force from ten men to eight men, while still turning out the same number of shoes. Forgetting for the moment about the possible stimulatory effects of buying a new labor-saving machine,* let us see what happens to purchasing power and employment if the shoe manufacturer simply goes on selling the same number of shoes at the same prices as before, utilizing the new lower-cost process to increase his profits.

Suppose our manufacturer now spends his increased profits in increased consumption. Will that bring an equivalent increase in the total spending of the community? If we think twice we can see why not. For the increased spending of the manufacturer will be offset to a large extent by the decreased spending of the two displaced workers.

Exactly the same conclusion follows if our entrepreneur used his cost-cutting invention to lower the price of shoes, in the hope of snaring a larger market. Now it is *consumers* who are given an increase in purchasing power equivalent to the cut in prices. But again, their gain is balanced by the lost purchasing power of the displaced workers.

Incomes vs. employment

Thus we can see that the introduction of labor-saving machinery does not necessarily imperil *incomes;* it merely shifts purchasing power from previously employed workers into the hands of consumers or into

---

*This is not an unfair assumption. The labor-saving technology might be no more than a more effective arrangement of labor within the existing plant, and thus require no new equipment; or the new equipment might be bought with regular capital replacement funds.

profits. But note also that *the unchanged volume of incomes is now associated with a smaller volume of employment. Thus the fact that there is no purchasing power "lost" when a labor-saving machine is introduced does not mean that there is no employment lost.*

Is this the end to our analysis of labor-displacing technology? It can be. It is possible that the introduction of labor-saving machinery will have no effect other than that of the example above: transferring consumer spending from previously employed labor to consumers or to entrepreneurs. But it is also possible that an employment-generating secondary effect may result. Our entrepreneur may be so encouraged at the higher profits from his new process that he uses his profits to invest in additional plant and equipment and thereby sets in motion, via the multiplier, a rise in total expenditure sufficient to re-employ his displaced workers. Or in our second instance, consumers may evidence such a brisk demand for shoes at lower prices that, once again, our employer is encouraged to invest in additional plant and equipment, with the same salutary results as above.*

The moral is clear. *Labor-displacing technology can offset the unemployment created by its immediate introduction only if it induces sufficient investment to increase the volume of total spending to a point where employment also rises.*

The impact of automation

It is in connection with our foregoing discussion that the much talked-of threat of *automation* becomes most meaningful. By automation, we mean technological inventions that perform increasingly complex and often self-regulatory tasks, some on the factory floor and, more significantly, some previously associated with white-collar work. In the main, automation is clearly a cost-cutting and labor-saving kind of technology, although it has important applications for new products as well. But one aspect of automation requires our special attention. It is the fact that automation represents the belated entry of technology into an area of economic activity that until now has been largely spared the impact of technical change. This is the area of service and administrative tasks that we have previously marked as an important source of growing employment. Thus the threat inherent in the new sensory, almost humanoid, equipment is not only that it may accelerate the employment-displacing effects in the secondary (manufacturing) sector. *More sobering*

---

*Do not fall into the trap of thinking that the new higher demand for shoes, will, by itself, suffice to eradicate unemployment. To be sure, shoe purchases may now increase to previous levels or even higher. But unless their incomes rise, consumer spending on other items will suffer to the exact degree that spending on shoes gains.

is that it may put an end to the traditional employment-absorptive effects of the tertiary service and administrative sector.

What could be the implications of such a development? In simplest terms, it means that in the future, fewer people will be needed to produce the same quantity of goods and services. The absorption of labor from agriculture and manufacturing into the ever-expanding service sector would now slow down or come to a halt, since the service sector could increase its output without hiring a proportionate increase in workers.

This *could,* of course, mean massive unemployment. But it need not. Just as our imaginary society limited its demand to agricultural goods and solved its labor problem by cutting the workweek, so a society that no longer needed to add labor as fast as its demands rose could easily solve the unemployment problem by more or less equitably sharing among its members the amount of labor it *did* require. To be sure, this raises many problems, not least among them the wage adjustments that must accompany such a reapportionment of hours.* But it makes clear that, essentially, the challenge of automation is one of finding a new balance in out attitudes toward work and leisure, and an equitable means of sharing work (and income, the reward for work) in a society where technology is beginning to invade the last precincts of human skills. The solution will assuredly not be an easy one, although it is by no means inherently impossible.

Unemployment in the U.S.

We have spoken of unemployment heretofore in a somewhat detached and analytic fashion. Now it is time to look at the actual figures in the United States and to consider how unemployment can be actively and effectively combatted.

Table 11-9 gives us the important statistics. The terrible percentages of the Great Depression need no comment. Rather, let us pay heed to the level of unemployment in the 1960's. Here the record is mixed. During the early years of the decade we were troubled with persistent

---

*What society is trying to do in rolling back hours of work is to *share* work and incomes more equitably. This is good for those who would otherwise be unemployed, but it may not be so good for those who are lucky enough to have jobs at the time when unemployment becomes a problem. These workers will be glad to cut their workweek, but not so glad to cut their pay or to deprive themselves of increased pay in order to share incomes with their new workmates. In actuality, this source of potential conflict is softened because the process of shortening hours stretches out over fairly long periods and is often accompanied by rising productivity. As a result, hours may fall and weekly pay remain steady. But of course, if hours had not fallen, employed workers would have enjoyed a rise in pay.

levels of unemployment much too high to be healthy. In the later years, unemployment declined sharply, but there is the discomfort of tracing much of this decline to an increase in war spending.*

TABLE   UNEMPLOYMENT
11 • 9   IN THE UNITED STATES

Year	Unemployed (thousands)	Per cent of civilian labor force
1929	1,550	3.2
1933	12,830	24.9
1940	8,120	14.6
1944	670	1.2
1960	3,931	5.6
1961	4,806	6.7
1962	3,911	5.5
1963	4,070	5.7
1964	3,786	5.2
1965	3,366	4.5
1966	2,875	3.8

What is the cause of this unemployment? There is no single cause. All of the possible reasons for unemployment that we have studied in our text have a relevance to the current situation. In part, our labor participation rate has been high, especially among women, thereby swelling the job-seeking labor force. In part, our total GNP has not been large enough. In part, we have experienced a considerable amount of labor-displacing investment. In some industries, wages may have risen too fast. And other reasons that we have not specifically studied may be added as well, primary among them being discrimination against the Negro.

Combatting unemployment

The uncomfortable level of unemployment in the U.S. and the prospect of a rising tide of young job hunters during the next decade have naturally turned attention toward combatting unemployment. Our previous analysis should enable us to understand many current proposals.

1. *Increasing demand.* We have learned that as a general rule, anything that increases the total demand of society is apt to increase employment. This is particularly true when unemployment tends to be widespread, both in geographic location and industrial distribution. Then

*In addition, we have recently become aware of a serious failure to count the full numbers of the unemployed in Negro districts. In some places, Negro unemployment reaches levels of catastrophe.

the expansion of GNP, whether by the stimulation of private investment or consumer spending or government expenditure or net exports should prove the single most reliable means of creating more employment.

There is, however, a problem here. Doubtless, a vast amount of employment could be created if aggregate demand were enlarged; for instance, the systematic reconstruction of our cities, a task that is becoming an increasingly pressing necessity, could by itself provide millions of jobs for decades. So could the proper care of our rapidly-growing older population, or the provision of really first-class education for large segments of the population that lack it.

The problem is that these programs require the generation of large amounts of *public demand,* and this requires the prior political approval of the electorate. If this political approval is not forthcoming, the generation of additional demand will have to be entrusted to the private sector — that is, to individual entrepreneurs in search of a profit.

Can private enterprise, without a massive public investment program, generate sufficient demand to bring about full and lasting employment? One cannot be dogmatic about such questions, but there is at least some historical reason to be uncertain. Let us not forget that the years from 1900 to 1965 saw the greatest flowering of new products and processes ever seen — the automobile and the truck, the whole field of consumer durables, office machinery, new metals and materials and fabrics, radio and movies and television, to name but a few. Yet at the end of that period the total requirements for labor in all the goods-centered industries had risen by *only a little over 2 percentage points.* During the era of the greatest increase in factory production ever known, there was virtually no increase in the demand for factory labor — indeed, if we take into account the sharp decline in the number of hours worked per week over the period, there was an actual decrease in the need for human effort to turn out goods.

To be sure, there was a vast migration of labor into the private service sector, as well as into public service. But at least in recent years, the number of jobs opening up in all private employments has not nearly kept abreast of the increase in the labor force. Between 1950 and 1960, for example, private enterprise accounted for only one out of every ten new jobs created in the economy.[1] All the rest were created in the public or the private not-for-profit sector (universities, hospitals, etc.).

To this sobering trend in employment creation, we must also add the potentially serious, although as yet untested, effects of the new technology of automation, particularly as it may cut into job needs in the tertiary sector. Hence there seems to be good reason for caution in assuming that the private sector, unaided by public programs of investment,

[1] Eli Ginzberg, *The Pluralistic Economy* (New York: McGraw-Hill, Inc., 1965), p. 144.

will be able to offer as much employment as the growing labor force demands. The likelihood is that a large enough aggregate demand will require the substantial use of public expenditure, whether for urban renewal and welfare services or for other ends.

2. *Wage policy.* But suppose that a very high aggregate demand is maintained, through public or private spending. Will that in itself guarantee full employment?

The answer is that it will not if the spending creates only higher incomes for workers who are already employed, rather than new incomes for workers who are unemployed. Thus if we want to maximize the employment-creating effect of spending, whether private or public, we need to hold back wage raises at least until the unemployment has fallen to a socially acceptable level.

But if raising wages can impede the process of job creation, can cutting wages encourage it? The question is not a simple one, for lower wages set into motion contrary economic stimuli. On the one hand, lower wages cut costs and thereby tempt employers to add to their labor force. On the other hand, lower wages after a time will result in less consumption spending, and will thus adversely affect business sales. The net effect of a wage cut thus becomes highly unpredictable. If businessmen feel the positive gains of a cut in costs before they feel the adverse effects of a cut in sales, employment may rise—and thereby obviate the fall in consumption spending. On the other hand, employers may *expect* that the wage cut will lead to lower sales, and their pessimistic expectations may lead them to refrain from adding to their labor forces, despite lower costs. In that case, of course, employment will not rise. On balance, most economists today fear the adverse effects of wage-cutting more than they welcome the possible job-creating effects.

It seems, then, that maintaining wages in the face of an economic decline and restraining wage rises in the face of an economic advance is the best way of encouraging maximum employment. It is one thing, however, to spell out such a general guideline to action and another to achieve it. To maintain wages against an undertow of falling sales requires a strong union movement. But once times improve, this same union movement is hardly likely to exercise the self-restraint needed to forego wage raises, so that additional spending can go into the pockets of the previously unemployed. This poses another dilemma for a market society in search of a rational high employment policy, and there is at this moment no solution in sight.

3. *Remedying structural unemployment.* Not all unemployment is due to insufficient demand. Some can be traced to "structural" causes—to a lack of "fit" between the existing labor force and the existing job opportunities. For instance, men may be unemployed because they do not know of job opportunities in another city, or because they do not have

the requisite skills to get, or hold, jobs that are currently being offered. Indeed, it is perfectly possible to have structural unemployment side-by-side with a lack of manpower in certain fields.

A sharp debate has raged in the United States concerning the importance of structural reasons (as contrasted with a general deficiency of demand) in accounting for the present level of unemployment. Many observers have pointed out that the unemployed are typically grouped into certain disprivileged categories: race, age, lack of training, and unfortunate geographic location. The aged and the young, the Negro and the unskilled, the displaced West Virginian coal miner or Massachusetts textile worker are not quickly pulled into employment by a general expansion of demand. The broad stream of purchasing passes most of them by and does not reintegrate them into the mainstream of the economy. Hence stress is increasingly placed on measures to assist labor mobility, so that the unemployed can move from distressed to expansive areas, and on the retraining of men for those jobs offered by a technologically fast-moving society.

Retraining is, unfortunately, much easier when it is applied to relatively few persons than when it is proposed as a general public policy affecting large numbers of unemployed. Then the question arises: for what jobs shall the unemployed be trained? Unless we very clearly know the *shape* of future demand, the risk is that a retraining program will prepare workers only for jobs that may no longer exist when the workers are ready for them. And unless the *level* of future demand is high, even a foresighted program will not effectively solve the unemployment problem.

4. *Reducing the supply of labor.* Finally, the possibility exists of attacking unemployment not from the demand side, but from the supply side, by cutting the workweek, lengthening vacations, and using similar measures. Essentially, the possibility held out by shortening the workweek is that a more or less fixed quantity of work will then be shared among a larger number of workers. This is entirely feasible and possible, provided that *the decrease in hours is not offset by an increase in hourly pay rates.* In other words, once again a rational wage policy holds the key between success and failure. Shorter hours, coupled with higher hourly wage rates, will merely raise unit costs (unless productivity rises quickly enough to compensate). This will certainly not contribute to increased employment. Shorter hours *without* increased hourly rates, on the other hand, may make it necessary for the employer to hire additional help in order to continue his established level of output.

Shortening hours of work can be a policy of despair. If people do not wish to change their working habits—the number of hours per week or the number of years in their lifetimes—then the cure for unemployment is surely to expand the demand for labor and not to diminish its supply.

If private demand is inadequate to this task, then, as we have said, public demand may serve the purpose instead.

But an attack on unemployment that seeks to reduce the supply of labor, rather than to expand the demand for it, need not be a program of retreat. It can also become part of a deliberate and popularly endorsed effort to reshape the patterns and the duration of work as it now exists. Thus it may be possible to reduce the size of the labor force by measures such as subsidies that would induce younger people to remain longer in school or by raising Social Security to make it attractive for older people to retire earlier. Such policies can be useful not only in bringing down the participation rate and thus reducing "unemployment," but in affecting changes in the quality of life that would find general public approval.

The long-run prospect

We have done no more than cast an eye over the spectrum of possibilities before us. The likelihood is that we shall have to cope with the employment program by using not one, but a variety, of techniques. The large numbers of youths coming rapidly onto the labor market present a severe problem that must be met by extensive programs of training; and the belated entry of the Negro into full economic equality will require not only training but education—of whites as well as Negroes. So, too, the advent of an end to war spending would require the redeployment of skills and hands not only from one region to another, but from one industry to another. All this will require policy measures that are keyed to dealing with structural rather than aggregate unemployment.

But it is likely, particularly if we achieve a stable or even declining military budget, that we will also need to encourage aggregate demand if we are to absorb the full supply of job seekers coming onto the market. This will require fiscal and monetary measures aimed at helping private enterprise expand—policies that encourage entrepreneurs to borrow and invest and to take risks for the future.

At the same time, as we have indicated, there will very probably be a need for large programs of public expenditure. Here the question that seemed so academic at the end of the chapter on the government sector comes to life, for the issue is sharply posed in relation to not only the *ends* to which government expenditure should be aimed, but also the *means* by which fiscal policy can be given its greatest leverage.

Last and perhaps most distant is the possibility that we stand at the threshold of an age when technology will as last invade those areas of production that have heretofore escaped duplication by machine, and that the whole supply of human labor will require readjustment in the face of this radically changed environment. It is certainly likely that over the longer run, some further contraction will take place in the normal workday or workweek, and very likely in the worklife of the normal individual. This may be no more than a prospect for the future, but it is one to which we would be wise to direct our thoughts now.

Summary

1. *Participation* in the working force has slowly increased over the long run. This is the net result of three forces: the *large-scale entry of women* into the labor force after child-bearing, offset by the *later entry and earlier retirement of males.*

2. Participation in the short run mirrors economic opportunity. *The labor force is elastic* and responds to increases in job openings. As a result, *it is possible for employment and unemployment* (meaning an active, although unsuccessful, search for work) *to increase at the same time.*

3. The demand for labor reflects not only the total spending of the economy, but also the structure of demand of that economy. In the United States, *this pattern of demand has slowly but substantially shifted* from products of the soil to products of manufacture, and even more strikingly to services of various kinds.

4. Along with this shift in demand has come an uneven impact of technology. Machines have very greatly boosted the productivity of the primary and secondary sectors, while relatively much less affecting the output per person of the tertiary sector.

5. As a consequence of these patterns of demand and of technology, *employment has been steadily shifted out of farming into manufacturing, and even more importantly into service and administration.* It is the prospective entry of new machinery into the tertiary sector that now poses the greatest problems for employment.

6. Large-scale unemployment is generally caused by *inadequate total demand.* This unemployment may be aggravated, or its cure made more difficult, both by changes in technology, such as the trend to automation, and by irregularities in the *population age structure*—in particular by the prospect of large numbers of youths coming onto the labor market during the next decade.

7. Technology can both displace labor and create a demand for it. *Demand-creating technology increases employment through the creation of a substantial volume of new investment.* Labor-displacing technology does not diminish incomes but can shrink employment in particular industries.

8. Unemployment can be combatted in several ways, of which *increasing aggregate demand* is probably the single most important way. However, because of the labor-displacing properties of modern technology, it is uncertain that private demand alone can create and maintain full employment. Public expenditure will also probably be required.

9. The creation of additional employment requires a *wage policy* that prevents increased spending from swelling the incomes of the already employed, rather than giving new income to the unemployed. *Wage-cutting, on the other hand, is an uncertain and possibly dangerous mode of increasing employment,* since the adverse effects of lowered consumption may more than offset the positive effects of lowered costs.

10. *Structural unemployment* requires much more specific remedies than those

provided by aggregate demand. Training and education programs are the main weapon against this kind of joblessness.

11. There is a long-term trend toward *leisure* in all advanced countries, and it is probable that this trend will continue. One way of alleviating unemployment is to convert it into leisure; i.e., by lengthening the period of schooling, advancing the age of retirement, shortening the workday or week, and so on. This is probably a direction in which the economy will slowly move.

Questions

1. How do you account for the fact that there are more people per hundred who want to work today than there were 70 years ago, when the nation was so much poorer? How much does the monetization of labor have to do with this? How much is it a change in "life styles," especially for women? What do you expect for the very long run—say 100 years from now?

2. How can employment and unemployment *both* rise at the same time? What would you consider to be a useful definition of unemployment, one that could be easily used by interviewers in the field?

3. What do you think accounts for the shift in demand from primary to secondary and tertiary products? In particular, what do you think is the reason for the steady growth of services as a kind of output that society seems to want?

4. Suppose that technology in the 1890's had taken the following turn: a very complex development of machines and techniques for improving public and private supervisory and administrative techniques, very clever devices that performed salesmen's and clerks' services, but almost no improvement in agricultural techniques. What would the distribution of the labor force probably look like?

5. What is the relation between leisure and unemployment? Is a man who is retired before he wants to stop working "at leisure" or "unemployed"? Can one make a clear distinction between the two, or does it depend very largely on social customs, and other things?

6. Suppose that an inventor puts a wrist radio-telephone on the market. What would be the effects on consumer spending? What would ultimately determine whether the new invention were labor-attracting or labor-displacing?

7. Suppose that another new invention halved the cost of making cars. Would this create new purchasing power? What losses in income would have to be balanced against what gains in incomes? What would be the most likely way that such an invention could increase employment? Would employment increase if the demand for cars were inelastic, like the demand for farm products—that is, if people bought very few more cars despite the fall in prices?

8. Unemployment among the Negro population in many cities in 1967 was worse than it was during the Great Depression. Among Negro adolescents, it reached 25 to 30 per cent. What steps would you propose to remedy this situation?

9. Would raising wages, and thereby creating more consumption demand, be a good way to increase employment?

10. Do you believe that there exists general support for large public employment-generating programs? Why or why not? What sorts of programs would you propose?

11. How would you encourage private enterprise to create as many *jobs* as possible?

12

The problem of growth

There remains for us to consider but one subject in our introduction to macroeconomics: the subject of growth. Actually, we have already been concerned for many pages with the main problem, if not the explicit theme, of growth. From the very beginning of our study, investment has been at the center of our focus. Up to this point, however, we have thought of investment mainly as the process by which savings were offset so that a given level of expenditure could be maintained, or in the preceding chapter, as the key to the dynamic process by which employment was sometimes created and sometimes destroyed. In all these considerations, *fluctuations* in the level of investment were all-important, a slowdown spelling recession and unemployment, an acceleration leading to the opposite.

Now we must see the process of investment in a somewhat different perspective. Whether it proceeds slowly or fast, investment consists in the addition of real wealth to the stock of wealth of the nation. Thus, so long as there is *any* net investment, our stock of capital is growing; and with a growth in our capital, there should come a growth in our capacity to produce. In this way we can see that the process of investment leads inevitably to a consideration of economic growth, and it is to this subject that we now turn.

The structural requirements of growth

How does growth take place? Through investment, we know. But how does investment take place? How does a society actually find the resources to devote to capital-building? In our rich, industrialized economy, such a question may seem pointless. We simply use our industrial equipment to make more industrial equipment. And for the necessary labor we simply employ the people who are already working in steel and other capital-goods industries.

But the matter-of-factness with which we answer the question hides from us the real structural significance of growth. For when we turn our gaze abroad or backward in time and ask how a poor society grows, the question is not so easy to answer. Such societies do not have steel mills waiting for orders, nor labor forces that are already deployed in capital-goods industries. How do they, then, create capital?

The process is by no means an obvious one. Suppose we have a very poor society (like an extremely underdeveloped nation) in which 80 per cent of the population tills the soil, equipped with so little by way of capital—mere spades and hoes—that it produces only enough to maintain itself and the remaining 20 per cent of society.

Who are the other 20 per cent? In reality, of course, they might be government officials, landlords, and others, but we will simplify our model by assuming that the whole 20 per cent is occupied in making the simple spades and hoes (the capital goods) with which the consumption-goods sector works. Like the farmers, the toolmakers labor from dawn to dusk; and again like the farmers, they are so unproductive that they can produce only enough capital to replace the spades and hoes that wear out each year.

Now how could such a society grow? If we look again at the capital-goods sector, we find a clue. For unlike the consumption-goods sector, we find here not one but two distinguishable kinds of economic activity going on. In the agricultural side, everyone is farming; but in the capital-goods side, not everyone is making the spades and hoes with which the agricultural laborers work. No matter how we simplify our model, we can see that *the capital-goods sector must carry out two different tasks*. It must turn out spades and hoes, to be sure. But part of the capital-goods labor force must also turn out a different kind of capital good—a very special kind that will produce not only spades and hoes, but also more of itself!

Is there such a kind of equipment? There is indeed, in a versatile group of implements known as *machine tools*. In our model economy, these may be only chisels and hammers that can be used to make spades, hoes, and more chisels and hammers. In a complex industrial system, machine tools consist of presses and borers and lathes which, when used ensemble, not only make all kinds of complicated machines but can also recreate themselves.

Capital formation

Thus we encounter the unexpected fact that there is a strategic branch of capital creation that lies at the core of the whole sequence of economic growth.*

How does growth now ensue? Our model enables us to see that it is not simply a matter of bringing in peasants from the fields to make more spades and thereby to increase their productivity. For they will not be able to make spades until they have laid the ground by an increase in output of this strategic branch: before spades can be made, chisels and hammers must be made. Before textile or shoemaking or food-processing or transportation equipment can be made, machine tools must be made.

Thus at the core of the growth process—whether in a very backward nation or a highly industrialized one—we can see *two* great structural shifts that must take place:

1. *A shift of effort* within *the capital sector to increase its own productive capacity.*

2. *A shift of effort from the consumption sector to the capital sector, to man the growing volume of equipment which emerges from the enlarged capital sector.*

Can we actually trace this process in real life? The shifts *within* the capital sector are not always easy to see, because there is usually some excess capacity in the machine tool branch. By running overtime, for instance, it can produce *both* more machine tools *and* more hoes and spades. Yet if we examine a society in the process of rapid industrialization, such as the U.S.S.R. (or for that matter, the United States in its periods of rapid wartime industrial buildup) we can clearly see the importance of this critical branch in setting a *ceiling* on the over-all pace of industrial expansion.

When we turn to the second shift, from the consumption sector into the capital sector, the movement in real life is very apparent. Table 12-1, for instance, shows us the proportion of the population engaged in agriculture for a number of industrialized nations at an early and a late stage of their transformations.

Here we see in reality the wholesale emigration that takes place in the

---

*This raises the perplexing question of how the machine-tool industry *began*, since it needs its own output to grow. The answer is that it evolved as a special branch of industrial production during the industrial revolution when, for the first time, machinery itself began to be made by machinery instead of by hand. A key figure in the evolution of the machine-tool industry was Maudslay, whose invention of the screw-cutting lathe was "one of the decisive pieces of standardization that made the modern machine possible." (Mumford, *Technics and Civilization*, p. 209.)

TABLE 12•1	PROPORTIONS OF LABOR FORCE IN AGRICULTURE

	Early 19th century (per cent of labor force)	1950
France	63 (1827)	35
Great Britain	31 (1811)	6
Sweden	63 (1840)	19
United States	72 (1820)	11

Sources: Colin Clark, *The Conditions of Economic Progress* (London: Macmillan & Co., Ltd., 1960), pp. 512, 514, 518; B.R. Mitchell, *Abstract of British Historical Statistics* (Cambridge: Cambridge University Press, 1962), pp. 60-61; and O.E.C.D.

industrializing process (note that by 1811 Britain was already well on the road). Over the course of the nineteenth and twentieth centuries, these countries have lost two-thirds to four-fifths of their erstwhile farmers—not all to capital-building alone, of course, but to the whole industrial and commercial structure that capital-building makes possible. In this way, the process of economic growth can be seen in part as a great flow of human and material resources from simple consumption goods output to a hierarchy of industrial tasks—a flow that is even more dramatic in real life than we might have divined from our imaginary model.

The historical record

Thus, behind the phenomenon of growth we encounter a hidden structural shift of the greatest importance. Once the shift has taken place, however—once a large capital-building sector has been established—the process of adding to the stock of capital is greatly simplified. Indeed, we now get that long process of gradually increasing output that provides us with our ordinary starting point in the study of growth. In Fig. 12-1 we see the American experience from the middle of the nineteenth century.

How steady has been our average rate of growth? The answer is: astonishingly constant, whether we take an average over the past thirty-odd years since the Great Depression, or whether we go back to the earliest reliable statistics and calculate our growth rate since the 1870's (or even 1830's). As the chart shows, the swings are almost all contained within a range of 10 per cent above or below the trend. The trend itself comes to about 3.5 per cent a year in real terms, or a little over 1.5 per cent a year per capita.*

*This is a very good time to stress the dangers of intertemporal comparisons of GNP voiced in Chapter 2. In case you have forgotten, they are: (1) the *quality* of output varies greatly over a long span of time, favorably and otherwise; (2) part of GNP is *imputed* and

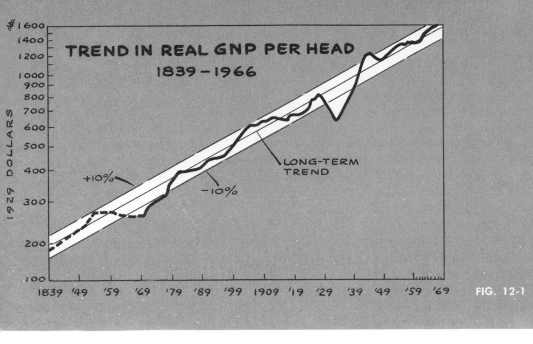

FIG. 12-1

How do we account for this long, steady ascent? In part, the answer cites the underlying forces of propulsion that come to light in a historic survey of American economic development. We will not examine that chapter of history now, although we will return to the forces of growth in a somewhat more analytical focus at the conclusion of this chapter.

But the second part of the answer is equally important. It is that year-by-year growth was *not* so smooth and steady as the long-term growth rates suggest. Take the years 1895 to 1905, very smooth-looking in Fig. 12-1. As Table 12-2 reveals, the advance was anything but steady.

TABLE RATES OF GROWTH
12 • 2

1895 – 1896	− 2.5
1896 – 1897	+ 9.4
1897 – 1898	+ 2.3
1898 – 1899	+ 9.1
1899 – 1900	+ 2.7
1900 – 1901	+11.5
1901 – 1902	+ 1.0
1902 – 1903	+ 4.9
1903 – 1904	− 1.2
1904 – 1905	+ 7.4

this portion varies over time; (3) there is a long-term *monetization of household tasks* that adds a deceptive component of growth; and (4) *not all of GNP*—and different amounts in different periods—*adds to well-being*. All in all, growth statistics should be used with caution in making comparative statements about output and welfare in two widely separated periods.

203

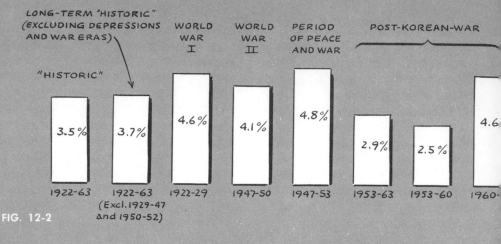

SHORT-TERM VARIATIONS IN THE RATE OF GROW

LONG-TERM "HISTORIC"
(EXCLUDING DEPRESSIONS   WORLD   WORLD   PERIOD
AND WAR ERAS)   WAR   WAR   OF PEACE   POST-KOREAN-WAR
                         I   II   AND WAR

"HISTORIC"

3.5%   3.7%   4.6%   4.1%   4.8%   2.9%   2.5%   4.6

1922-63   1922-63   1922-29   1947-50   1947-53   1953-63   1953-60   1960-
          (Excl.1929-47
FIG. 12-2 and 1950-52)

Or examine a more recent period, not year by year, but in groups of years. Here is the record of the U.S. economy — or rather, the records of the U.S. economy — between 1922 and 1964. As we can see, the rate of growth varied greatly in different periods.

Business cycles

This extraordinary sequence of ups and downs, rushes of growth followed by doldrums, introduces us to a fascinating aspect of the subject of growth — *business cycles*. For if we inspect the profile of the long ascent carefully, we can see that its entire length is marked with irregular tremors or peaks and valleys. Indeed, the more powerful the magnifying glass we apply — which is to say, the more closely we examine year-to-year figures — the more of these tremors and deviations we discover, until the problem begins to be which of these many vibrations to consider significant and which to discard as uninteresting.

The problem of sorting out the important fluctuations in output (or in statistics of prices or employment) is a difficult one. Economists have actually detected dozens of cycles of different lengths and amplitudes, from very short rhythms of expansion and contraction that can be found, for example, in patterns of inventory accumulation and decumulation, to large background pulsations of seventeen or eighteen years in the housing industry, and possibly (the evidence is unclear) swings of forty to fifty years in the path of capitalist development as a whole.

Generally, however, when we speak of "the" business cycle we refer to a wave-like movement that lasts, on the average, about eight to ten years. In Fig. 12-3 this major oscillation of the American economy stands forth very clearly, for the chartist has eliminated the underlying tilt of growth so that the profile of economic performance looks like a cross section at sea level rather than a cut through a long incline.

Reference cycles

In a general way we are all familiar with the meaning of business cycles, for the alternation of "boom and bust" or prosperity and recession (a polite name for a mild depression) is part of everyday parlance. It will help us study cycles, however, if we learn to speak of them with a standard terminology. We can do this by taking the cycles from actual history, "superimposing" them, and drawing the general profile of the so-called *reference* cycle that emerges. It looks like Fig. 12-4.

This model of a typical cycle enables us to speak of the "length" of a business cycle as the period from one peak to the next or from trough to trough. If we fail to measure from *similar* points on two or more cycles, we can easily get a distorted picture of short-term growth — for instance, one that begins at the upper turning point of one cycle and measures to the trough of the next. Much of the political charge and countercharge about growth rates can be clarified if we examine the starting and terminating dates used by each side.

Causes of cycles

What lies behind this more or less regular alternation of good and bad times?

Innumerable theories, none of them entirely satisfactory, have been advanced to explain the business cycle. A common business explanation is that waves of optimism in the world of affairs alternate with waves of pessimism — a statement that may be true enough, but that seems to describe the sequence of events rather than to explain it. Hence economists have tried to find the underlying cyclical mechanism in firmer stuff than an alternation of moods. One famous late-nineteenth century economist, W. S. Jevons, for example, explained business cycles as the consequence of sunspots — perhaps not as occult a theory as it might seem, since Jevons believed that the sunspots caused weather cycles that caused crop cycles that caused business cycles. The trouble was that subsequent investigation shows that the periodicity of sunspots was sufficiently different from that of rainfall cycles to make the connection impossible.

Other economists have turned to causes closer at home: to variations in the rate of gold mining (with its effects on the money supply); to fluctuations in the rate of invention; to the regular recurrence of war;

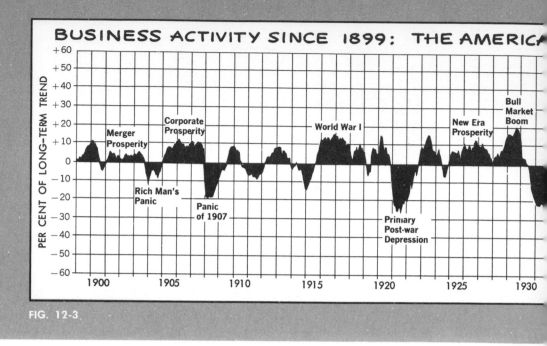

FIG. 12-3

and to yet many other factors. There is no doubt that many of these events can induce a business expansion or contraction. The persistent problem, however, is that none of the so-called underlying causes itself displays an inherent cyclicality—much less one with a periodicity of eight to ten years.

Then how do we explain cycles? Economists today no longer seek a single explanation of the phenomenon in an exogenous (external) cyclical force. Rather, they tend to see cycles as our own eye first saw them on the growth curve, as *variations in the rate of growth that tend to be induced by the dynamics of the growth process itself*. As we shall see, our knowledge of macroeconomics will quickly give us the clue to the mechanism at work.

The mechanism of business fluctuation

Let us assume that some stimulus, such as an important industry-building invention, has begun to increase investment expenditures. We can easily see how such an initial impetus can generate a cumulative and self-feeding boom. As the multiplier and accelerator interact, the first burst of investment stimulates additional consumption, the additional consumption induces more investment, and this in turn re-invigorates consumption. Meanwhile, this process of mutual stimulation serves to lift business expectations and to encourage still further expansionary spending. Inventories are built up in anticipation of larger sales. Prices "firm up" and the stock market rises. Optimism reigns. A boom is on.

What happens to end such a boom? There are many possible reasons

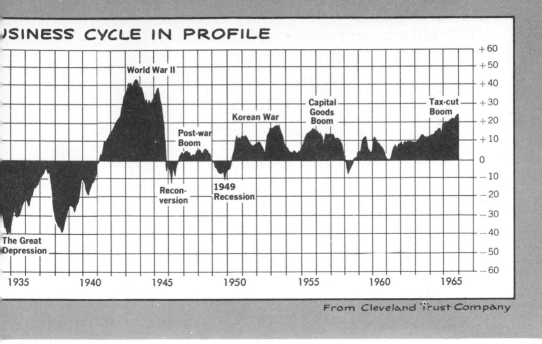

USINESS CYCLE IN PROFILE

World War II

Capital Goods Boom

Tax-cut Boom

Korean War

Post-war Boom

Recon-version

1949 Recession

The Great Depression

+60
+50
+40
+30
+20
+10
0
−10
−20
−30
−40
−50
−60

1935   1940   1945   1950   1955   1960   1965

why it may peter out or come to an abrupt halt. It may simply be that the new industry will get built, and thereafter an important stimulus to investment will be lacking. Or even before it is completed, wages and prices may have begun to rise as full employment is neared, and the climate of expectations may thereupon become wary rather than hopeful. (Businessmen have an old adage that "what goes up must come down.") Meanwhile, perhaps tight money will choke off spending plans or make new projects appear unprofitable. Investment may begin to decline because consumption, although still rising, is no longer rising at the earlier *rate* (the acceleration principle in action).

It is impossible to know in advance what particular cause will retard spending, but it is all too easy to see how a hesitation in spending can turn into a general contraction. Perhaps warned by a falling stock market, perhaps by a slowdown in their sales or an end to rising profits, businessmen begin to cut back. Whatever their initial motivation, what follows thereafter is much like the preceding expansion, only in reverse. The multiplier mechanism now breeds smaller rather than larger incomes. Downward revisions of expectations reduce rather than enhance

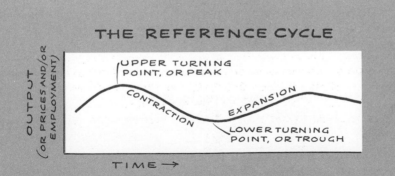

THE REFERENCE CYCLE

OUTPUT (OR PRICES AND/OR EMPLOYMENT)

UPPER TURNING POINT, OR PEAK

CONTRACTION

EXPANSION

LOWER TURNING POINT, OR TROUGH

TIME →

FIG. 12-4

the attractiveness of investment projects. As consumption decreases, prices fall and unemployment begins to show up. Inventories are worked off. Bankruptcies become more common. We experience all the economic and social problems of a recession.

But just as there is a "natural" ceiling to a boom, so there is a more or less "natural" floor to recessions.* The fall in inventories, for example, will eventually come to an end: for even in the severest recessions, merchants and manufacturers must have *some* goods on their shelves and so must eventually begin stocking up. The decline in expenditures will lead to easy money, and the slack in output will tend to a lower level of costs; and both of these factors will encourage new investment projects. Meanwhile, the automatic stabilizers of government fiscal policy will slowly make their effects known. Sooner or later, in other words, expenditures will cease falling, and the economy will tend to "bottom out."

Business cycles and growth

Thus, business cycles appear as accelerations and decelerations to the underlying momentum of growth. But why growth? How do we know that the peak of one cycle will be higher than the peak of the previous one? What accounts for the underlying tilt to the whole cycle chart?

The essential reason is one that we are very familiar with. Even in the doldrums of recession (except for a very few severely depressed years) the economy manages to lay down a net increment of wealth in the form of investment, and this investment then adds its leverage to that of the entire stock of capital with which society works. So, too, every year, the labor force tends to grow as population increases, adding another component of potential input to the economic mechanism.

This does not mean, as we well know, that the economy will therefore *automatically* utilize its full resources. Unused men and unused machines are very well known to us in macroeconomic analysis. But the steady addition to the factors of production does mean that the *potential* of the economy will be steadily rising. *Growth is thus introduced into the system by the steady addition to its basic instruments of production, both human and material.* The question we then face is to see how much of this potential source of output we will use.

---

*In retrospect, the tremendous and long-lasting collapse of 1929 seems to have been caused by special circumstances having to do with speculation and monetary mismanagement, rather than by any inherent characteristics of the system.

Actual vs. potential GNP

As Fig. 12-5 shows, all through the 1950's and 1960's potential output ran well ahead of the output we actually achieved. Indeed, between 1958 and 1962 the amount of lost output represented by this gap came to the staggering sum of $170 billion, or nearly $1,000 per person. Even in 1964, a very prosperous year, the President's Council of Economic Advisers reported that we could have added another $25 billion to $30 billion to GNP—more than $300 per family—if we had brought unemployment down from 5 to 4 per cent and had also found jobs for the larger labor force that would have sought work in a climate of full employment.

Reaching full employment growth

How can we reach full employment growth? The main answer, as we know very well by now, lies in *increasing the volume of expenditure*. If we are suffering from a rate of growth that is inadequate to give us our potential output, the best way to augment that growth is to add to one or more of the streams of expenditure that propel us forward.

But which one? The consumption stream is basically a passive economic force that will reflect, but will rarely initiate, changes in the pace of activity. The export stream, although important, is too small to give a major boost to our economy. The choice lies between increasing the rate of gross private domestic investment and that of government expenditures.

Or rather, the route to full employment growth lies in encouraging

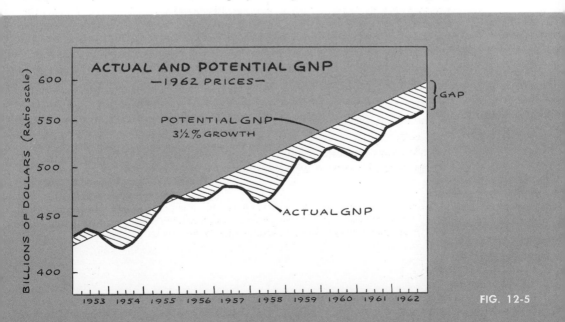

FIG. 12-5

both private investment and government expenditure, for it is wrong to see the two as rival claimants for national resources as long as some of those resources, human and material, lie unused. So far as encouraging private expenditure is concerned, economists have learned a great deal about the use of tax incentives or accelerated depreciation or low interest rates to help induce businessmen to make capital outlays. Yet, in the end, the volume of private capital spending remains always beyond direct control. It is the quantity and quality of invention and innovation on which the pace of investment depends more than on anything else; and although we can encourage research and development activities, both public and private, we cannot guarantee that a flow of usable and profitable products and processes will be steadily fed into the business world.

There is much more that we can do to speed up growth by using the public sector. The fact that increased spending for Vietnam effectively closed the gap between actual and potential GNP in 1966 is proof enough that we can grow at faster rates by using the stimulus of public expenditure. The trouble is that the imperatives of peace have always rated less high than those of war. Thus the avenues of public expenditure by which growth might be speeded up—the repair and rebuilding of the cities, the cleansing of the air and water, the provision of comfort and health for the aged and unwell—have heretofore been only half-heartedly tried. The use of public expenditure as a tool to lift our rate of growth near to the full employment mark is one that we must still learn to use boldly and effectively.

Long-run growth

Yet, in the long run, the problem of unemployed resources may not be the most important problem we face. For when we look a few decades ahead, we begin to see that even the trajectory of full employment growth sets limits to our economic grasp. For instance, in 1960 a rather conservative Commission on National Goals established by President Eisenhower laid down a set of "goals"—from enhanced consumption through a variety of improved public and private programs—to be achieved by 1975 in some fifteen areas of national economic activity. Recently, the National Planning Association "costed out" these goals to see how many of them we were likely to reach. Its conclusion was *that even if output grew at 4 per cent a year (14 per cent faster than the traditional 3.5 per cent rate), our GNP in 1975 would fall short by $150 billion of achieving the aspirations of the Eisenhower Commission!* GNP would then amount to $981 billion (in 1962 prices), whereas the cost of the desired goals would come to $1,127 billion. Only by raising

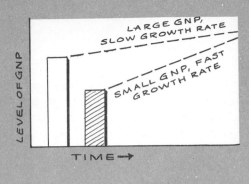

LEVEL OF GNP

LARGE GNP, SLOW GROWTH RATE

SMALL GNP, FAST GROWTH RATE

TIME →

THE DIFFERENCE THAT GROWTH RATES MAKE

FIG. 12-6

the national growth rate to 5.5 per cent (which would mean working the economy under a wartime-like forced draft) could we fulfill the program envisioned by the commission.

As this example makes clear, changes in growth rates of "only" a percentage point make very large differences in the absolute amount of output after a few years.* Indeed, if GNP grew at a 3 per cent rate instead of a 4 per cent rate, the short fall to the commission's goal would increase from $150 billion to $375 billion. When we look to the future, in other words, it is not the present level of GNP that determines the outlook nearly so much as the rate at which that GNP will grow, as Fig. 12-6 illustrates.

Causes of growth: extensive investment

Thus we must think of growth not only as a means of remedying the underuse of resources, but as setting the trajectory that will define for us the scope of our realizable potential. But this changes our focus from one of merely increasing expenditures to one that asks the more fundamental question of how our capacity to produce can be increased.

One answer to that fundamental question is obvious enough. The simplest way for an economy to raise its output is to increase its use of human and material resources—in more technical terms, *to increase factor inputs.* Indeed, total inputs *must* grow if the new members of the community are to get as least as large a share of output as the older members.

*Recently, Professor Kenneth Boulding pointed out that before World War II no country sustained a growth of GNP per capita of more than 2.3 per cent, whereas since World War II at least one country—Japan—has achieved and held a rate of growth of per capita GNP of 8 per cent. Writes Boulding: "The difference between 2.3 per cent and 8 per cent may be dramatically illustrated by pointing out that [at 2.3 per cent] children are twice as rich as their parents—i.e., per capita income approximately doubles every generation—while at 8 per cent per annum, children are six times as rich as their parents." However, Boulding doubts that such rates of increase can be long maintained, for they would soon bring us up against absolute barriers of resources that would throttle growth back to a much slower pace. (*The Public Interest,* Fall 1966, p. 38.)

We cannot grow very successfully, however, if we try to use only the existing capital equipment for employing new members of the work force. The peasants who are born into our model underdeveloped economy, must be given spades—and this means, as we know, that there must be a prior increase in the output of hammers and chisels. In a highly developed industrial economy, an expanding labor force must be matched with new capital of all kinds (which requires additional machine-tool output). Failure to keep the capital-labor ratio constant will result in a steady falling-behind of the newer members of the labor force and a consequent diminution of growth.

Productivity

Yet it is apparent that merely to match each new worker with as much equipment as his predecessors' is something like running to stay in place. This kind of *extensive* investment which "widens" the amount of capital wealth is essential if we are not to fall behind, but it does not result in our forging ahead. For that, we must *gain* output per capita—we must achieve more output for each unit of input, rather than maintain the previous level. The efficiency or *productivity* of our factors must be enhanced.

As we learned in the preceding chapter and as Table 12-3 reiterates, our inputs *have* been getting steadily more productive, both in industry and agriculture. On the average, during the 1950's and the mid-1960's, our labor productivity (our rate of output per man-hour of input) increased by some 2.9 per cent a year, averaging industry, where it has been slower, and agriculture, where the rate has been very high. How important this increase in productivity has been in making possible our national growth is apparent in Fig. 12-7.

TABLE 12•3   INDICES OF REAL OUTPUT PER MAN-HOUR: 1947 = 100

	1947	1964 (prelim.)
Agriculture	100	267
Manufacturing	100	159

The chart shows that increases in productivity account for by far the larger part of our aggregate economic growth since World War II. The low labor input figure is, of course, partly the result of a rising rate of unemployment during many of these years, when we were not putting to work as many of our increased numbers of workers as we might have.

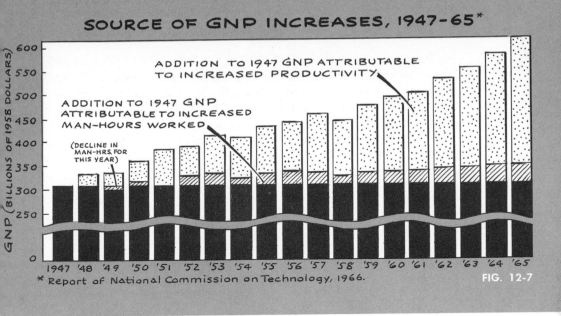

SOURCE OF GNP INCREASES, 1947-65*

ADDITION TO 1947 GNP ATTRIBUTABLE
TO INCREASED PRODUCTIVITY

ADDITION TO 1947 GNP
ATTRIBUTABLE TO INCREASED
MAN-HOURS WORKED

(DECLINE IN
MAN-HRS. FOR
THIS YEAR)

GNP (BILLIONS OF 1958 DOLLARS)

1947 '48 '49 '50 '51 '52 '53 '54 '55 '56 '57 '58 '59 '60 '61 '62 '63 '64 '65

* Report of National Commission on Technology, 1966.

FIG. 12-7

But even if 1947 rates of employment had been maintained, the role of productivity-increases would still have been predominant.

Causes of improved productivity

What accounts for the increase in labor productivity? Generally, we can distinguish four principal sources.

1. *Increased skills and education.* In the short run, the dexterity, skills, and adaptability of the labor force make a tremendous difference in the amount of output obtainable from a given capital apparatus. Fiascoes of production testify to the absence of these determining influences in underdeveloped areas where modern plants must often be opened without a trained work force. In the longer run, it is not so much skills as general education that determines the output per individual worker. Contemporary studies place more and more stress on the productivity gains to be had from education, and attribute as much as one-fifth of the total U.S. growth rate to the steadily rising "stock" of education incorporated in the average worker.

2. *Economies of large-scale production.* A second source of increased productivity per unit of input is the magnifying effect of mass production on output. Typically, when the organization of production reaches a certain critical size, especially in manufacturing, so-called "economies of scale" become possible. Many of these are based on the possibility of dividing complex operations into a series of simpler ones, each performed at high speed by a worker aided by specially designed equipment. It is

213

difficult to estimate the degree of growth attributable to these economies of size. Certainly during the era of railroad-building and of the introduction of mass production, they contributed heavily to growth rate. In a careful study of the contemporary sources of U.S. growth, Edward F. Denison estimates that new economies of large-scale production add only about 10 per cent to our annual rate of productivity increase.*

3. *Deepening of capital.* We have talked of the "widening" of capital, as each new worker was given the necessary equipment to put him on a productive par with his fellows. Now we must add the concept of the "deepening" of capital, or increasing amount of capital with which each worker is equipped. Clearly, if we give each worker more machinery and other types of capital goods to work with, we should expect him to be able to increase his output for each hour's work. Over the long course of economic growth, increased productivity has required the slow accumulation of very large capital stocks per working individual. Thus investment that increases capital per worker is, and will probably continue to be, one of the most effective levers for steadily raising output per worker. But unlike the steady widening of capital, the deepening of capital is not a regular process. Between 1929 and 1947 there was no additional capital added per worker! This was, of course, a time of severe depression and thereafter of enforced wartime stringencies. Since 1947, the value of our stock of capital per worker has been growing at about 2.7 per cent a year. As we shall see, immediately following, however, the *size* of this additional stock of capital is of less crucial importance than the *productivity* of that capital—that is, its technological character.

4. *Technology.* We have just mentioned the fourth and last main source of increases in productivity—technology. During the past half century, GNP has consistently grown faster than can be accounted for by increases in the work force or the size of the capital stock. (Even during the 1929–1947 era, for instance, when capital stock per worker remained fixed, the output of GNP per worker grew by 1.5 per cent a year.) Part of this "unexplained" increase can be attributed to some of the sources of growth we have itemized above—mainly education and training, and economies of scale. But contemporary economic investigation increasingly attributes the bulk of the "bonus" rate of growth to the impact of new technology.

The term is, admittedly, somewhat vague. By "new technology" we mean new inventions of the demand-creating kind we have talked about, innovations of a labor-displacing (but productivity-enhancing) kind, the growth of knowledge in the form of research and development, changes

*The Sources of Economic Growth in the United States (New York: Committee for Economic Development, 1962).

in business organization or in techniques of management, and many other activities. What is increasingly apparent, however, is that the search for new products and processes in the main force behind much productivity-enhancing investment. Thus while investment has become less important for growth simply as a means of adding sheer quantities of capital to the labor force (although that is still a very important function, particularly in construction), it remains the strategic variable as the carrier of technological change.

Changing patterns of growth

It is time to sum up what we have covered. We have seen that long-term growth proceeds from two sources: *more* input and more *productive* input, and we have been concerned with studying some of the main facets of both kinds of growth. Perhaps we can summarize our findings in Fig. 12-8, comparing the sources of growth in two eras of our past.

Note the declining importance played by increases in numbers of workers or sheer dollar value of capital, and the increasing importance of the "intangibles" of education and technology. To a number of observers, this shift implies that we have been slowly moving into a new phase of industrial organization in which productivity will more and more reflect the application of scientific knowledge, rather than the brute leverage of mechanical strength and power. Whether this "post-industrial" society will grow at a faster or slower rate than in the past is a question that we will not be able to answer for many years.

The value of growth

Will we want to grow as fast as possible in the future? It is tempting to assume that growth is in itself an economic goal of the highest priority,

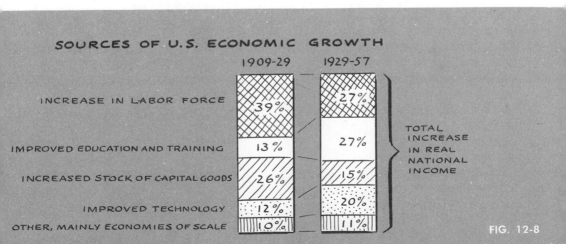

SOURCES OF U.S. ECONOMIC GROWTH

	1909-29	1929-57	
INCREASE IN LABOR FORCE	39%	27%	
IMPROVED EDUCATION AND TRAINING	13%	27%	TOTAL INCREASE IN REAL NATIONAL INCOME
INCREASED STOCK OF CAPITAL GOODS	26%	15%	
IMPROVED TECHNOLOGY	12%	20%	
OTHER, MAINLY ECONOMIES OF SCALE	10%	11%	

FIG. 12-8

but the matter is not quite that simple. Insofar as it brings material benefits to millions who still experience the meanness of poor food and tawdry surroundings, economic growth surely comes as an unalloyed gain. The question is, however, whether the increases in output in an affluent society will go to those whose need is greatest, or whether they will be dissipated for other purposes. Spending for arms and rockets to the moon, for Cadillacs that cruise the streets above crowded subway systems, for luxury apartment houses that look out over the slums—this also counts in the national books as "growth." It is all too possible to make a fetish of growth and to fail to inquire into the quality of the life that growth brings or the social shortcomings it conceals.

These reflections on the purpose and application of growth bid fair to assume greater and greater relevance in the years ahead. Already we have reached a stage in our national economic development when the poorer families in the nation are no longer immediately helped by the normal process of growth. The majority of the poor in America are not the employed, who *will* benefit from the growth they help create. The poor today are the aged, the sick, the racially disprivileged, the inhabitants of rural backwaters, whose link to the productive mechanism is insubstantial or lacking entirely. If they are to share in the proceeds of an expanding economy, measures must be taken to direct a portion of our annual increments of output into their hands. Otherwise, growth is likely to increase the disparity between the affluent and the disfavored, bringing not a sense of greater national well-being, but a heightening of social tensions and unrest.

Yet, with all these caveats, it is well that we conclude our study of macroeconomics with a sense of the great possibilities hinging on the trajectory of growth. Enormous opportunities for self-realization reside in the vast productive potential toward which we are moving; and however much it may test us to put that potential to good use, the irrefutable fact is that we must gain it before we can put ourselves to the test. Perhaps in the end, the purpose of the study of macroeconomics is to help create an economically literate and concerned citizenry who will urge and support the policies that will give us high growth and the wise use of the affluence that will result from it.

Summary

1. Growth in output derives from *investment that adds to our stock of capital wealth.* In an industrialized society, this investment is achieved by utilizing an existing capital-goods sector. But in a poor society, the process is much more difficult.

2. In such a poor society, we can see that the *capital-goods sector consists of two subsectors:* one producing capital goods that, in turn, make the equipment

used in the consumption-goods sector; and the other making machine tools, capital goods that can create more capital goods.

3. *Thus growth requires two shifts:* (1) the machine-tool capacity of the capital-goods sector must be enlarged and (2) resources must be shifted from the consumption sector to the capital goods sector.

4. United States growth has shown a *persistently steady rate* of 3.5 per cent—1.5 per cent per capita—for well over a century. From *year to year*, however, the *rate of growth is very uneven.*

5. We can discern *many cyclical patterns* in the year-to-year variations. The most important is "the" *8–10 year business cycle.* We designate its main features as upper and lower turning points (or peak and trough), expansion and contraction.

6. Many causes have been suggested to explain the business cycle, but none has been wholly satisfactory in accounting for its *cyclicality* or in explaining why its *periodicity* is 8 to 10 years.

7. Economists today explain the cycle as *variations in the rate of expansion.* The interaction of the multiplier and the accelerator explain the expansive and contractive phases. Upper turning points are usually caused by one or more of the many economic strains induced by the expansion itself; lower turning points tend to come about from the "bottoming out" of the contractive spiral.

8. Actual growth often falls behind *potential growth* or full employment growth. The wastage in output is best avoided by maintaining a high rate of aggregate demand.

9. Potential growth depends on deeper causes. One of these is the *amount of labor input and the extensive investment* needed to maintain labor/capital ratios. A second and more important cause is *improved productivity.*

10. Productivity, in turn, results from many sources. Among the most important are: *increased skills and education, economies of large-scale production, deepening of capital equipment,* and *technological advance.* Increasingly, growth has resulted from enhanced education and technology rather than from more inputs of labor or capital.

11. Growth is not an end in itself, but only a *means to an end.*

Questions

1. Describe carefully the shifts in labor needed to begin the process of growth in a very simple economy. Are such shifts visible in an advanced economy?

2. What is the special property of machine tools? Is there a very simple article of output that is also capable of the dual uses of machine tools? How about the seed corn held back by a farmer?

3. How do you explain the fact that the year-to-year growth of the United States is so much more irregular than the long-term growth?

4. Describe the course of events in a "typical" business cycle? How does such a cycle get started? How does it build up? What is likely to bring it to an end? How does the decline come about? What stops it?

5. Do you think that the policies needed to minimize the fluctuations of the business cycle are the same as those needed to accelerate long-term growth?

Discuss what you would do to improve stability and to augment potential output.

6. What is extensive investment? What is intensive investment? Which is more conducive to growth?

7. Why is productivity so important in achieving growth? What are its main sources? What would you recommend as a long-term program to raise American productivity?

8. What do you think are the main purposes to which growth should be directed? How would you arrange for growth to be directed to these ends?

Statistical
Appendix

Statistical Appendix

Gross National Product: Annually, 1929–66
(millions of dollars except constant dollars in billions)

	1929	1930	1931	1932	1933	1934	1935
Gross national product (billions of 1958 dollars)	203.6	183.5	169.3	144.2	141.5	154.3	169.5
Gross national product (current dollars)	103,095	90,367	75,820	58,049	55,601	65,054	72,247
Personal consumption expenditures	77,222	69,880	60,464	48,589	45,795	51,335	55,699
Durable goods	9,212	7,155	5,485	3,646	3,469	4,213	5,111
Nondurable goods	37,686	34,022	28,956	22,741	22,257	26,691	29,322
Services	30,324	28,703	26,023	22,202	20,069	20,431	21,266
Gross private domestic investment	16,228	10,260	5,618	960	1,401	3,334	6,411
Fixed investment	14,514	10,612	6,766	3,440	2,965	4,069	5,337
Nonresidential	10,560	8,273	5,041	2,709	2,402	3,205	4,138
Structures	4,959	4,015	2,343	1,219	931	1,050	1,234
Producers' durable equipment	5,601	4,258	2,698	1,490	1,471	2,155	2,904
Residential structures	3,954	2,339	1,725	731	563	864	1,199
Nonfarm	3,779	2,208	1,647	693	520	812	1,119
Farm	175	131	78	38	43	52	80
Change in business inventories	1,714	−352	−1,148	−2,480	−1,564	−735	1,074
Nonfarm	1,836	−83	−1,608	−2,590	−1,370	195	376
Farm	−122	−269	460	110	−194	−930	698
Net exports of goods and services	1,148	1,032	516	407	358	601	128
Exports	7,034	5,448	3,641	2,474	2,402	2,975	3,265
Imports	5,886	4,416	3,125	2,067	2,044	2,374	3,137
Government purchases of goods and services	8,497	9,195	9,222	8,093	8,047	9,784	10,009
Federal	1,261	1,372	1,495	1,456	2,000	2,981	2,919
National defense	....	....	....	....	....	....	....
Other	....	....	....	....	....	....	....
State and local	7,236	7,823	7,727	6,637	6,047	6,803	7,090

1936	1937	1938	1939	1940	1941	1942	1943	1944	1945	1946
193.0	203.2	192.9	209.4	227.2	263.7	297.8	337.1	361.3	355.2	312.6
82,481	90,446	84,670	90,494	99,678	124,540	157,910	191,592	210,104	211,945	208,509
61,912	66,507	63,920	66,834	70,824	80,575	88,501	99,330	108,255	119,701	143,400
6,304	6,925	5,686	6,670	7,766	9,647	6,947	6,572	6,718	8,044	15,757
32,857	35,224	33,953	35,116	37,017	42,853	50,753	58,597	64,348	71,903	82,374
22,751	24,358	24,281	25,048	26,041	28,075	30,801	34,167	37,189	39,754	45,269
8,486	11,783	6,475	9,264	13,133	17,909	9,811	5,741	7,135	10,576	30,609
7,226	9,241	7,389	8,853	10,950	13,440	8,060	6,371	8,120	11,610	24,230
5,619	7,308	5,365	5,927	7,549	9,506	5,951	5,013	6,843	10,087	16,986
1,645	2,442	1,897	1,953	2,287	2,928	1,886	1,342	1,841	2,802	6,778
3,974	4,866	3,468	3,974	5,262	6,578	4,065	3,671	5,002	7,285	10,208
1,607	1,933	2,024	2,926	3,401	3,934	2,109	1,358	1,277	1,523	7,244
1,510	1,807	1,923	2,791	3,218	3,703	1,934	1,198	1,132	1,385	6,728
97	126	101	135	183	231	175	160	145	138	516
1,260	2,542	−914	411	2,183	4,469	1,751	−630	−985	−1,034	6,379
2,066	1,726	−1,046	316	1,902	4,049	652	−577	−575	−595	6,350
−806	816	132	95	281	420	1,099	−53	−410	−439	29
115	297	1,291	1,066	1,719	1,289	6	−2,049	−1,830	−613	7,494
3,539	4,553	4,336	4,432	5,355	5,925	4,791	4,416	5,298	7,240	14,735
3,424	4,256	3,045	3,366	3,636	4,636	4,785	6,465	7,128	7,853	7,241
11,968	11,859	12,984	13,330	14,002	24,767	59,592	88,564	96,544	82,281	27,006
4,935	4,664	5,409	5,105	6,015	16,882	51,875	81,148	89,002	74,179	17,234
....	....	....	1,249	2,214	13,750	49,363	79,743	87,433	73,507	14,738
....	....	....	3,856	3,801	3,132	2,512	1,405	1,569	672	2,496
7,033	7,195	7,575	8,225	7,987	7,885	7,717	7,416	7,542	8,102	9,772

	1947	1948	1949	1950	1951	1952	1953	1954
Gross national product (billions of 1958 dollars)	309.9	323.7	324.1	355.3	383.4	395.1	412.8	407.0
Gross national product (current dollars)	231,323	257,562	256,484	284,769	328,404	345,498	364,593	364,841
Personal consumption expenditures	160,704	173,555	176,803	191,009	206,266	216,679	229,969	236,494
Durable goods	20,394	22,677	24,628	30,477	29,648	29,334	33,248	32,836
Nondurable goods	90,471	96,215	94,545	98,110	108,753	113,950	116,792	118,278
Services	49,839	54,663	57,630	62,422	67,865	73,395	79,929	85,380
Gross private domestic investment	33,984	46,014	35,687	54,081	59,340	51,932	52,593	51,724
Fixed investment	34,446	41,306	38,762	47,292	49,044	48,799	52,146	53,267
Nonresidential	23,387	26,866	25,092	27,903	31,810	31,810	31,615	34,155
Structures	7,499	8,815	8,483	9,249	11,159	11,399	12,652	13,061
Producers' durable equipment	15,888	18,051	16,609	18,654	20,651	20,216	21,503	20,552
Residential structures	11,059	14,440	13,670	19,389	17,234	17,184	17,991	19,654
Nonfarm	10,367	13,574	12,836	18,608	16,423	16,424	17,233	18,951
Farm	692	866	834	781	811	760	758	703
Change in business inventories	−462	4,708	−3,075	6,789	10,296	3,133	447	−1,543
Nonfarm	1,298	2,976	−2,209	6,000	9,057	2,146	1,068	−2,129
Farm	−1,760	1,732	−866	789	1,239	987	−621	586
Net exports of goods and services	11,529	6,440	6,149	1,779	3,671	2,226	386	1,828
Exports	19,737	16,789	15,770	13,807	18,744	17,992	16,947	17,759
Imports	8,208	10,349	9,621	12,028	15,073	15,766	16,561	15,931
Government purchases of goods and services	25,106	31,553	37,845	37,900	59,127	74,661	81,645	74,795
Federal	12,544	16,515	20,112	18,403	37,652	51,779	57,034	47,377
National defense	9,071	10,734	13,268	14,091	33,584	45,928	48,664	41,198
Other	3,473	5,781	6,844	4,312	4,068	5,851	8,370	6,179
State and local	12,562	15,038	17,733	19,497	21,475	22,882	24,611	27,418

1955	1956	1957	1958	1959	1960	1961	1962	1963	1964	1965	1966*
438.0	446.1	452.5	447.3	475.9	487.7	497.2	529.8	551.0	580.0	614.4	652.6
397,960	419,238	441,134	447,334	483,663	503,734	520,097	560,325	590,503	631,712	681,207	743,300
254,381	266,675	281,432	290,069	311,207	325,241	335,152	355,057	374,982	401,356	431,465	465,900
39,639	38,920	40,795	37,881	44,306	45,294	44,180	49,540	53,928	59,353	66,057	70,300
123,309	129,262	135,589	140,152	146,623	151,295	155,903	162,557	168,632	178,877	190,596	207,500
91,433	98,493	105,048	112,036	120,278	128,652	135,069	142,960	152,422	163,126	174,812	188,100
67,374	70,016	67,850	60,901	75,304	74,826	71,699	83,018	87,140	92,959	106,559	188,000
61,421	65,321	66,515	62,392	70,547	71,257	69,677	77,014	81,274	88,293	97,478	104,600
33,613	43,714	46,355	41,613	45,096	48,410	47,032	51,667	54,284	60,714	69,679	80,200
14,310	17,246	17,980	16,585	16,661	18,127	18,385	19,207	19,469	21,011	24,864	27,900
23,804	26,468	28,375	25,028	28,435	30,283	28,647	32,460	34,815	39,703	44,815	52,300
23,307	21,607	20,160	20,779	25,451	22,847	22,645	25,347	26,990	27,579	27,799	24,400
22,685	20,925	19,498	20,146	24,806	22,233	22,043	24,753	26,411	27,017	27,249	23,800
622	682	662	633	645	614	602	594	579	562	550	5,000
5,953	4,695	1,335	−1,491	4,757	3,569	2,022	6,004	5,866	4,666	9,081	13,400
5,486	5,075	801	−2,339	4,765	3,336	1,743	5,290	5,081	5,260	8,146	13,700
467	−380	534	848	−8	233	279	714	785	−594	935	−300
2,009	3,967	5,729	2,206	147	4,046	5,621	5,130	5,897	8,490	6,957	5,100
19,804	23,595	26,481	23,067	23,489	27,244	28,575	30,278	32,339	36,958	38,993	43,000
17,795	19,628	20,752	20,861	23,342	23,198	22,954	25,148	26,442	28,468	32,036	37,900
74,196	78,580	86,123	94,158	97,005	99,621	107,625	117,120	122,484	128,907	136,226	154,300
44,090	45,586	49,538	53,594	53,659	53,531	57,408	63,389	64,244	65,182	66,827	77,000
38,557	40,330	44,225	45,902	46,049	44,946	47,825	51,582	50,760	49,985	50,143	60,500
5,533	5,256	5,313	7,692	7,610	8,585	9,583	11,807	13,484	15,197	16,684	16,500
30,106	32,994	36,585	40,564	43,346	46,090	50,217	53,731	58,240	63,725	69,399	77,200

*1966 constant dollar figures rounded at nearest millionth.
Note: 1929–1965 data from U.S. Dept. of Commerce, *The National Income and Product Accounts of the United States, 1929–1965, Statistical Tables.*
1966 data from U.S. Dept. of Commerce, *Survey of Current Business,* October, 1967.

Index

Index

A

B